D0864448

THE FUTURE OF THE HOLOCAUST

Also by Berel Lang—

Art and Inquiry
The Human Bestiary
Faces, and Other Ironies of Writing and Reading
Philosophy and the Art of Writing
Act and Idea in the Nazi Genocide
The Anatomy of Philosophical Style: Literary Philosophy
    and the Philosophy of Literature
Writing and the Moral Self
Mind's Bodies: Thought in the Act
Heidegger's Silence

Edited Volumes

Marxism and Art: Writings in Aesthetics and Criticism
The Concept of Style
Philosophical Style: An Anthology about the Writing and Reading
    of Philosophy
Philosophy and the Holocaust
The Philosopher in the Community: Essays in Memory of Bertram Morris
The Death of Art
Writing and the Holocaust

The Future of the Holocaust

BETWEEN HISTORY AND MEMORY

Berel Lang

Cornell University Press ITHACA AND LONDON

First published 1999 by Cornell University Press
First printing, Cornell Paperbacks, 1999

Printed in the United States of America

Library of Congress Cataloging-in-Publication Data

Lang, Berel.
    The future of the Holocaust : between history and memory / Berel Lang.
        p.   cm.
    Includes bibliographical references and index.
    ISBN 0-8014-3588-9 (cloth : alk. paper). — ISBN 0-8014-8569-x (pbk. : alk. paper).
    1. Holocaust, Jewish (1939–1945)—Causes. 2. Holocaust, Jewish (1939–1945)—
Influence. 3. National socialism. 4. Holocaust, Jewish (1939–1945)—Moral and
ethical aspects. I. Title.
D804.3.L357   1999
940.53′18—dc21   99-20088

Cornell University Press strives to use environmentally responsible
suppliers and materials to the fullest extent possible in the publishing
of its books. Such materials include vegetable-based, low-VOC inks
and acid-free papers that are recycled, totally chlorine-free, or partly
composed of nonwood fibers. Books that bear the logo of the FSC
(Forest Stewardship Council) use paper taken from forests that have
been inspected and certified as meeting the highest standards for
environmental and social responsibility. For further information, visit
our website at www.cornellpress.cornell.edu

Cloth printing   10   9   8   7   6   5   4   3   2   1
Paperback printing   10   9   8   7   6   5   4   3   2   1

FSC FSC Trademark © 1996 Forest Stewardship Council A.C.
        SW-COC-098

For the Stamms

—Bessie, Mae, Sarah, Julius, Sully, Charlotte—

a world in a generation

Contents

Preface

With the exception of Chapter 3, which appeared earlier, the essays in this book were written between 1990 and 1998, addressing issues and topics I considered more generally or only indirectly in *Act and Idea in the Nazi Genocide* (1990) and in *Heidegger's Silence* (1996) but like those books impelled by the fact of the Nazi genocide itself. It may nonetheless seem that the essays collected here have moved away from the historical center that in those books I attempted to bring as close to philosophical scrutiny as history, on its side, and philosophy, on the other, would permit. The result may seem a mediated and abstract view filtered through lenses set in the "*post-*Holocaust": the more than half century since the end of World War II and the Third Reich's war within that war against the Jews. There undoubtedly is a distancing effect in the "meta-" issues taken up in these essays: analyzing the structure of Nazi "intentions" by considering those intentions under general categories of historical explanation (including the category, itself disputed, of "corporate" decisions); questioning the claim of "Holocaust-uniqueness" by questioning the criterion of uniqueness itself; measuring the uneasy relation between history and memory as that affects the still-unfolding cultural representations of the "Final Solution"—from monuments to public school curricula—within the Jewish and the German communities. A similarly abstractive effect is suggested by the moral analysis of acts and values that come into view as the Nazi genocide, which is in the most obvious sense past, is viewed as also claiming a place in the continually new present—sometimes dramatically, as in the evocation of revenge or the (inverse) prospect of forgiveness, but also, more restrainedly, in considering the reconstitution of "normalcy" within the Jewish and German communities. And last, as I venture in conclusion to judge what "lessons" may be drawn from the event of the Holocaust: a formulation I recognize to be a version—not much less offensive—of the question posed in this volume's title, which asks what (or whether) the future of "the Holocaust" is. The one justification for risking these locutions seems to me the larger offense—and danger—of their omission.

I confess my own uneasiness at this shift in focus. I do not in any event mean with it to claim precedence for historiography over the history of the Holocaust, for privileging the echoes of memory or image over the contingent decisions and acts—the character—of the individual agents in that event, for reifying the abstractions of philosophical ethics as they so often appear apart from the practices that occasion them. There is much to be said in respect to the writing of ethics—and not nearly enough *has* been said—about the relation between moral principles and the specific decisions or acts they (supposedly) determine; between the common ahistoricism of ethical theory and the artifice of the examples on which its proofs and counterarguments typically depend. Notwithstanding the topics considered here that push in the opposite direction, I have attempted to hold history at the center of the essays—for the sake of the facts revealed by historical analysis and on which everything said or written about the Holocaust turns, but still more for the recognition of history itself *as* a fact. Other orders of priority will no doubt continue to contribute to analyses or "theories" of the Holocaust, but these secondary frameworks—keyed to theology or political theory or art or historiography (that is, the *theory* of writing history)—do this always at some cost. The advances even during the last few years in uncovering what are by any standards still rudiments of the history of the Nazi genocide (e.g., the role of the Wehrmacht in carrying out the "Final Solution" and the conduct of the "neutral" bystander countries of Europe during that time) underscore the ways in which new findings are still capable of shifting what have already, quickly, become normalized interpretations and angles of vision.

The basic issue concerning the Holocaust to which these essays return even when the directions they take seem to move away from it thus remains the question "What happened?" together with the historicized version of Kant's transcendental question that asks *how* what happened "was possible." So too, even from a distance, the studies here continue the inquiry about the causal mechanisms of decision making and conduct in Nazi Germany— that is, among the initiators and perpetrators—and about the responses to those genocidal actions by those against whom they were directed, by the individuals and nations who actively fought the Nazis, and by the "bystander" countries and individuals. If, to understand and judge the Holocaust, more is required than the assembly of historical data, surely the analysis demands no less. Thus too, in my view, what appear openly as meta-historical representations of the Nazi genocide—moral, philosophical, aesthetic—also return to the historical configurations that precede them. Even the parodic group of figures who deny that there *was* a Holocaust strengthen the claims of this source. Calling attention to that event by their denial, they remind everyone (including, one supposes, themselves) of its enormity. Also they concede that *if* the Holocaust had occurred, it would have marked a distinctive moment in moral history; their denial that it did occur is in this sense at least as much a psychological or epistemic problem as a moral or historical one.

On the other hand, the grist that keeps history's mill running does not suffice for understanding. The facts of the Holocaust speak for themselves as much as facts ever have, but the judgment still remains to be made of how far those facts extend, which among them are more compelling—or "telling"—than others, what led up to that occurrence in the past and now reaches from it into the present (and toward the future). Thus, in the retrospective essays presented here on topics that can only be addressed retrospectively, I try to show how the past, from which the topics addressed set out, at once loses its initial edge and sharpens a new one as it is brought to bear on the present and then also on the future—both of the latter more indeterminate than the past. Like every future, this one too—that is, the future of the Holocaust—is unpredictable, not because we do not know enough (although that too), but because, as for all futures—including at one time the future containing the event of the Holocaust itself—this one, too, is open, with varied possibilities standing before it. Even after that future has become actual, then, it will not *have* to have become what it is. This does not mean that that future will include no reference to the past, but that the former cannot be reduced to the latter. And all this despite what seems equally undeniable—that the grip of the past is never dislodged from what happens subsequently. For anyone who doubts the two sides of this elementary but stubborn foundation for a philosophy of history, the Holocaust itself is proof: the evidence of its occurrence is matched in weight by the evidence that it *need* not have occurred—that in addition to the impersonal contingencies of history that fell into place along the way, human and voluntary intervention at crucial moments in its unfolding would almost certainly ("almost," because the indeterminacy of history extends this far as well) have altered its outcome. To this extent, then, the offense of drawing "lessons" from the Holocaust in a way that depicts that event as something like a classroom exercise is exceeded only by the denial that anything is to be learned from it—the latter, in my view, a slightly less flagrant version of "Holocaust-denial" itself.

The framework of these essays thus views the Holocaust as historically actual and for the future, still possible. The representation of that event as past could not, even if we wished it to, remain fixed or unchanging; from the perspective of the future, the implication seems unavoidable that if the Holocaust occurred once, it can occur twice. And anyone who writes about the Holocaust without an awareness of these contextual—and more important, ethical—points of reference endangers his writing and his audience, and, of course, himself. More abstractly, this means that no view of the past is fully determinate *and* that the past will in some form reappear in the future whether we wish it to or not. In this sense, we are unable not to incorporate the past in our present; together with this, however, we face the danger of mythologizing the past—yes, including the past of the Holocaust—by freezing it inside history, immobilizing it in our understanding (and so also immobilizing our understanding), or by conceiving of it as disembodied; that is, as outside history altogether.

There should be no doubt then of the difference between the center and the periphery of any study of the Holocaust—and I hope that none will be raised by the essays collected here, notwithstanding their emphasis on external and in some cases distant facets of its representation rather than on the event itself. The very designation of "The Holocaust," it should be recognized, reflects this difference between center and periphery insofar as it requires at least tacit quotation marks: the corporate and sacrificial echoes of the literal term constitute if not a barrier at least a filter that shades the individual agency and the *anti*-sacrificial events designated by it; this is why, for direct reference, I prefer to cite the "Nazi genocide." Nor should there be any doubt that the historical center of the Holocaust will continue to have the last word in understanding not only the causal complexity of that event but also its moral darkness; the representations of the Holocaust articulated in the post-Holocaust have continually pointed to this source. This applies as we find evidence in the post-Holocaust no less than in the Holocaust itself for Marx's harsh assertion that "the truth is always present but not always in truthful form." For also spectators—including those who safely write or read about an event from afar, long after the fact—have a responsibility to that subject in the recovery of its past and then also in judging its present and shaping its future.

I do not mean with these strictures to legislate a single role for the Holocaust in common—universal—consciousness or memory. Here there is a sharp difference, it seems to me, between memory and history. For although in history—that is, at the level of chronicle—the Holocaust is already fixed, what follows from it remains to be seen or, more strongly, made. It is one thing, for example, to note the enormity of the Holocaust as a single historical event alongside but independent of others; it is another thing to hold it implicated in the shape of a moral history of mankind which before that event had hardly been recognized as a history at all. That such a history does exist, one in the constitution of which the Holocaust had a significant part, is my thesis in the first section of this book, which then also shapes the two sections following it. This is not in itself an ethical theory, but a theory of ethical history, marking the location of the Holocaust in moral chronology (under a different heading: the history of evil) and then also in the moral imagination. All of these appear then as concepts in process for which "the Holocaust" has made a significant difference in post-Holocaust consciousness and, one might hope, conscience.

History's physical elements—its body in time and space—ensures a continually growing distance between new generations of writers and the Holocaust as a subject. But thought and understanding have their own means of sustaining the material past, by holding biology and even history at bay through the reach of the moral imagination. The "unthinkable" Nazi genocide not only occurred but also was thought; it has since been re-thought and thought still again (and again)—and the danger would be greater in failing to continue this process than in sustaining it. The unavoidable fear of misrepresenting the Holocaust is a shadow of the danger cast by the event itself.

CONVERSATIONS and correspondence with many colleagues and friends in the course of writing these essays contributed to them, no doubt in some ways of which I am not aware, but certainly in ways that I am. I mention this (and their names) not to disperse accountability but to thank them—and also, of course, to urge the discussion on. If common cause were ever needed to further the ideal of solidarity in confronting a cruelly isolating event—isolating even in its study—surely that applies to the subject addressed here. So, mingling degrees, kinds, and occasions, my thanks to: Aharon Appelfeld, Omer Bartov, Yehuda Bauer, Hedva Ben-Israel, Richard Bernstein, Garry Brodsky, Avner Cohen, Felmon Davis, Morris Eson, Saul Friedländer, Wolfgang Gombocz, Carol Gould, Moshe Greenberg, Raul Hilberg, Karsten Harries, Geoffrey Hartman, Binyamin Harshav, Sara Horowitz, Sam Kassow, Joel Kraemer, Lawrence Langer, Herbert Linden-berger, Leslie Morris, Gerald Myers, Bert Nepaulsingh, Peter Novick, Cynthia Ozick, Elchanan Reiner, Alan Rosenberg, Richard Stamelman, Laurence Thomas, Forrest Williams, Leni Yahil, and Yael Zerubavel. Danny

Leifer, Nathan Rotenstreich, and Marx Wartofsky remain in memory as valued interlocutors. Over many years I have benefited from Hayden White's bounties of historical imagination and intellectual generosity. Ariella Lang and Jessica Lang, who provided me earlier with an incentive for trying to bring the subject of these pages into *their* memories, were by the time of this writing valued consultants. For the book as a whole and in its parts, my wife, Helen S. Lang, has been a resourceful, acute, and tireless reader. (That is, *re*-reader).

I am grateful for support of this work through fellowships from the American Council of Learned Societies and the Center for Judaic Studies at the University of Pennsylvania, and by grants from the State University of New York at Albany. Audiences at the State University of New York at Albany, the University of Chicago, the University of Pennsylvania, and the United States Holocaust Memorial Museum also contributed to this book.

Versions of several chapters have appeared previously, and I thank the publishers for permission to present them here in revised form. The essays and sources are: "The History of Evil and the Future of the Holocaust," in Peter Hayes, ed., *Lessons and Legacies* (Evanston, Ill.: Northwestern University Press, 1991); "Genocide and Omnicide: Technology at the Limits," in Avner Cohen and Steven Lee, eds., *Nuclear Weapons and the Future of Humanity* (Totowa, N.J.: Rowman and Allanheld, 1986); "The Second Time? The Fifth? Arguing the Holcaust's Uniqueness," *History and Theory* (1996); "Intentions and the 'Final Solution,'" *Journal of Social Philosophy* (1992); "Revoking and Sustaining the Past: Two Views of Forgiveness," *Tikkun* (1996); "Holocaust-Memory and Revenge: The Presence of the Past," *Jewish Social Studies* (1996); and "For and Against the 'Righteous Gentiles,'" *Judaism* 46 (1967). The excerpt from "For Adolph Eichmann" in *Collected Poems* by Primo Levi, translated by Ruth Feldman and Brian Swann (1988), appears with permission of Faber & Faber.

BEREL LANG

Hartford, Connecticut

THE FUTURE OF THE HOLOCAUST

Introduction: Between History and Memory

Or should it be "Between Memory and History"? In other words, which comes first? And then, of course, which would be the other, the later one? Well, surely, the beginning is in memory; that is, with our own: inside us, what makes us us, the early sounds and smells and shapes that are all we know of ourselves in our first moments, as we set out there with no inkling of an "other" or "it" apart from the still-vague "I" which encompasses them (would not the *first* pronoun be "we" rather than "I" or "it"?). Only then do we go outside, recognizing what stands apart and so asserts its independence; so then too we begin to find and (because of that) to look for an external order different from the one we find in ourselves and which also depends on ourselves. In this way, memories—and as they constitute it, memory as such, growing out of the individual marks that compose the aleph-beth of a self—turn outward and then into history, accumulating as the impulses of memory become icons, reminders, with their surface then taking on the patina of usage; so those marks themselves become depersonalized, public, objective, even—first in a small way but then increasingly—monumental.

On the other hand, and no less certainly: is it not clear that history is where we begin, even (or especially) as we are *not* aware of its course? Something has first to happen in order to be remembered, even if we recognize the happening only after memory has been at work and even if the remembering, when that happens, may not get it quite right. The first happening is history, an outside whether seen from the inside or not. Otherwise history would be indistinguishable from creations of the imagination or dreamworld or, more simply, of desire. And then, also, there has to be something

1

to remember with or by, themselves elements of history. Nerve cells, synapses, categories of the mind (causality, identity): these cannot be only remembered, they have to be *there* if memory is to have a purchase, serving memory as limbs—hands and legs–which, however disjointed, memory requires to keep pace with the ever-growing past.

But to find the order of genesis for these experimental chronicles is as futile as any claim about their logical order. And the difficulty of establishing such a dialectic of representation—inside memory, outside history (or is it outside memory and inside history?)—is all the more pointed when it is "The Holocaust" that appears between history and memory. Few historical events have been so radically driven inside bodies and minds; few have expressed the effects of external force so openly and systematically. Certainly at the point from which we now observe the Nazi genocide against the Jews, a half century after the decisions and acts constituting it ended, history and memory mingle in a contested present, quarreling between as well as within themselves: Whose history is it? Whose memory is to be credited (or honored)? Are the causes of that history also the reasons of memory? And are there not also "reasons" of history and "causes" of memory? To say nothing about the prior question of what these happen to be; that is, the particular causes and reasons of the Holocaust. But also, finally, why *not* expect just such dissonance when what is at issue is not only what happened in the past and whose past it is, but also whether that past also has a future and what it will be. Memory, we know with certainty, is contingent (if only by recalling the occasions when "memory fails"); and history, too—its representations as well as what they are "of"—grows: outward and sometimes larger, sometimes by contracting and becoming smaller. Contrary to Hegel's dream of totality, the whole either is or is not what is real—and so too, then, the question of its parts.

Yet the factual outline of the Holocaust in its broadest strokes is clear—already laid bare by the anima of historical discourse: intelligible, detailed, connected. At least as fully accessible as any other complex historical event. The conscientious effort by one nation among others to make a group of people who lived with or near them to "disappear from the earth," as Himmler, a principal visionary among its agents, proclaimed their common purpose. An effort which came so close to success that the failed results remain themselves the strongest proof of the design known still by its code name, the "Final Solution." But of course not only its outcome defines the history. The question of what impelled the Nazi genocide, what chains of causality produced and sustained it, continues to be filled in by new findings, reaching in directions that had earlier been obscured by the impact of the event itself—an even more formidable filter than the Nazis' own attempts at concealment. In the expanding space of retrospection, those directions have continued to spread, encompassing now almost without exception the "nations of the world"—reaching beyond the immediate agents and victims also to the bystanders who from positions of supposed neutrality or detachment now also appear to have stood on one side or the other (or both); to the corporate and transnational institutions (churches, political parties, professional societies, and business corporations) who had earlier tried to persuade others as well as themselves that what they did or did not do in the war had indeed reflected the discretion and principles of moral responsibility. If at an earlier time it was possible for historians to turn their hands to purely "local" events, the Nazi genocide established the future implausibility of such inclinations: the ligatures disclosed by that event which connected historical to moral truth and (even more rudimentarily) to its geography settled once and for all the inseparability of the slightest, most out-of-the-way villages (Osweicim, Sobibor, Belzec) from the largest national capitals (Berlin, Warsaw, London, Washington). Politics may indeed be and remain local—but not history.

Predictably, this enlarged space for analysis has in one of its consequences also nourished an impulse for normalization and interpretation. After the stark lines of "the Holocaust," which in its immediacy appeared as simple murder, were collectivized under that rubric, they have also, as in any corporate designation, come to be attenuated, at times qualified. There is the weight of new information (and questions) about chains of command, the elements and variables of social and political intention and act: how orders were given and obeyed, what institutional interests were expressed or contested, how micro-histories—individual biography, material need or psychological fear, self-interest—fed the overarching larger one. The *writing* of history, furthermore, is always directional (whether or not this is true of history as such). In their transformations of chronicle to description, the simplest formulas of historiography have a distancing effect; grammar itself, the shift of tenses from present to past, is a form of mediation. This is no less the case on a view like Croce's which sees the writing of history as "always contemporary." However they can otherwise be described, the Nazis were part of German history, which in turn was and remains part of European history; the Jews of Europe were also part of those same histories—and also have their place within Jewish history. The pitfalls that threaten attempts to locate the Holocaust on this expanding canvas are evident: the choice between seeing too much—with the Holocaust one atrocity among many, where no single event would make much difference to the whole; or seeing too little, where individual events occupy so much space that they block out even the imaginary whole, let alone the extent of their own place in it. Com-

pressed between these two alternatives, also the historiography of the Holocaust has if not a lesson to teach, at least a problem to pose for the writing
of all history.

And yet also the inner surface of history, the acts of appropriation or
rejection intrinsic to memory, remain as alive now as in the earliest post-
Holocaust days when the events themselves still echoed. Memory, in contrast
to the chronicles of history, is always *someone's*: so universities, idealizing im-
personality and objectivity, build departments of history, not departments
of memory. Certainly the moving impulse of memory is not for the accuracy
professed by historians: accounts of perception reveal not only discrepan-
cies between points of view but such lapses and dissonance that it is impossible to believe that they are not intrinsic to the effort behind them rather
than only a common failure to live up to more impersonal ideals. It also
seems clear that neither the vividness nor the intensity of memory is motivated only in reaction to external events. Indeed such reactions appear often as an element of memory itself, as likely to result in repression as in
dramatization; they are in any event expressive and purposeful, turning the
past into the future exactly at the point where memory is "produced." History, so far as it figures in this process, is subordinate; that is, after the fact
of memory itself.

The aging and deaths of those who were in direct touch with the Holocaust—here there is no distinction among victims, perpetrators, bystanders—progressively erode a central strand of memory. The outpouring of
Holocaust-testimonies in the last two decades is an expression of this
prospect. The voices that after years of silence began to speak reflect an
awareness of time closing in, the consciousness that memories not now
recorded will be lost to history *and* memory. It is as if individual memories
here take on a collective burden—to contribute to the whole from a sense
of solidarity which they had not earlier imagined to be possible, with many
of those voices so badly wounded that at first their speaking out had not
seemed even desirable. But also something more than the awareness of a
last chance has intensified the expression of Holocaust-memory as it extends now to a second or third generation of "survivors" who have come to
articulate events of the Holocaust as if those events were part of their own
past and (now) of their present. In one respect, in fact, this retroactive connection has a sharper edge than for the survivors who at least began life in
a different world, one from which genocide was absent, in which that occurrence was quite inconceivable. For the post-Holocaust generations, whatever their direct relationship to victims or survivors (or perpetrators), that
absence was dismissed before they were born; they do not remember the

world without it. The possibility of genocide and so also its present immanence has become a world-inheritance. Even those unconscious of this
addition bear it also as a birthmark that, like any other such "mark," may
suddenly, at any time, come to the surface.

Many of the lines drawn between memory and history are as much con-
structs as the features identified on either side of that division. In its usual
terms, history is primarily external—open for understanding or judgment
to anyone who makes the effort; by contrast, memory is typically posses-
sive—someone's or some group's: expressive, purposeful. But history is no
more immune to the internal motivation of memory than memory is indifferent to the external challenge of history. The title assumed by the United
States Holocaust "Memorial Museum" underscores both the strains and the
affinities of this division. For that title at first glance seems an oxymoron: On
the one hand, the "memorial"—a willed identification, bridging the past
and present, on the parts of both creators and viewers, with the dead thus
being recalled: it is *their* memorial, as a gravestone "belongs" to the person
named on it to which the viewers then attend and "pay respect." But on the
other hand, the "museum" joins a diverse and distanced assembly: so also,
the museums of natural history, of science and industry, of the solar system
(that is, the planetarium), even Mme. Tussaud's "Waxworks." However intense the turn of either creator or viewer to the particular content of a museum, there is no requirement of a will for identification, for joining the future to the past in them.

The very concept of museums, as they flourished during the nationalist
age of conquest and acquisition, attested to the new forces of commercial
desire and power, anticipating the artifice of detachment and action at a
distance which then came to control them. This conjunction is epitomized
in the great art museums of the world: physical contact with their objects
becomes a taboo, and not only because it is held to be irrelevant (also ir-
reverent) to the experience of their objects. Looking from a distance is emblematic of the true character of the museum; the objects displayed thus
also come to seem as if they were created to make museums possible rather
than the other way round. When John Dewey criticized the "Museum Theory of Art," he objected to precisely this encrypting process of aestheticization (with the irony that it was the aestheticization of *art* that was at issue);
that criticism of the ideology of the museum still carries conviction.

Yet the two sides of memory and history are forced together in the
"Memorial Museum." And although it might be supposed that it is the distinctive character of the Holocaust itself that supports this particular conjunction, the import of the linkage in the U.S. Holocaust Memorial Museum

discloses a more general one. It displays openly and pointedly what other memorials and museums also intend but with more restraint: the convergence of history and memory in the present.

I do not mean with these comments to equate or to conflate history and memory—to imply that in the end they have the same elements, the same motives, the same consequences (even if in different proportions). Nor do I suppose that history and memory are two aspects of a single phenomenon, mirroring each other through the lenses of different interests. The differences between them are those between the general and the particular, between the abstract and the concrete, between the static and the transient. Efforts to reduce these pairs to one or the other of their terms have consistently failed, and there is no reason to believe that the relation between memory and history in the aftermath of the Holocaust will be elided any more readily.

WE HAVE heard cautious reference in the aftermath of the Holocaust to a "surfeit of memory," in Charles Maier's phrase.[1] But that phrase itself reinforces the very distinction between memory and history—as "surfeit" implies the existence, by contrast, of a proper or just amount; what is objectionable thus occurs when whatever animates memory (individual or group) displaces or overwhelms other efforts, specifically (here) the prospect of history. The dangers of succeeding in this reduction are evident—displayed most explicitly in the phenomenon of Holocaust-denial where the "surfeit" comes not from recollection but from repression. For the issue here is the same: that the will to shape or reinforce an identity becomes determinant of impersonal or transpersonal history. Here, as in the more standard examples of sentimentality or kitsch, the effects of reduction are evident institutionally (as in the sometime struggle in Holocaust discourse over "whose" Holocaust it is), and personally or individually as well, where aestheticization or emotive designs—nonreferential and ahistorical—dominate at the expense of understanding and so conclude in *mis*representation.

The issue here does not originate exclusively or even principally with the individual. Quite apart from the theoretical question of the status of human nature: which comes first, the one or the many, the individual or the group, the present or the past?—we recognize supposed resolutions of the evident tension between history and memory. So Pierre Nora looks back with nostalgia at a time when memory sufficed for the shaping of culture; that is, as memory premodernly created and sustained from the inside out—"a bond

---

[1] Charles S. Maier, "A Surfeit of Memory? Reflections on History, Melancholy and Denial," *History and Memory* 5 (1993): 136–152.

tying us to the eternal present"—and so with continuity and identity assured. But all this, we learn, has now become victim to the dissociation of self, the casualty of a breakdown in the inherited tradition, in the received wisdom, in natural hierarchy. So our "hopelessly forgetful modern societies" turn instead—second-best, as good as last—to history, to that "intellectual and secular production" which admittedly provides a "representation" but is burdened by the intrinsic limitations of all representation, beginning with its artifice.[2] Memory, on this account, is internal, "spontaneous"; history by contrast is external, contrived, impelled mainly by the will, since the fall into history is anything but up. Is it only coincidence that for Yosef Yerushalmi this same pattern is exemplified notably in the Jewish turn from memory which, as he describes it, had served well from its origins to the beginning of modernity but was then—*now*—driven to the artifice of history?[3]

Ad hominem as any such comment must be, we can hardly avoid noticing that these two historians themselves write from history rather than from the nostalgic ideal of memory that they prefer to recall. The position they defend goes from the (allegedly) new dominance of historical texts back to the (implied) loss of memory—since, as their common argument goes, if memory had sufficed, why should it ever have been superseded? But this inference is based on more than history alone, and the metaphysical or moral considerations that figure in it have broader implications than the one on which they settle.

It is difficult to dispute the claims of change in the modern sense of time—with time a common ingredient, perhaps the single one, of both memory and history. Tradition, no doubt, has recently lost much of its authority, with the past now so remote that it has no present consequence or so fully absorbed into the self-absorbed present that it loses its character as past. What these invidious accounts of history omit, however, is that memory, even if it once was a preeminent influence, was also a construction, however involuntary—and that history, now viewed as self-conscious and contrived—ideological, tendentious, manipulative—remains also expressive beyond that. The most self-conscious self cannot jump out of its own skin—a lesson that any history of history (or of historians) is forced to admit. And if, in history's terms, this limitation is intrinsic—the inability of ob-

[2] Pierre Nora, "Between Memory and History: Les Lieux de Memoire," *Representations* 26 (1986): 7–8. It is noteworthy that where Maier sees in the "surfeit of memory" an end to "Enlightenment aspirations to collective institutions" (p. 148), Nora finds a danger in current "universalism" to which the nation-state of the eighteenth and nineteenth centuries was (in his view) opposed. A common nostalgia, then, for what turns out to be two different pasts.
[3] Y. Y. Yerushalmi, *Zakhor: Jewish History and Memory* (Seattle: University of Washington Press, 1982).

jectivity to objectify itself—it hints also at a residue of matter in memory's design, even if that design *aims* to subordinate to the will any claim or constraint of fact (that is, of "fact").

The model that thus appears in this account is of a progressive displacement: memory first looking from the inside out, history then (second) looking from the outside in—with the former having been exhausted and then superseded by a substitute which acquires strength from memory's desuetitude (the consciousness of the existence of others, the sense of their inevitability and immovability). And then, too, the second stage heralds its own inadequacies—as history, consuming its own oxygen, then finds itself gasping for breath. The common representation of human history as modeled on the impersonal stratifications of geological history omits only such small considerations as will, intention, social and personal identity; that is, the ingredients of memory.

This "Displacement Model" of the relation between memory and history, however, is not the only one to which the evidence points.[4] I propose in fact an alternate "Dialectical" model in which also memory has its outside and also history an inside, with the two now joined not by splitting the differences between them—the inviting, liberal resolution—but by asserting those differences: an at once reactionary but also, it seems to me, still more progressive resolve. When Maurice Halbwachs held up to view the phenomenon of collective memory, he introduced more than only another category of social analysis; what was most innovative in his conception of collective memory was the relationship it posited between the individual and the group. For although nineteenth-century nationalism had already registered its claim against the liberal and Enlightenment arguments for the individual's priority over the nation or the people (or as then emerged, the race), memory was a more recalcitrant element to integrate because of its apparently personal, that is, individual, origins. Halbwachs's reversal, then, according to which individual memory was in certain respects a function of collective memory rather than the other way around, both identified a new causal factor in social topography and added weight to the side of memory in the continuing tension between it and history.[5]

Even when later authors incorporated the turn to collective memory initiated by Halbwachs, however, they typically ignored its connection to his-

---

[4] A more equivocal version of the Displacement Model is suggested by Jacques LeGoff, who differs from Nora, however, in finding the displacement of memory by history a *desirable* turn: "Memory is the raw material of history." Jacques LeGoff, *History and Memory*, trans. S. Rendall and E. Claman (New York: Columbia University Press, 1992), p. xi.

[5] Maurice Halbwachs, *On Collective Memory*, ed. and trans. Lewis A. Coser (Chicago: University of Chicago Press, 1992).

tory—collective or individual. And it is here, I suggest, that the dialectic of memory and history is most fruitfully placed—as memory then becomes externalized, and as history, taking its turn, is internalized. On this Dialectical Model, it takes (at least) two to remember; that is—in a corollary of Wittgenstein's private language argument—that the act of remembrance is not only a construct (as Nietzsche had memorably described it) but also a *social* construct, depending for its expression on a principle of exchange and collaboration. No one memory, in other words, without two—a ready counter to the received view expressed in statements such as Amos Funkenstein's, that "memory is a mental act, and therefore it is absolutely and completely personal."[6]

On the other hand—here we find ourselves in the aftermath of Halbwachs's work—the implications of this collectivization of memory posed an immediate challenge to the corporate, and for the nineteenth century, the scientific ideal of impersonal or at least transpersonal history. For if memory is first a group-representation rather than the act of an individual that is then joined or contracted with others, the conclusion follows that the sharp division otherwise alleged between the parochialism of collective memory— tendentious, linked to the inspiration of a particular group whose memory it is—and the objectivity or externality of history could not be sustained. This does not mean that the two are simply elided with no difference left between collective memory and group history, as the inside moves outside and the outside moves inside. It means that the pressures on each are more nearly equal than has been supposed; that history, however intense its desire to escape its local origins, to *become* déraciné, remains indebted to memory—and that memory, whatever the claims of ownership or tutelage made for or by it, incorporates and inscribes in its own right the impersonal aspiration of history. History without memory, in other words, is empty; memory without history is blind. And since history is not, certainly need not be, empty, and memory is not, certainly need not be, blind, it is the conjunction of the two, each evoking a response in the other, that then establishes and interprets the detail of social topography.

I HAVE suggested that for contemporary reflection the Holocaust marks a distinctive (distinctive, not unique) moment in the analysis of the relation

---

[6] Amos Funkenstein, "Collective Memory and Historical Consciousness," *History and Memory* 1 (1989): 6. Although in arguing against a binary opposition between history and memory, Dominick LaCapra proposes a version of what I call here the Dialectical Model, he views the mechanism of causality—at least in respect to the Holocaust—as based on psychological "trauma" and in this respect seems to me to reiterate the "private memory" view. See LaCapra, *Memory and History after Auschwitz* (Ithaca: Cornell University Press, 1998), chap. 1.

between history and memory. To some extent this is a historical accident, or perhaps better, coincident; namely, that the Nazi genocide directed against the Jews was in itself a public event, deliberately and systematically set in motion, enacted, and recorded; that it was initiated by and impinged on groups of people for whom founding structures of history and collective memory and of the dialectic between them were themselves influential traditions. The "post-Holocaust" has both elaborated and been moved by this set of circumstances. The intended genocide "succeeded" only in part: the Jews did not "disappear from the earth." And the German people and their new leaders to whom Hitler in his last will and testament—drawn only hours before his death in the Berlin bunker—bequeathed the goal of completing the destruction of the Jews, chose (or were able) neither to do that nor to follow him to his grave. The supposed Bystanders who "observed" the Holocaust as it unfolded have in the aftermath found themselves increasingly implicated: both as individuals who recognize now that they had options on which they did not act and through their governments (including the "neutrals" like Switzerland and Sweden) who in retrospect turn out to have had the power but neither the inclination toward nor the principles of agency.

For them all, then—and finally, in this accounting hardly anyone in the Western world is left untouched—the post-Holocaust has projected an internal memory forced to take direction from an external history, with each then within the uneasy grasp of the other. Attempts have been made from both sides to compress one of these into the other, to act as though the other did not exist, or if it existed, as though it did not matter. Both of these impulses thus meet continuing opposition; for neither, whether singly or together, as Saul Friedländer notes, has a single narrative yet become "Master." The effort in respect to German history to vanquish memory through history has been impaled on the two horns of a dilemma: either to normalize the Holocaust so that it becomes one element in an indistinguishable sequence of complex events in the history of a modern state—or to view it as an ahistorical aberration (a fit of insanity) within that history. For Jewish history, the impasse has come from the other direction—in the conflicting impulses to subordinate history to memory, placing the Holocaust in a collectivized ritual of catastrophe which now, in the post-Holocaust, discloses the continuity of that "lachrymose" past which began with the destruction of the first Temple—*or* to join this one conglomerate and doleful memory with a second triumphal one (the establishment of the State of Israel) in respect to which it is associated by more than only historical contiguity.

The proportions of the latter two events by themselves would ensure that their consequences would stand first as memory—backward and forward, but in any case as internal, shaping contemporary Jewish identity. Conjoined, their effect in memory (and then in commemoration, and then still later as history) has been overpowering. So the narratives in which they appear as joined reinforce each other, impelling each other forward in a combination of memory and social identity—attached to the Zionist theme of a consummation which, despite (in part, because of) the Holocaust's enormity, contributed to the creation of a Jewish state; turned (and not only in religious sources) to an older, more sustained memory of exile and suffering in anticipation of an ultimate redemption. In this connection, memory has the advantage over history of repetition forward as well as backward.

That there are such different complementary effects in history and memory does not prove that the two are joined; neither one of them wills accommodation with the other, and for individuals and nations alike, one or the other may at times be successfully repressed or ignored—especially, it should be noted, as individuals or nations look to the future and such metaphysical notions as "destiny" (where there is no practical difference between "manifest" and "latent"). At any rate, the issue between history and memory is not simply a matter of choice. The writers of Germany history have already had an effect on German collective memory; for many of those authors, this is a central purpose. And the efforts at what has come to be called "post-Zionist" history are in their turn surely intended as instances of what Foucault termed "counter-memory"—moved by their intention to demythologize the past, thus to disrupt the contours of both particular memories and the more general, naturalizing effects of memory as such.

To be sure, the "future of the Holocaust" does not depend exclusively on the shapes assumed by German history or Jewish memory or on the relationship between them—*or* by the countervailing forces of German memory or Jewish history. There is after all, Western or World History of which both German and Jewish history have been part—albeit a smaller part than either may recognize. There is, furthermore, an emergent collective memory with expanding boundaries. One example of this is the way that the two "World Wars" (with the Holocaust as part of one of them) have come to be conflated under unifying categories like "industrialized killing" or the rise of totalitarianism. Also from these conceptual shifts, then, the future of the Holocaust has been affected by the erosive effects of temporality in terms of both history and memory: in respect to history, as the framework it provides has the result of lengthening the whole, in respect to memory as the motivation by which it calls up specific moments has the effect not of expansion but compression. These contrasting impulses are nonetheless intrinsic and complementary—nature's own "last word" impressed on history and memory alike.

The phrase, the "future of the Holocaust," is offensive even as a manner of speaking: offensive to memory as it suggests the likelihood of change—including, as soon as one thinks in such terms, also revision and forgetfulness; and perhaps even more fundamentally, as it implies that what appears still as an unforgivable enormity must nonetheless, as the future acts on it, take its historical chances, inviting oblique rather than direct glances, diminished in the role of its historical efficacy, and in any event underscoring the fact of its historical contingency. The phrase may thus seem an affront also in its implication of the provisional nature of even the most comprehensive and dispassionate historical accounts, reminding their authors and readers that they too are in the hands of history, not the other way round. And then, too, there is a still deeper offense in reference to the future at all—since admitting the legitimacy of a question that asks what future there is for the Holocaust, and so whether it *has* one, may seem to allow for challenge to the fact of its occurrence. Wherever we mark the line between history and memory in respect to that event, however, the line itself stands also as emblematic of their meeting. Even if we are at times troubled by a "surfeit" here (perhaps on both sides), that too would occur only insofar as we find ourselves at once outside and inside each of them. And who, after all, would not wish to have had less cause for either the history *or* the memory of the Holocaust? But who now, taking or giving account of that event, would deny the necessity of both?

I

THE HOLOCAUST INSIDE AND OUTSIDE HISTORY

1

Degrees of Genocide—and Evil

The term *genocide* has become so much a part of our moral vocabulary, so commonly attributed and bearing such weight that we might well wonder what served in its place before it was coined by Rafael Lemkin in his 1944 book, *Axis Rule in Occupied Europe*. Was the moral or political universe *so* different before that moment? To be sure, that a name is invented at a certain time does not mean that what it designates did not exist before. Lemkin believed that the act of genocide had ancient precedents in addition to the Nazi genocide in which he and his family were immediately caught up and which he himself had predicted even earlier.

The question of the history of genocide continues to provoke discussion, especially in relation to the claims about the Nazi genocide as unprecedented or unique (which I discuss in Chapter 5). That historical and empirical question warrants continued analysis, but whatever view one holds of it, there can be little disagreement about the emotive connotation that the charge of genocide has acquired in the fifty years of its history—with the implication unmistakable now of sustained destruction in the act's consequences and of extraordinary malevolence in its agents and their intentions. Even the word's sometimes indiscriminate application to events that hardly warrant it reflects this impulse to extremity. Genocide has plainly become the most serious charge in the world's moral vocabulary; it is as close to being a curse as an ostensibly descriptive term can be.

One reason for the force now associated with the term is probably to be found in the etymological connotation in the Greek *genos* (in *geno*cide) of a *natural* group or tribe. For although the charge of genocide, in its current usage, is not restricted to attacks on groups distinguished in or by nature, a primary association persists in the concept of genocide of the attempt to destroy a group or groups that span generations and that thus include all their members, from the aged to infants and then extending with the same deliberation to generations yet unborn. Genocide thus attacks group members who could not be responsible for the identity ascribed to them as well as those who are quite incapable of acting on that, or any, assertion of identity. In contrast to even wanton or mass murder, it denies in principle any exception to its aim of destruction.

A second factor in this connotation is the effect of genocide in destroying the *genos*, or group, apart from as well as in its members—first recognizing the group as an entity (whether natural or social) and then acting against it. The revulsion to this aspect of genocide amounts to more than the analogous, possibly related reaction against the extinction of biological species because the destruction of a human group qua group attacks the grounds of its members' identities beyond their individual histories. In this sense, genocide involves a twofold killing: once at the physical level of individual or "mere" nature and then again in the destruction of a "second nature," the constructed social or collective identity that is no less integral to human existence than the biological self it joins. The tradition of political liberalism has relied heavily on the doctrine of natural rights, according to which "inalienable" rights (such as life or liberty in the U.S. Declaration of Independence) are located in the individual. Without judging the question that this doctrine typically begs of whether the human self is intrinsically individual or private rather than social, I suggest that the intensity conveyed with the charge of genocide implies the existence of something like a group "right" which genocide transgresses—and which in this sense appears to be as natural or fundamental as the more often privileged individual rights. (The justification for *any* right claimed as "natural" faces serious theoretical difficulties; my point here is that the concept of group rights is at no greater disadvantage in respect to those difficulties than is the concept of individual rights.)

Added to the evidence of the historical occurrence of genocide, these aspects of its conceptualization point to wrongdoing or evil as having as much claim to a developmental history as its more often cited counterpart in moral enlightenment. Unlikely as it sounds, we discern here historical "progress" in both these contradictory directions at once, each of them the product of imaginative innovation and moral (more precisely, on its second side, immoral) design. If, as is often argued in evidence of moral progress, cultural attitudes toward slavery have since its classical and biblical apologetics progressively moved against that practice, the increasing occurrence and inventiveness of genocide seem undeniable on the other side. As the first individual murder—emblematically, Cain's attack on Abel—was one decisive moment in the history of wrongdoing, so the event and still more, the idea of the murder of a group as a group marks another, more "advanced" stage.

The latter claim, however, underscores a problem that confronts all efforts to quantify moral actions or qualities. By what measure can any one instance of such action be judged more heinous—"wronger"—than another? For even on the assumption that acts causing the loss of life differ qualitatively from other, more retrievable acts—and even here, of course, quantitative distinctions are not irrelevant—the question of how to draw distinctions within that first group seems intractable. Evidently, atrocities vary in their mechanisms as they do in their extent; but on what grounds can we distinguish them by degrees of moral enormity when it is precisely the common feature of this enormity that marks them in the first place? And thus, too, for the main issue posed here: Is there any way that is not either self-defeating or morally offensive to distinguish degrees of genocide—any way that does not lead directly to competing claims of victimization and the political arguments invariably associated with those claims? Even if one does arrive at some such plausible distinctions, the question often directed against the claim of Holocaust-uniqueness recurs here as well. Just as we ask what difference the Uniqueness-Claim would make even if it were true, so we might consider what purpose could be served in understanding the phenomenon of genocide by drawing distinctions among its degrees or kinds.

For the victims of murder, in the most obvious sense, its consequences are as one; differences of degree or kind—or motive or even means—change nothing in their fate. Still more basically, to suppose that the judgment of murder (or genocide) can be computed by comparing the numbers of victims or the motives of perpetrators exacts a heavy moral price of its own. More than only judicious detachment is required to measure the value of one life (or one million lives) as something like, or exactly, *half* that of two (or two million). The definition of genocide itself has not been and should not be based on the number of victims alone—even if, on the other side of this plain truth, there seems an equally plain one that would say that of course there is a difference between genocide (or any act) directed against a group numbered in the ten's and an act that affects a group numbered in the millions. (There is no conceptual reason, in any event, why the smaller group should not constitute a *genos* or why a very large group—for example, the inhabitants of a single large city—should; this contrast points to the difference between genocide and mass murder.)

Differences in degree, kind, and culpability, however, are constantly asserted in characterizing acts of murder, not only for legal verdicts but also for the moral judgments that invariably underlie such verdicts and the legislation on which they are based. Types of individual murder are distinguished by degrees, which range from acting with premeditation or "malice aforethought" through lesser orders and then move on to other, related categories such as manslaughter or criminal negligence. The moral differences behind these legal distinctions measure, on the one hand, the degree of responsibility or culpability in the agent and, on the other hand, the physical, and to some extent the moral, injury suffered by the victims; both of these are distinguishable from if not entirely independent of the fact that, where deaths are involved, the material outcome is identical. If we ask why legal systems prescribe such distinctions—quantifying values that from a moral perspective seem unquantifiable—the most obvious explanation adduces still other moral grounds; namely, that the consequences of not doing so are even more objectionable: this omission would then equate all instances of wrongdoing, irrespective of motive, deliberation, or means. This view is, we recognize, the intent of Draconian justice—which is problematic exactly because it refuses to acknowledge differences either in the scope of consequences or in the measure of intention, thus punishing all violations with equal severity just because of their common status *as* violations of the law. Even the biblical commandments which come—all of them—with divine authority, are viewed as nonetheless standing in a hierarchical order; violating different commandments incurs correspondingly different measures or types of punishment.

Even if one grants an analogy in these terms between individual murder and genocide, however, the practical objection can still be raised that the prosecution of genocide as a crime requires, in practical terms, not only a national but also an international juridical system and code of law. Because genocide remains beyond the reach of all such systems, except in the most rudimentary and makeshift form, the effort to analyze its varieties may be worse than useless insofar as it suggests the impossibility of punishing or finding a remedy for that violation. (The current effort to establish an international court and body of law with authority to address and judge the crime of genocide is a brave attempt to remedy the practical impediments to such a process; the United States' refusal to sign the international agreement—one of the few countries to do so–suggests the difficulties that even its signatories would be likely to raise in its enforcement.) But the counterargument to this objection turns its own terms against itself: precisely because the magnitude and indistinctness of genocide has been a factor in hindering the formulation of international law, that goal will be reached, if it is at all, only by drawing tangible and verifiable distinctions among its kinds or degrees. As in the development of all legislation, furthermore, the effect of such analysis and of the legislation itself will almost certainly have implications for possible measures of prevention.

Thus, for the term genocide to be more than an all-purpose metaphor for heinous wrongdoing will require an effort to distinguish among its degrees—even if those distinctions too must set out from its initial, common, and indisputably vague definition. The U.N. Convention on Genocide, adopted by the General Assembly in 1948, remains notably imprecise (and heavily qualified with conditions attached to it by almost all of its signatories) on certain crucial issues, but it remains the basic document from which subsequent analysis still sets out. That convention defines genocide in terms of two principal modalities: by specifying the types of *group* subject to genocide and by distinguishing the types of *action* directed against those groups that would violate the law. The types of group cited by the convention include "national, ethnical, racial, or religious" groups (not political groups, which were excluded—on political grounds—after intense debate at the U.N.). Among the six acts that count as genocidal under the U.N. definition are killing itself, causing serious bodily or mental harm, inflicting conditions of life calculated to bring about its destruction, imposing measures intended to prevent births, and the forcible transfer of children from the group. This second modality is further qualified (and confused) by stipulations that the actions cited may be directed against the group that is attacked "in whole or in part"; furthermore, the actions taken must be explicitly intended as genocidal.

I mention here only certain questions evoked by the first of these modalities, for example, the issues of whether a minimum number of members is required for the definition of a group, whether the ascription of group identity must be made by group members as well as externally by their persecutors, and how certain marginal instances of group identity (for example, familial ties or voluntary social or professional organizations) are to be judged. These considerations bear on the distinction among degrees of genocide as well as on the concept of genocide itself—as in the difference between the self-ascription of identity and the imposition of that identity by others. It is, however, more directly in the distinction among features of the acts of genocide that the most serious differences among degrees become evident. I propose three examples that indicate how the conceptualization of genocide by degrees articulates certain individual occurrences of genocide which otherwise might not be noted at all; they thus conduce to a more systematic account of the phenomenon.

The U.N. Convention stipulates that for an act to be judged genocidal, it must have been committed with the *intention* of committing genocide.

Clearly, proof of premeditation, in genocide as for any other wrongful act, would indeed, prima facie, add to the weight of judgment against it. Historical examples have also occurred, however, in which groups or populaces have been annihilated not as the result of an explicit prior design but by a coincidental if not arbitrary combination of independent factors that reinforce each other. (These then may combine with negligence or denial on the part of their agents even after the consequences begin to become evident; the latter feature, however, although relevant, remains ancillary). This seems to have been the pattern, for example, in the destruction of the indigenous South American population after the Spanish conquest, where, in something more than a hundred-year period, an estimated 90 percent of the populace (on the order of forty million) died as the result of a combination of disease introduced from abroad (mainly smallpox), economic deprivation, and direct attack. The combined result of these factors, then — even if we acknowledge the absence of a prior, overall design — was the virtual annihilation of a group, which qualifies under the U.N. definition. That effect, moreover, came to be known at the time at least in broad outline, but this awareness did nothing (or very little) to alter the conduct of those responsible for the policies that led to those consequences. It may seem offensive, on this basis, to reduce the charges against the perpetrators here to a lesser count such as criminal negligence, and at some point (here as elsewhere) negligence itself may be judged to be, in some sense, deliberate or premeditated. It also seems clear, though, that at certain points in this process and for some of the agents responsible for it, unintentional genocide or genocide by negligence (the group equivalent of individual manslaughter) would be a pertinent category — and a serious one, because it is after all still the general charge of genocide that is being applied here. Not much comfort is gained in moral terms by the reduction in degree of such a charge. (It is worth noting that the "Functionalist" analysis of the Nazis' "Final Solution," which took up one side of the "Historikerstreit"—to be considered in Chapter 4—proposed a version of the causal origins of the Nazi genocide based almost exactly on such "unintentional" terms.)

A second distinction in degree that the U.N. Convention on Genocide avoids is the relation between physical and cultural destruction (although this issue is explicitly raised in the two U.N. conventions, on Human Rights and on Minority Rights, respectively). To be sure, although physical destruction implies cultural destruction, the converse does not hold. Insofar as its culture defines the life of a group, however, there seem to be at least as compelling reasons for including ethnocide as a variety of genocide as there are for establishing it as an independent category, with the implication that it is different in kind from genocide. The difference between physical and cultural destruction is clear; but also the latter—implemented, for example, by bans on language, education, or religious practice, and, more extremely, by the forced dispersion of a populace among an alien host—is calculated to bring about the end of group identity and so of its existence. Numerous historical instances can be cited in which members of one religious group have been forced to choose between conversion to another religion and death. It is clearly the case, furthermore, that the threat of death is tacitly present in the background of much if not all ethnocide (as in the dispersion through "relocation" of ethnic groups, such as the Chechens and the Balkars under the Stalin regime in the USSR); this would be an additional reason for including it under the rubric of genocide. (The inclusion in the U.N. Convention on Genocide of the "forcible transfer of children" as indeed an instance of genocide comes close to making this connection, but the convention stops short of detailing the elements of group social identity as such.) To be sure, the differences among levels at which ethnic repression may be applied—ranging from prohibitions against using ethnic names or against speaking a particular language to quotas of exclusion in employment or educational institutions to "forcible transfer"—will make it difficult to judge when the line of ethnocide has been crossed. As for any other objection that turns to the "slippery slope" argument for support, the fact that certain instances of ethnocide are beyond doubt is all that would be required for its characterization as a category of genocide. Some cases may occur that are difficult to decide on the basis of the applicable norms or laws, but this is a common difficulty, after all, of much legal reasoning.

A third example of the applicability of degrees and kinds: For most instances of genocide that have been alleged or conceived as possible, the group attacked is identified with a specific geographical area. Often this limitation has been tacit or presumptive, reflecting a lack of mobility in the group threatened or the inability of their attackers to pursue them beyond the attackers' own borders. Whatever the practical reasons, however, a difference in principle exists between the intention to destroy a group within a defined area and the intention to destroy it irrespective of where its members may be—the intention asserted, for example, in the 1943 Poznan speech by Himmler, mentioned earlier, to make the Jews "disappear from the earth"; that is, not out of this or that place, but out of existence. This declaration of intent proved to be no mere figure of speech, and its literal force (not Himmler's alone, after all) argues for another distinction within the general range of genocide: between allowing at least the possibility of continued group existence, even if it is relegated to an actual or even prospective "elsewhere," and explicitly precluding that possibility. It may well be that the latter extreme position of intending not only local but universal annihilation would have been made part of other genocidal efforts if that course of action had been conceived as possible, but it was not. The combination first of envisaging the possibility and then of attempting to make it actual, as the Nazis did in the "Final Solution," makes an obvious difference in the character of the intention itself: the difference between the denial of existence as such and the denial of existence only in a specific place. In this example as well, distinctions of degree are relevant, even within the single category of premeditated or intentional acts.

This brief outline does not propose a specific order for the differences or degrees of genocide; my immediate concern is to show how (and that) distinctions of this sort advance the analysis of genocide in respect to understanding its historical occurrence and character and to the moral assessment we are required to make of it. The drawing and application of such distinctions is obviously a macabre exercise; it is also open to abuse and misapplication, and not least of all to special pleading. Furthermore, it invites disturbing arguments that are impossible to settle about which historical and collective wrongs are greater or lesser or which groups have suffered more or less than others—distinctions that are always invidious and almost always tendentious. But to infer from these objections that all such comparisons are impossible or improper is also to refuse to acknowledge in genocide what is recognized as commonplace and essential in the analysis of other crimes (namely, differences of degree or kind). The consequence is to conflate acts of disparate sorts in a way that, without in the least mitigating their heinousness, adds the liability of historical and moral obscurantism and, in the end, misrepresentation. It would furthermore impede efforts to discover in the history of genocide those causal connections or sources that might be used in identifying "early warning" indicators of genocide and thus of proposing measures that might be effective in preventing its occurrence; both of these areas are the subjects of numerous recent analyses of genocide. What originates in an effort to draw moral distinctions for the sake of illuminating judgment and understanding might thus, carried forward, help to avert the very events that impel the distinctions in the first place.

To be sure, reaching agreement on the value of distinguishing degrees of genocide (and on a specific order of its kinds) would not establish how distinctions or comparisons are to be made in *moral* terms. Does the specific number of lives destroyed make no difference in judging the acts or the agents responsible? Is there no moral difference between mass murder and genocide even if the same number of deaths were caused by each of them? If the value of a single human life has no calculable material equivalent, then what is the moral difference between that and the destruction of many, even millions of lives?

It seems clear that distinct conceptual issues are implicated in these questions, and although the problem of "degrees of evil"—in contrast to "degrees of genocide"—may remain intractable even when the two problems are held apart from each other, no resolution of such questions would be possible without the distinction itself. Lurking behind all the questions is the traditional theological and metaphysical "problem of evil"—and the special weight (allegedly) given that problem by the enormity of an event such as the Holocaust. How, in a divinely ordered world—whether governed by an omnipotent and beneficent God or by a principle of goodness that, in the Platonic tradition, serves the same function—could evil on the scale of this event occur? How would it be—is it—possible?

But at least one part of the response to this formulation seems clear and unequivocal: far from resolving or being resolved by any traditional answers to the "problem of evil," the Holocaust changes nothing in the force (or weakness) of the issues that underlie this problem. For it is the possibility of evil in its merest form that first raises the problem for theological or metaphysical conceptions of a benevolent God. Large-scale evil such as the Holocaust, in other words, is no more problematic in theological or metaphysical terms than its slightest instance; genocide, no more an issue—in Dostoyevsky's example—than the single tear of an innocent child. If we find a justification for the latter, other, much "larger" manifestations of evil may be justified as well—and unless we find a justification for the slightest instance, we will not be able to find a justification for any other. The tradition of theodicy, originating in biblical principles and elaborated in its philosophical exposition by figures ranging from Plato to Leibniz, faces this "problem" squarely. For them, the quotations marks are necessary to identify its provisional character: there is no justification at either the slightest or the weightiest levels of wrongdoing or evil because, quite simply, there is nothing to justify: God and/or Reason have seen to that. In the universe so constituted, evil is not a positive presence at all, but only an indicator of absence or privation; its "occurrences," then, are only apparent and thus also, as they are called evil, misrepresented: evil has no positive existence, and therefore the question of comparison or degrees of evil is moot. There is nothing to compare—even between the single tear of a child and the Holocaust.

This conclusion, which asserts that even an occurrence such as genocide has a rightful place in the larger scheme of things, is a harsh "truth" for its proponents to live with; certainly it poses a severe test for theodicy and thus for any authentic or searching expression of faith, whether turned to traditional religious sources or to the like-minded optimism of philosophical rationalism. Religious thinkers who are committed to the principle of an omnipotent and beneficent God have recognized the difficulty in this, although they have not always been willing to confront it directly. Indeed, among the writings that address the Holocaust in religious terms, the proportionately smallest number come from the most orthodox or fundamentalist sources (of whatever denomination). The same difficulty presumably also explains why many putatively religious narratives drawn from various histories of atrocity, including the "Final Solution," emphasize miracles of rescue and survival—notwithstanding the irony that such emphasis implicitly calls attention to the much greater number of occasions on which miracles did not occur, as well as to the still more fundamental question of how, in the first place, the circumstances that required such "miracles" could be explained or justified.

Understandably, wanton or (still more) intended suffering and destruction such as that evident in the Nazi genocide underscores the problem of evil for religious belief, at times leading to its breakdown. Examples of this are known from the Holocaust, as are also examples of commitment that withstood the challenge. For the heroic rescuers among the "bystanders," as well as for certain heroic figures in the Jewish community, religious commitment sometimes motivated them, sometimes not; a similar diversity held also among the perpetrators, although it was, after all, an ostensibly Christian Europe in which the Holocaust occurred. If few theological accounts have been directed to explaining the latter connection, there have been even fewer sociohistorical accounts. This absence is, if anything, more significant than the first.

But this denial of the status of evil in terms of degrees—the denial of the latter as analytically relevant—is only one among a number of both conceptual and practical distinctions bearing on the phenomenon of evil that need to be borne in mind. A further distinction is required between judging the agent and judging the consequences of his (or their) actions. If moral evaluation takes only the latter into account—as in the varieties of Utilitarianism or "consequentialism"—the possibility of a computational model becomes inevitable; the comparison of acts of wrongdoing would then liken them by a calculus of numerical terms (two lives versus one, two million versus one million, and so on). This is not the place to argue about the general problems raised by this position, but the objections to the Utilitarian view when consistently maintained as the single determinant of moral judgment are overwhelming (and became evident early to John Stuart Mill, leading to his revision of Bentham's formulation of the doctrine).

On the other hand, the opposite extreme, as in Kant's emphasis not on consequences but on the intention of the moral agent, faces an analogous criticism of the danger of reductionism. To will to violate the moral law (assuming that this can be determined apart from the act) is not—except by stipulation—identical with the violation itself—and surely it stretches common understanding to equate all such violations (or intentions), to regard each instance of "contradiction" of the Categorical Imperative as equal to every other. Here in fact the legal codes serve as a useful corrective to moral fundamentalism. For as in most legal codes, distinctions are drawn on the basis of a combination of harm done (consequences) *and* the role of intention or deliberation, so it also seems that moral judgment, answering both to weight of experience and the need for sustaining social structures, will involve distinctions based on a similar combination of circumstances. The difference between premeditated and accidental wrongdoing is a moral as well as a legal one, as is the difference between large-scale and individual murder. The phrase "crimes against humanity," introduced in the Nuremberg trials primarily in response to the Nazi genocide, was criticized then as ad hoc and vague; it is no longer ad hoc, although it remains, and will almost certainly continue to be, imprecisely defined. But that there are and have been such crimes and that they differ in quality from individual wrongdoing, no matter how malevolent and cruel, seems indisputable. The Nazi genocide of the Jews demonstrates this difference, and although our recognition of this differentiation does not settle the question of where the lines can be drawn among instances or kinds or degrees of moral culpability, it provides all the evidence that might be required about the need for making, and then applying, such distinctions.

2

The Progress of Evil:
The Past and Future of the Holocaust

True lastingness is constantly in the future.
—Franz Rosenzweig

Since efforts are still needed to describe for the present the events of the Nazi genocide of the Jews, it may seem premature and even offensive to ask about the future of those events—as if they might later be assessed quite differently from the way they are now or even that they might more simply be erased. But as soon as such possibilities are considered, the importance of raising the question of "the future of the Holocaust" becomes clear. One consequence impelled by this prospect bears on the Nazi genocide considered on its own terms—that is, for the detailed reconstruction of those events and of the contemporary responses to them. This task is most immediately historical in character; it falls not only on the social, political, and economic historians who are central to such efforts, but also on the social scientist and the literary and cultural critics, all of whose works contribute to describing the events of the genocide as it occurred and the roles assumed by or imposed on its agents, victims, and bystanders.

This form of historical address has been taken up by many writers and commentators, and I mention it here only to suggest the importance of a projection into the future even for such accounts that focus designedly on the past. I mean to assert more by this suggestion than the general histiographic principle that requires for historical discourse, together with the assembling of data, also is an act of imagination into the *historian's* future—a projection that is required, after all, wherever evidence is interpreted (that is, wherever it is found to disclose a pattern in the causal structure). I mean rather to emphasize that even for present consideration of the Nazi genocide, certain versions of its future are already clear; anticipation of these alternatives as future bears also on the present analysis of the genocide, which in a different, all-too-obvious sense is past and concluded.

To be sure, new information about the Nazi genocide will undoubtedly continue to be gathered. Future accounts, however, are unlikely to be affected in any radical way by such additions—in part because the single factor least likely to be changed by new findings is also the weightiest one, that is, the "disappearance" of between five and six million European Jews and in part because the pattern of future alternatives reflects logical as well as historical distinctions that are already visible. The pattern available to historiography in this convergence of historical and logical alternatives is clear: in the view from the future, the occurrence of the Nazi genocide will be affirmed, or it will be denied, or—between those possibilities—it will be reconceived in a way that defines a middle ground between the two.

There is, to be sure, nothing startling in this statement of alternatives (although this, too, attests to our familiarity with the alternatives as actual): affirmation, in institutions ranging from historical scholarship and artistic expression to the openly rhetorical forms of social incorporation in monuments and museums; denial, in the extreme form of exclusion, but also, more noncommittally, by those people who remain or who will be unknowing of its occurrence (the reference to "Holocaust" in E. D. Hirsch's itemization of knowledge required for "cultural literacy"—it appears there between "Sherlock Holmes" and "The Holy Grail"—vividly displays this precariousness);[1] and then the reconceptualization, in the revisionist forms that press in from each of the two sides—from the side of denial, as the genocide is represented as a (perhaps) regrettable but in any event justifiable act of self-defense and from the side of affirmation in the view, for example, that the Jews were somehow the causal agents as well as victims in the genocide—that to a greater or lesser degree they brought their fate on themselves.[2]

What difference does it make to see these alternatives, already active in the present, as projected into the future? In one sense, this recommenda-

---

[1] E. D. Hirsch, *The Dictionary of Cultural Literacy* (Boston: Houghton Mifflin, 1993).

[2] For an account of the former of these "revisionist" efforts, see the exchange between Martin Brozsat and Saul Friedländer, "A Controvery about the Historicization of National Socialism," *New German Critique* 44 (1988), 81–126. The second, very different group of writers, who in varying degrees inculpate the Jews in their own destruction, come from varied ideological and historiographic directions, including not only Hannah Arendt's extravagant claims in *Eichmann in Jerusalem* (New York: Penguin, 1980), but also Raul Hilberg's conception of "anticipatory compliance" in his classic, *The Destruction of the European Jews* (New York: Holmes & Meier, 1985).

tion amounts to a variation on Kant's categorical imperative directed now at the historian: write the historical account of the Nazi genocide, this maxim directs, as though you were legislating every future view of its subject. Even this near-truism, however, might have consequences that are less than obvious. It has passed unnoted or at least undisputed, for example, that the reliance in contemporary forms of discourse (including history) on the experimental method of science, with the latter's expectation of future revisions, has substantive and not only rhetorical implications for the way in which what is written is formulated. Even the most dogmatic or ideologically motivated writings have come to reflect this expectation; the results are evident in all the academic or scholarly disciplines that have taken scientific discourse as their model—that is, in all the disciplines.

There is also, however, a subtler implication of the projection into the future that bears on representations of the Nazi genocide—and this is as a reminder that the events thus represented were indeed, fundamentally, historical. To envisage them in the present from the point of view of the future makes it more difficult to conceive those events in their own time as not having posed a question to the future. It underscores, in other words, their status as contingent rather than necessary, involving factors that may be too extensive to enumerate but not too extensive to conceive and which thus include the element of human agency with its accompanying implication of individual and/or corporate responsibility. It is not that this historical factor would otherwise be indiscernible, but that to view the events from the perspective of the future underscores the role of contingency, which, because of the pressure of "hard" facts, is often elided, if not simply denied, in historical writing—in writing about the Nazi genocide hardly less than elsewhere.

To be sure, anomalous events may occur historically as they do biologically; furthermore, many historians of the Nazi genocide already avoid claims of its "uniqueness" or the related assertion of its "incomprehensibility" on the ground that such claims have the effect, whether intended or not, of distancing the occurrence of the genocide from history altogether. The importance of addressing the events of the Nazi genocide as historical, however, with the justification for this not only in its material causes but also in its superstructure—in the language it created and employed and in its moral and ideological conceptualization—warrants continued emphasis because of the danger of the alternative. In this sense, such emphasis outweighs even the danger that with historicization the Nazi genocide may come to seem so normalized, so thinly dispersed in the *alltäglich* world, that any attempt to distinguish it as having unusual historical importance is open to question as a matter of principle as well as of fact.

What this proposal comes to in practice is this: from the point of view of the future—on a modal conception of history that includes possibility and contingency as categories—the work of the historian in detailing the events of the Nazi genocide is itself contingent, with the historian, through his or her writing, present now as agent. The historian is in this sense responsible for his or her historical representation—a claim that would convey only a verbal platitude and indifferent moral weight if not for the fact that it links the writers of history to the ascription of responsibility *within* the events about which they writes. Insofar as the events of the genocide are now known largely through the accounts provided by historians, with the factor of contingency evident both in those representations and in the events represented, the historian shares in the responsibility found (or denied) there. From the standpoint of the historians, this becomes a condition of their own future, now joined to the future of the events that are their subject.

A second, more specific reason for considering the future of the Nazi genocide as a means of facing it in the present is that the turn in this direction poses unavoidably the question of *which* history (or histories) the Nazi genocide is to be viewed as a part. Formulated in this way, the question suggests an intrinsic perspectivalism for the writing of history ("which history?" or even "whose history?"); and at the level of practice, this conception of historiography as characteristically pluralistic seems unexceptionable. Without judging whether history can ever claim more than this (for example, as intending history "in itself"), and even admitting the approximate boundaries of "particular" histories, it is evident that distinctions among such particular histories are commonly assumed. The place of the Nazi genocide in the context of Jewish history differs in its proportions (not necessarily as incompatible—although that too is a possibility—but as different) from its representation in a history of Germany or in a history of Russia and still more, and more obviously, from that in a history of Madagascar. The literary categories of implied author or authorial point of view make a scholarly difference in these instances; this difference is further accentuated in historical accounts of the Nazi genocide that embed it not in national or ethnic frameworks, but in contexts defined topically or conceptually, for example, in the histories of rhetoric or of socialism or of demography—in all of which the Nazi genocide also warrants a place.

The means for identifying such particular histories are not a priori or fixed, but the conventions they depend on are substantial enough to indicate that they are not arbitrary. I propose here to relate the events of the Nazi genocide to another of these histories, which is in certain respects more problematic than the ones mentioned, but whose subject has arguably been more constant and consequential a presence than anything the other histories have been histories "of." This is the history of moral judgment and conduct—more restrictively, the side of that history that I would represent as the history of evil. It is in relation to the latter history, I suggest, that a view of the future of the Holocaust becomes more portentous for its—and our—present.

This formulation may seem to have skipped ahead of the argument by several steps, and these need to be mentioned, at least to the extent that they presuppose a concept of evil itself. Without claiming this definition as adequate, I suppose here a "minimalist" conception of evil in which harm is done to a person or group deliberately and without putative justification (or with the justification for it incommensurate with the outcome)—that is, with either the consciousness of it as a wrong or with the capacity, and so the responsibility, for achieving that consciousness. Without distinguishing specific measures of responsibility, furthermore, I assume that this general conception of evil applies both to the corporate "act" and to individual agents of the Nazi genocide. Notwithstanding disagreements about the status of the intentions or of the deliberation involved in that genocide, some acknowledgment of their relevance is admitted in all but the extreme accounts that deny its occurrence altogether. For purposes of this discussion, even a minimal acknowledgment of this relevance provides a basis for relating the two phrases that are joined together in this chapter's title.

The effort to link the question "What is the future of the Holocaust?" to the history of evil encounters difficulties in explaining the second part of that conjunction as well as the first. For it is by no means obvious that there *is* a history of evil—and some evidence argues to the contrary. One item of prima facie evidence for the latter view is especially notable here: no histories of the phenomenon of evil, in point of fact, have been written—not of evil as historical idea or as practice, not in terms of its evolution or development, not even in the simplest form of chronicle. In contrast to specific institutions such as slavery, warfare, and means of punishment and in contrast to such related (inverse) ideals as natural rights, freedom, or even love, all of which have been recognized as "having" histories or as being part of other histories, evil has not been viewed as a historical phenomenon at all.

This absence or omission, again, is no more than prima facie evidence: that no history of evil has been written does not prove that there is no such history to be written. But the explanation of this absence must at least consider the requirements that must be met for something to "have" a history, and also the way in which evil (allegedly) fails to meet them. There are, it seems to me, two principal reasons why evil has not been conceived historically—why philosophers, theologians, and imaginative writers (as well as historians "proper") have regarded it as one of the small class of phenomena for which any representation as historical is so improbable as to deter even the attempt. These reasons are at once conceptual and moral; they correspond, in fact, to the two principal theories of moral evaluation in the history of ethics: moral judgment as determined by the intentions of the agent and moral judgment as determined by the consequences of an act.

In the conception of history implied by intentionalist theories, the conditions for evildoing are fully—and finally—realized in its first occurrence. From the standpoint of intentions, how an act turns out does not matter morally; it is the will to do wrong or at least the will not to do what one is obligated to do that counts. In this sense, because the will as a faculty is all of one "kind," all evildoing is identical and thus complete. If the intention is present, the potentially large differences in consequence among particular acts do not enter in. To be sure, varied accounts are given of exactly what such a widespread common intention would be; these range from the claim of an innate human impulse to one of a deliberate (but still common) project of the imagination. Overriding such differences in content, however, is the view of evildoing in each occurrence as the exemplification of an original form: desire, fear, or even idea. And in these terms, there is no reason to ascribe a history to evil, because evil is fully present whenever it appears, early or late, small or large.

The reference to such an "original" form is an obvious echo of the most radical version of this view—that of "original sin," as it prefigures all other wrongdoing. Even a less dramatic reading of "the Fall"—such as the account of the events in Eden given by the Jewish tradition—argues to this same effect. For on the latter reading, too, knowledge of good and evil comes to Adam and Eve at a moment; neither they nor their descendants have more to learn about *that*, the knowledge itself appearing as at once complete and irrevocable. Whatever else constitutes the moral knowledge thus acquired, two of its features are unmistakable: there is nothing to add to it, and there is no forgetting or escaping it.

It is not difficult to infer the motivation for this account in which history begins and ends in a single moment. Dominant in it are the issue of theodicy for the monotheistic traditions of religion and the analogous conflict between reason and wrongdoing for the rationalist tradition in philosophy: how to account for evil, given the existence (in the former) of a beneficent and omnipotent God and, in the latter, given a reality that is essentially rational. In the end, no resolution of the "problem" of evil (in effect, the pseudo-problem of evil) may be possible on either of these accounts, and the rationalist tradition is forthright in conceding this when (as in Plato, for example) it flatly denies the reality of evil altogether. Even when, in the biblical narrative, the existence of evil is acknowledged, moreover, its origin is traced to a single historical point—presumably on the grounds that the difficulty in explaining one moment would only be compounded if there were other ones that required explanation as well. This practical reason joins a second, more substantive assumption—that a single and common ground is decisive in all evildoing, namely, the intention or will to do it. Insofar as the latter serves as the necessary and sufficient condition for evildoing, the explanation it provides for any particular instance of evil applies in principle and equally to *all* its manifestations. In these terms a narrative detailing a number or even a typology of instances of wrongdoing would, nonetheless, be irrelevant as history, because the instances in that variety would disclose only incidental variations on a single–essential—theme.

The disposition of the second—utilitarian or consequentialist—argument against ascribing a history to evil is related to the first. To measure evildoing by its consequences requires an inclusive moral calculus into which any possible consequence can be translated. The difficulty of formulating a calculus both general and specific enough to cover the multiplicity of human actions has, however, proved formidable. One source of the difficulty, again, is itself a moral judgment. There is an obvious difference between an act that causes the destruction of one life and another that causes two deaths, a difference that becomes larger as the numbers increase. But some might nonetheless object that to measure degrees of evil by such numerical differences denies the absolute value ascribed to any single life and challenges the basis of value itself: is quantity to be the decisive feature in judging the "quality" of evil? Few utilitarians after Bentham have been willing to accept the implications of the latter claim; and the reluctance to do so has had the effect of flattening the dimensions necessary for a history of evil. Here, too, that potential history is undermined at its source.

These plausible reasons for denying the history of evil do not, however, outweigh other grounds for asserting such a history as real. It is these other grounds and the conceptual framework based on them that connect the "future of the Holocaust" to an understanding of the Holocaust in the present. This connection becomes apparent on both "external" and "internal" readings (and writings) of history.[3] In external history, the subject, judged from the outside to have a fixed identity or "self," appears in different historical settings which disclose that identity more fully. It is in this sense that evolutionary histories are written of biological organisms and that the histories of language or of medicine are also conceived.

---

[3] For the distinction between "external" and "internal" history, see R. G. Collingwood, *The Idea of History* (Oxford: Clarendon Press, 1946), pp. 213–215.

The last of these examples provides a useful analogue to the history of evil. The goal or "final cause" of medicine—the maintenance or recovery of health—is the center around which its history turns; the written history of medicine is then an external—metaphorically, a technological—rendering of the means devised over time to reach the end assumed in each of its moments. In the case of medicine, its history is often regarded as progressive (based, for example, on life expectancy). In other external histories—for example, the history of art or the history of biology—the possibility of a progressive ("whiggish") interpretation is itself a theoretical issue. Whether a particular external history is judged to be cumulative or not, however, the identity of the historical subject is presupposed, and the written account then details variations over time in its appearance and their connections to other histories.

Does evil have a history in this "external" sense? Admittedly, it is more difficult here than for other histories to identify individual events that serve as chronological markers (and thus as evidence that there *is* such a history). But for evil, too, individual factors are distinguishable within the concept of violation or transgression—in motivation, in the role of intention or premeditation, in the conceptualization of the victim; it is also possible to identify differences among these factors as they occur *historically*. Consider again the statement made about the Nazi genocide against the Jews by Himmler in the "secret" speech to the S.S. at Poznan in October 1943 which has already been referred to: "The hard decision had to be made that this people should be caused to disappear from the earth. . . . I myself believe that it is better for us—us together—to have borne this for our people, that we have taken the responsibility for it on ourselves (the responsibility for an act, not just an idea), and that we should now take this secret with us into the grave."[4]

On the face of it, this complex statement is dispassionate, reflective. According to it, the "Final Solution" was indeed intended as genocide—the disappearance of "this people." It was, moreover, intended selflessly, not for personal gain but as a matter of principle. The principle itself remains unstated in the immediate context, and Himmler acknowledges that in "act" and "idea," it may be so difficult for others to comprehend (even among his German compatriots) that it ought to remain a secret permanently—further evidence of the selflessness required. The totality of the "Final Solution," in other words, is meant to encompass the fact of the event itself.

---

[4] On this and the other Poznan speeches, see Bradley F. Smith, *Heinrich Himmler* (Stanford: Hoover Institution, 1971).

Comparisons are always to some extent tendentious. But it is not tendentiousness that distinguishes Himmler's words from, for example, the statements that Suetonius attributes to Caligula or to Nero, who stand out among the Twelve Caesars (and in history since) for their regimes of terror and brutality. Himmler's statement is a moral world apart from the latter, distinguished even in its own terms by its "principled" basis. It differs from the professions of Caligula or of Nero as much as does selflessness from egoism, as totality from partiality, as genocide from murder—even murder on a large scale.

I do not mean to suggest that the historical distance between these examples is impassable, that there are no later echoes of the chronologically earlier one or earlier anticipations of the later one. Obviously some cases even in antiquity, such as Cato's call for the destruction of Carthage, come close to the ethos expressed by Himmler. But for that, too, as more clearly in the other example, a significant difference in the imagination of evil is asserting itself. It is probably too extreme to claim that Himmler's statement *could* not have been uttered at the time of the Roman Caesars or of Cato, but a good measure of the difference between Himmler's intention and that of the others is indeed historical—a function of changes in the material context and also, more fundamentally, in the conceptualization of evil itself. That the difference has an authentic historical referent is further substantiated by the fact that the changes that thus appear are not only differences in the external sense of variations on a theme, but also are internal, as they reflect an intensification or fuller realization of their subject, that is, of evil. The debate continues today as to whether the Nazi genocide is indeed the first historical instance of genocide. It cannot be reasonably doubted, however, that the "Final Solution" was an instance of genocide—nor can it be doubted (and this is more important for the claim of a history of evil) that, as a phenomenon, genocide is a more dominant presence for social existence in the twentieth century than it has ever been before. In connection with this, Himmler's statement, however distinctive in its own context, also epitomizes a more general change.

A similar claim, although only indirectly related to Himmler's statement, applies to the phenomenon of torture, as that, too, stands as a representation of evil. Even allowing for both the increase in populations and the means of gathering and maintaining historical reports, the evidence suggests that the occurrence of torture in the twentieth century exceeds that in any previous historical period. There is probably no way to fully establish this comparison, but the implications of its claim gain in force when joined to the fact that what served earlier as a utilitarian "justification" for torture (i.e., the perceived need to obtain information) has been increasingly displaced in the twentieth century by the availability of new technology. In almost all circumstances now, drugs are capable of "extracting" desired information as certainly as any other means. The implication then of resorting to such other means as torture implies that something more than the obtaining of information is intended by its use.

Given such chronological differences, not only does evil appear then to "have" an external history—varying in its proportions over time—but a history that is arguably a progressivist one as well, in which the twentieth century has "advanced" over previous ones. In that "advance," marked in its most recent stage by the phenomenon of genocide and the persistence and spread—and gratuitousness—of torture, the "Final Solution" is a significant datum.

A second sense in which a subject might have a history is "internal"— where the subject has no fixed identity or essence, where its character changes and yet remains recognizable, and where the *process* of this development then defines the subject historically. The development involved here is much like that of a consciousness seen to deliberate on the future in light of its past, as in the historical genres of biography or autobiography. There is something problematic, to be sure, about citing a "consciousness" that impels historical events in which the agent is not a person, but also in these broader contexts, the metaphorical reference to an internal identity is often useful. To write English parliamentary history or the history of the American Civil War requires taking account of decisions made by individuals, and there is no need to posit a literal corporate consciousness to represent the sum of those decisions metaphorically. (An obvious danger—the more notable in respect to the Nazi genocide—lies in attributing a corporate essence to an historical subject (e.g., as in categories such as "French history" or "German history"). Individual agents who contribute to group decisions or acts introduce the element of contingency and with this the unfolding of corporate decisions similar to the history of a self. Like the latter, the former are at once contingent—not determined externally—and deliberate: effecting change in their own character without denying its identity. It is in these terms also that we speak of the history of artistic movements such as realism or romanticism, or of the history of ideologies such as marxism or liberalism.

And so, too, I argue, for the history of evil. Consider again the comparison cited earlier. The difference between the representation of the Nazi genocide in Himmler's statement and Suetonius's account of murder and torture under the Caesars is—the common horror notwithstanding—a world apart; it is much sharper, in any event, than the quantitative disparity between the two, although also that is evident. More fundamentally, the difference involves a reconceptualization of the subject itself—recognizable in the familiar distinction between extrinsic and intrinsic "goods" or purposes. For in Himmler's statement, and in the act of genocide it refers to, the goal intended is not designated as the means to another end, and still less as a matter of personal interest or desire—both of which dominated the acts of Nero and Caligula. In it, what is undertaken becomes a matter of principle, chosen deliberately not only to accomplish a particular end but also with an awareness of its quality *as* evil. Here evil, perversely, becomes part of the intrinsic "good"; in this sense, it resembles the ideal proclaimed by Milton's Satan, "Evil, Be thou my good!"—now expressed, however, by a human, not a mythical agent.

Admittedly, to demonstrate this distinction in terms of the Nazi genocide requires more evidence than is provided by the statement quoted from Himmler. Certainly, the opposing claim has often been made and could, in fact, draw on Himmler's speech itself: that the "Final Solution" was conceived by the Nazis instrumentally, for what they "perceived"—wrongly and criminally, but nonetheless "honestly"—as the means to another end, in the interests of the German people and, at a longer distance still, in the interests of mankind. On this account, the Nazis at least believed that the Jews were a threat, socially and racially; Nazi policies would then have been the means of averting this threat—a form of self-defense—which ought now to be judged with that mitigating consideration in mind.

Against this defense, the argument has to be made: that the Nazis often, even in their own terms, acted *against* instrumental considerations; that neither their campaign of extermination against the Jews nor the means employed is adequately explained on instrumental grounds alone, nor can their willingness to risk losing the more general war in order to carry on that campaign; that the imagination and will for evil that characterized the means used—the rarified intentions evident in such creations as orchestras in the death camps, the edifying slogans that were part of those camps (such as "*Arbeit macht frei*" at the entrance to Auschwitz), the imaginative means of degradation that invariably accompanied the act of extermination (what Primo Levi refers to as "useless violence")—are inexplicable on utilitarian grounds alone.[5] Perhaps most important among these considerations is the emphasis on secrecy that figures in Himmler's speech and that was a constant aspect of the "Final Solution"—in the "language rules" governing public and even private references to the genocide, and in the extraordinary ef-

---

[5] For an elaboration of this interpretation, see Berel Lang, *Act and Idea in the Nazi Genocide* (Chicago: University of Chicago Press, 1990), chap. 2; see also Ron Rosenbaum, *Explaining Hitler* (New York: Random House, 1998), pp. 208–215

forts to conceal or to destroy the evidence of its occurrence. This too might be explained on prudential or utilitarian grounds, but the same evidence could be construed as involuntary, in the form of shame, an awareness of the wrong being done and an incorporation of that wrongfulness then in the act itself.

It seems to me that the evidence for the latter contention is strong—sufficiently strong, in any event, to ensure that the claim for a conception of the evil at work here as based on "principle" becomes at least as plausible as the instrumental explanation that is more commonly given. And to take the matter even this far introduces a significant marker in the "internal" history of evil—where evil has moved from extrinsic or instrumental acts to acts undertaken in the name of principle, where a decision has been made for the practice of evil with the recognition that it is evil (not necessarily doing it *because* it is evil, although that also emerges here as a possibility). As with any historical shift, it is not necessary to demonstrate that this one came into existence fully formed or that there had been no earlier anticipations of it. It is enough to recognize that in the general historical context of occurrences of evil, the Nazi genocide epitomizes, if it does not disclose for the first time, a radical possibility that was, in its historical setting, so deliberate and deeply rooted that it cannot be written off or explained away as an aberration. It is better understood as evidence of the "achievement" of another stage—conceptually as well as chronologically—in the history of evil. The evidence that evil indeed has a history thus also provides a standard by which the particular events that constitute that history can be assessed.

EVEN if everything proposed so far were granted for the sake of argument, with the Nazi genocide viewed now from the standpoint of the future, in the context of a history of evil, the question would still persist of what difference this makes to an understanding of the Nazi genocide in the present. In one obvious sense, nothing in that event would have been altered: the motives, the strategies, the numbers of victims—and of the perpetrators—remain the same. But two implications emerge that do bear on the representation of the Nazi genocide—past, present, and future. The first refers to the place of the genocide "in" the history of evil; here the danger that the genocide might simply be absorbed as only another item in a lengthy and menacing sequence of events is balanced by a conflicting possibility that requires the conception of an evolving history of evil. There would be both reason and desperation in the claim that with the Nazi genocide the internal history of evil had at once been asserted and found its end—that this history was now complete, reaching a boundary by which any future instance of evil would be measured. Like the limit set by the speed of light, an outer limit would now have been defined for moral violation. Other instances of wrongdoing would henceforth be measured and judged in relation to this end point. Even with this conclusion, however, evil would at least have had a history and the Nazi genocide would stand as both a literal and symbolic marker within it.

The hope that this should indeed be the case joins a sense of moral horror to a conception of history: Could there, among the possibilities of evildoing, be a more extreme exemplification than that of acting on evil as a principle, as this was exemplified—on the claim presented here—in the Nazi genocide? Yet, the context of history in which that question now arises also compels recognition that this difficulty, too, is historical—a practical deferral that is itself subordinate to the imagination's distinctiveness as unpredictable. Insofar as evil is subject to the work of the imagination, we know enough to be wary of predictions of its end—of the claim in any context that there is nothing more that the imagination can imagine.

The basis for this caution is more than an acknowledgment of logical possibilities. Aristotle formulated a conception of justice that a number of philosophers have plausibly transposed into contemporary terms—although he himself found no incompatibility between that conception and the practice of slavery, which all current versions of justice—by authors who would not otherwise venture claims of precedence over Aristotle as a philosopher— reject. As Aristotle's conception came to be further defined in its later explication, however, a similar process may also apply to evil in its role as principle. It is more than only a truism to say here with Edgar in *King Lear* (turning his meaning slightly), "The worst is not so long as we can say this is the worst." To ask about the "future of the Holocaust," then, is also to recognize this other possibility of further "development"—a possibility that in no way diminishes the enormity evident in the Nazi genocide. One might argue, in fact, that to insist on viewing the genocide within the context of the history of evil makes its enormity more unavoidable than it is in those other accounts which, displacing it from history, tend also to obscure its humanly moral significance.

A second aspect of the future of the Holocaust is also apparent, once the present and the future are related to each other in the framework of the history of evil. This is the alteration of moral consciousness which, as a consequence of the Nazi genocide, now marks the present and future off from the past, altering the history of evil in a way that affects the social history of mankind more generally. As Cain's murder of Abel symbolized a new and literal fact of social existence, one that would thereafter be a constant element in the construal of all human relations and institutions, so the events of the Holocaust and the act of genocide at their center articulate a fact that can now never be absent from considerations of social or moral existence, however unaware or indifferent people may be individually to those events. Genocide informs the future with a new and now constant imminence; to think seriously of the future is also to recognize this one among its grounds in the present.

In this sense, the history of the Holocaust is fixed, beyond the reach even of the extreme efforts of historical revision. For there, too, the phenomenon of genocide has become real. The revisionists deny that the Nazi genocide occurred—not the enormity it would have been if it *had* occurred. A premise of the revisionists, too, in other words, is the evil in genocide; also for them, willing or not, the possibility of what they deny is undeniable. Through the memories incorporated in social institutions, moreover—for example, in the United Nations Convention on the Crime and Prevention of Genocide—the prospect of the future is held up to constant view. The role of the mark of Cain that was intended to symbolize the evil that one person could do to another by murder is usurped now by genocide—as the victims of evil become not individuals but groups, and groups that are defined not by a decision or act of their members (individually or collectively) but externally, by the same force that would then destroy them. No less important, the premeditation that is only a possible and occasional feature of individual murder appears as a necessary condition for genocide: here knowledge and the will meet. The mark of Cain was meant at once to identify the murderer and to preserve his life in order to attest to that identity. There is yet no equivalent mark of genocide: the division between the two Germanies that had served as an analogous symbol has been erased (although the uneasiness stirred by this change attests to its role as symbol). For the present, then, memory must serve as its own mark—but this itself can be assured only if evil does indeed have a history and only if the Holocaust itself has a future.

3

Genocide and Omnicide:
Technology at the Limits of Ethics

Are we not always living the life that we imagine we are?
— Thoreau

It may seem at first glance that genocide and omnicide have no special causal or conceptual relation to each other aside from the terrible prospect that they mark out together of gratuitous killing—murder—on a large scale. Omnicide, shaped as a concept and pressed on our consciousness by the specter of nuclear war, threatens the extinction of mankind, perhaps of all life; genocide, fearsome with its elevation of annihilation to an impersonal and arbitrary principle that considers individuals only as the members of a *genos* or group, seems nonetheless to be cut to a lesser scale, an occurrence that mankind has already, in fact, survived at least once and may even have learned from. That the twenty-first century faces the continuing prospect of both these threats could, even with a clear recognition of their enormity, be viewed as no more than an unfortunate coincidence, further complicating an already complex historical period, but not bearing in any fundamental way on the cultural structures or the ethical norms of that or subsequent times.

If the history of past responses to extreme situations is a guide, moreover, the occurrence of these two phenomena might be expected to make little difference, even for ideological or theoretical reflection. They would be unlikely, for example, to affect the belief in theodicy shared by traditional religions with modern science, according to which history is rational, progressive, in the long run working for the good; on these accounts, all problematic events, whether as slight as a traffic accident or as large as a holocaust, will eventually be explained and justified. For skeptics, too, the conjunction of genocide and omnicide might serve as no more than confirmation of what they already had assumed: the constant failing—the unhappy consciousness—of man, only reinforced now by the irony that as man has increasingly gained control over nature through his technological ingenuity, he has found himself increasingly victimized by that same power, the slave once again asserting himself as master.

But the fact remains that such appeals to abstract theory refuse to take history seriously: we quickly recognize, from what they do not say as well as from what they do, that no historical occurrence or set of events would be admitted by them as counterevidence to their conclusions (in this sense, there *is* no difference between a traffic accident and a holocaust). And although metaphysical "first principles" may underlie even the most rudimentary attempts to identify the relationship between historical and moral analysis, surely we do better to begin from the immediacy of such analysis than from the abstractions to which it may eventually drive us. A person living after 1945—that is, after the "Final Solution" had been attempted and after the atomic bomb had demonstrated what *its* future might be— will hardly, either by ignorance or denial, escape the consequences of living in a social and conceptual space that, for the first time in history (so I claim) includes these two extraordinary moral phenomena: the possibilities and thus also—politically, psychologically, morally—the imminence of genocide and omnicide.[1]

The complexities of historical causality make it unlikely that we shall ever fully understand why those phenomena have obtruded themselves as or when they have or what the connection between them is. It is not evident, to be sure, that even *with* such understanding, we could be certain that either or both these mechanisms of mass murder will not become part of— perhaps the end of—human history; the most optimistic predictions must yet admit some probability that they will impinge on man's future no matter *what* he does, individually or collectively. Nor can there be much comfort in the remote possibility—since accidents do happen—that the dangers thus posed may be averted even if we do nothing to prevent or evade them, if we move into the future as heedless of the constrictions of historical possibility as we did into the past and, it has still to be said, into the present. Between these alternatives of historical determinism and random chance, however,

---

[1] I refer to the "phenomena" of genocide and omnicide in a way that may seem to ignore the fact that genocide has occurred in the twentieth century (and perhaps before), where omnicide may seem to be only threatened or possible. But these modalities are not so easily distinguished.Genocide, as defined in the U.N. Convention does not presuppose completion of the act of collective murder but only the evident intention to do so; and the point I emphasize is that the will to risk omnicide in itself raises the question of intentions and thus of moral judgment on it *as* an act.

there is a point on which understanding and practice converge, where conceptual and practical analysis may make a difference in focusing on the fact and the relation of the possibilities of genocide and omnicide.

I propose to consider here two principal issues that bear on this topic. The first is the question of how we can account for the recent appearance, within a period that by one standard of measurement extends over only some five years, from 1940 to 1945—almost simultaneously and yet both for the first time—of the threats and, more than the threats, the realities of genocide and omnicide. The second is the question of what the implications are of the occurrence (is it too strong to say the *invention*?) of these phenomena beyond their most immediate and blatant consequences if realized: what happens to the societies and their cultures—their minds and their bodies—for which genocide and omnicide appear even as only possibilities?

These questions are themselves open to question. The first depends on a presupposition that must itself be argued: that genocide and omnicide are indeed phenomena of the twentieth century—in effect, that they are new social facts and that it is in part because of this novelty that they may bear so forcibly on the societies that must now confront them. To be sure, even if precedents could be found for the two threats—if not exact precedents, close analogies—this would not necessarily alter the likely significance of their present role: the setting of the "global village" in which they now appear is clearly different from any prior social or political structure and would by itself ensure the need for their reexamination. But the claim for their common and recent origin is pertinent in a number of ways, epitomized in one inference from them for the existence of a "negative" history of ethics—that the imagination and practice of evildoing, like those more commonly claimed for good, may also reveal a history of progress. And again: there are few points in human history of which the assertion can be made that a specific and readily distinguishable causal factor appeared for the first time, one that would act symbolically as well as practically, in prospect as well as in fact, and thus influence—beyond its immediate physical or material consequences—human consciousness and social practices more generally.

It is impossible to detail here in full the evidence for genocide and omnicide as recent historical developments, but the outline of that evidence can be made clear. Admittedly, Rafael Lemkin, who coined the term *genocide*, alleged a number of precedents to twentieth-century instances, as in Rome's destruction of Carthage and in Titus's (again, Rome's) attack on the Jews.[2] But as his own initial conception of the term was modified (for ex-

---

[2] Rafael Lemkin, *Axis Rule in Occupied Europe* (Washington, D.C.: Carnegie Endowment for International Peace, 1944). For subsequent analyses of the concept of genocide, see, e.g.,Uriel

ample, in the formulation of the 1948 U.N. Convention on Genocide),[3] so too, it seems, do those earlier alleged precedents need to be qualified in comparison to the Nazi genocide against the Jews that appears as its first full instance—in effect, as a standard or paradigm against which other putative instances must be measured. The purpose of the Nazi genocide was physical, not only cultural or religious or ideological, annihilation: the *genos*, itself defined in (purportedly) biological terms, was to be destroyed. Thus, it was not the group in association with a geographical area or in respect to a negotiable property (possessions, affiliations) that was threatened with extermination, but the group as such, wherever its members might be, with no option of conversion or substitution (e.g., paying a ransom). It is at least arguable—I believe that it is also demonstrable—that no other of the many alleged instances of genocide, in the harsh examples that range from Carthage to the Turkish massacre of the Armenians (1915–1917), answers exactly to these criteria. (Some Armenians, for example, were at times given the "option" of conversion to Islam, and the Turks did not in any event threaten them beyond the boundaries of Turkey itself.) Certainly, no instances of genocide has been as systematically and consistently elaborated by its perpetrators—that is, deliberated, implemented, and attested to—as the Nazi genocide against the Jews.

The analogous assertion of historical innovation in the prospect of omnicide is in one sense much simpler to demonstrate, in another sense more difficult. It is simpler in the sense that only with the technological achievement represented by the development of the atomic and hydrogen bombs, readily assignable in terms of chronology to World War II and its aftermath, does omnicide become part of social reality; from this limited point of view, there is no question of historical precedent. On the other hand, the latter thesis is complicated on other grounds, because although it might be argued plausibly that before the twentieth century even the idea of genocide in the extreme form noted had not occurred—surely not, in any event, as a serious practical option—there have been recurrent instances of apocalyptic thinking, one promised element of which was the end of mankind or perhaps of history as such. Noah's ark sailed against the background of this prospect in biblical thinking, and the Stoic doctrine of periodic conflagra-

---

Tal, "On the Study of the Holocaust and Genocide," *Yad Vashem Studies* 13 (Jerusalem, 1979): 7–52; George Andreopoulos, ed., *Genocide; Conceptual and Historical Dimensions* (Philadelphia: University of Pennsylvania Press, 1994); Frank Chalk and Kurt Jonassohn, *The History and Sociology of Genocide* (New Haven: Yale University Press, 1990); Helen Fein, *Accounting for Genocide* (New York: Free Press, 1979); Eric Markusen, *The Holocaust and Strategic Bombing: Genocide and Total War in the Twentieth Century* (Boulder, Colo.: Westview Press, 1995).
[3] For the background of the U.N. Convention, see Nehemiah Robinson, *The Genocide Convention* (New York: Institute of Jewish Affairs, 1960).

tions provided another version of an anticipated end. Premonitions such as these, moreover, were also often tied to human action, with the cataclysms held to be consequences (if only in the form of divine judgments) of human conduct; up to a point, in other words, they were within human control.

Notwithstanding these and other parallels (one might speak even of a psychological or cultural impulse for apocalyptic thinking, a collective death wish—or fear or threat, with all of these interrelated—that may also underlie them), a significant difference between the historical predictions of apocalypse and what I have referred to as the present "imminence" of omnicide is evident. It may be possible to describe or to explain the development of nuclear weapons in more abstract terms (theological or metaphysical), but ostensibly that development took place in a secular and instrumental context, at the instigation of governments and through the actions of individuals who are now (themselves or their successors) also in a position to decide when or how those weapons will be used, presumably for characteristically human reasons. If we ask who is in a position now to trigger a nuclear conflict that might result in omnicide—meaning a threat to civil and biological existence as we know it—a reply could, with little exaggeration, refer to almost every country on earth; even a response to this question that limited itself to nations that have, or are in a position to have, their own nuclear weapons would include at least three-fourths of the world's population.

The point here is that whatever the precedents in varieties of apocalyptic thinking for the idea of omnicide—an end of human history produced by the mass destruction of historical beings—never before has the capacity for initiating such an act been so generalized or widespread; never before has the capacity—and the knowledge of its existence—lain so immediately and readily within the power of human society, not only that of nations or other corporate entities, but also of relatively small groups of people and even of individuals; never before has the option of taking action that would be, literally, limitless in its consequences for human existence been so evidently a possible social "choice." So far as *any* geopolitical decisions are within the purview of governments and their citizenry, now also this one is among them.

This possibility, furthermore, is more than only a matter of technical capacity or potentiality. The planning for nuclear war—which can "safely" be assumed to be part of the planning of all the world's nuclear powers—entails acceptance of the possibility that such a war, however limited its initial aims, may result in a general conflagration—another and even more authentically "world war"—and thus also in omnicide (like genocide, which does not require the full annihilation of the *genos*, omnicide too might fall short of totality). Acceptance of the possibility of such escalation—which would be the greater enormity? admitting the possibility or the failure to anticipate it?—together with other features of such planning, even where the ostensible end is deterrence, amount to an *intention* for omnicide: the willingness to have it ensue as a consequence of other actions taken. This set of conditions supports the claim that as a world society, we face the prospect of omnicide for the first time. That the actual *use* of atomic bombs has so far occurred only in the cases of Hiroshima and Nagasaki more than fifty years ago; that the "Cold War" that followed the "hot" war has now itself, with the breakup of the USSR, lost its Manichean quality of dividing the world against itself; that nuclear deterrence has in some sense "worked," even in a community of nations for which international law continues to be observed only insofar as it serves individual national "interests"—all of these factors have contributed to a dulling of the consciousness of the line marked by the potential instruments of omnicide. No very deep or acute thinking is required, however, to recognize that that line exists now as it existed earlier, with the image of the mushroom cloud a constant if progressively less vivid part of collective memory; and indeed I suggest that this muted presence is even stronger evidence of the role of this possibility as a factor in our ongoing "construction" of social reality—a factor that is now simply taken for granted. Never has the possibility of total destruction rested so evidently in human—all too human—hands. Never have those hands had immediately available such an instrument for shaping—willing—the future; that is, for assuring an end to the future.

EVEN if the claims that genocide and omnicide (for one, the fact; for the other, the prospect) are innovations of the twentieth century were true, this would not in itself establish a relationship between them or between them and, except in the most general way, anything else in their then-common background. But I propose in addition to make the latter assertions as well: that the two phenomena are in fact interrelated and that it is more than accidental that they appeared when and as they did. They occur, in other words, within a single framework of causal implication.

It will be evident that no account of such relationships can expect to identify necessary and sufficient conditions for them; few historians would suppose this as a meaningful ideal for accounts of even much less complex phenomena. I mean, then, to outline a probable historical and conceptual connection between them, to call attention both to the present social context as it is affected by that connection and to the latter's origins. The basic features of this connection are themselves exemplified in the concept and practice of technology; for it can be shown that it is in large measure under the influence of that source that genocide and omnicide have assumed

their present shapes. Their dependence on technology is at once conceptual and material.

One point of contact between technology and the threat of omnicide is
so obvious as to be vacuous: the willingness to risk the destruction of mankind by a nuclear holocaust has presupposed the technological and scientific achievements required for the development of nuclear weapons. This
banality has even more general and significant implications, as it calls attention to the role of technology as a factor in setting the stage for and then
in shaping morally significant—nontechnological—decisions, and even
before that in the design and realization of morally significant ends. The
history of ethical values, it should come as no surprise, is closely related to
the history of the possibility of morally relevant actions. (It is a commentary
on the institutional bias of philosophy that writers on ethics have paid too
little attention to this connection to provide even a likely model of this relation: the social history of ethics is usually left to the anthropologists and
their studies of "primitive" ethical systems.) Two aspects in particular of this
connection are worth noting here: the first, an additional instance of the
way in which technology may provide a basis for change or innovation in
moral history; the second, where technology itself, both as a concept and as
an institutional structure, discloses a morally significant character.

With respect to the former aspect: just as technology has had an obvious
role in establishing the possibility of the threat of omnicide, it also figures
in the background of the Nazi genocide, and indeed of the concept of genocide as such. It is perhaps too strong to claim that without the technological
means then available, what we now see as the gradual evolution in Nazi
thinking toward the "Final Solution," culminating in the administrative formulation of that concept at the Wannsee meeting in January 1942, would
have been inhibited or even averted. There is no question, however, that
both the idea and the detail of technological accomplishment were important factors in the development of that conception and in its implementation. The death camps located in Eastern Europe that were the principal instruments of the Nazi genocide depended for their work of extermination
on a system of transportation and communication without which the very
conception of a "final" and centralized solution for the Jews of Europe—
that could provide, for example, a common registry and destination for the
Jews of Holland, Greece, or Hungary with those of Poland or Russia—
would have been a practical irrelevance, a brutal fantasy. That the means
used for the extermination itself were initially makeshift and (in terms of
their uses) inefficient pales beside the enormity of the purpose to which
those means were directed and also, in the end, to the efficient means of
murder that were eventually contrived. The phrase "death factories" that

has been applied to distinguish the six principal sites of systematic killing in Eastern Europe from the approximately ten thousand "concentration camps" scattered across the whole of Europe (extending in its westernmost outpost to the camps on the Channel isles) should be understood not as a metaphor but literally. Here the technological conceptualization of a factory was fully realized: within a relatively small—factory-size—area, "raw material" (that is, human beings) was turned into a single "product" (that is, death).

To be sure, the means that eventually led to this refinement were less dramatic and radical, but they too represented in progressive stages the appropriation of technological instruments and systems. The bureaucratic and mechanized administration of the "Final Solution" that enabled a figure as close to the center of its work as Adolf Eichmann to claim that he himself had not "taken part" in the killings, indeed that he had "nothing personal against the Jews," is itself a remarkable technological and social development. (This development includes the unusual changes in language use itself that have been shown to be correlated with technological development; also these innovations had an important role in the Nazi genocide.[4]) At issue here is action that is more than only social and *a fortiori* more than individual; thus we can understand Eichmann's statements (and his history) as reflecting only moral blindness or "thoughtlessness" (Hannah Arendt's term) only if we are also willing to say that such personal moral incapacity emerged and acted somehow independently of the bureaucratic apparatus, and this seems clearly incorrect. Bureaucracy itself, we know, has both a social history and a social personality—each tied closely to the history and character of technology.[5] The "organic" conception of the state, which is presupposed by fascism in its varieties and according to which each of its parts (or citizens) is a means directed toward realizing the whole, provides a natural home for the development of a bureaucracy that works most effectively (one of its aims, after all) when questions about purpose are detached from the individual act or agent.

---

[4] See, e.g., Nachman Blumenthal, "On the Nazi Vocabulary," *Yad Vashem Studies* I (Jerusalem, 1957), Kenneth Burke, "The Rhetoric of Hitler's *Battle*," in Burke, *The Philosophy of Literary Form* (Berkeley: University of California Press, 1973): 217–218; George Steiner, *Language and Silence* (New York: Atheneum, 1967), Berel Lang, "Language and Genocide," in Lang, *Act and Idea in the Nazi Genocide* (Chicago: University of Chicago Press, 1990). On the more general relation between language and technology, see H. D. Lasswell, Nathan Leites et al., *Languages of Politics* (Cambridge: MIT Press, 1965).

[5] See, e.g., Hannah Arendt, *The Origins of Totalitarianism* (New York: Meridian Books, 1958), chap. 7; Alvin W. Gouldner, *Patterns of Industrial Bureaucracy* (Glencoe, Ill.: Free Press, 1954); Henry Jacoby, *The Bureaucratization of the World*, trans. E. Kanes (Berkeley: University of California Press, 1973).

Finally, too, the idiom of germs and disease, which was a central theme in the Nazi justification for the genocide against the Jews—required to support the implication that the Jews were not human beings at all and thus did not have to be treated as human beings—was much more than just a rhetorical figure. It presupposed a conception of disease and of medical science that technological developments had made possible and that, before the late nineteenth century, could have been viewed even by its advocates as no more than an ominously useful fiction.

There is ample evidence that even these several and in some ways independent strands of technological development did not come together easily. The balance of evidence suggests that Hitler himself had not seriously intended the idea of genocide before the early years of World War II—that is, had not seen it as a genuine option.[6] Undoubtedly there are a variety of reasons, moreover, both for this delay and for the occurrence of the intention when it did arise. But it seems evident nonetheless that the technological feasibility of realizing that intention, of making it plausible both as idea and as practice, was a significant factor in its history; it is difficult even to imagine its occurrence in the absence of the features cited.

The limits of the claim I have been making so far should be recalled: it is not that genocide and omnicide are linked necessarily to the history of technology, much less to specific moments in that history. There is no a priori reason why some group or person in 942 should not have conceived a threat of genocide—and acted on it—of exactly the same sort that was to be made and acted on a thousand years later. But in point of fact this did not happen, not because the will to accomplish such ends would not have been present if the means were available but just because (at least) of the unavailability of the means. Certain quite specific technological advances preceded the occurrence of genocide and the threat of omnicide when they did arise that thousand years later, and prima facie, this connection is more than an accidental convergence.

The latter claim, one might object, is still not restricted enough. For even if the historical line traced were accepted, does it imply anything more than (circularly) that a nuclear war will be fought with nuclear weapons (in the same way that an army equipped with spears will fight with them), or that an industrialized nation may turn its technological resources to devising means of extermination as it might also turn those resources (even at the same time) to improving medical care; that is, for sustaining rather than destroying life? But, again, the argument presented is not that genocide and om-

---

[6] See on this issue Yehuda Bauer, *The Jewish Emergence from Powerlessness* (Toronto: University of Toronto Press, 1979), Chap. 3, and Michael Marrus, *The Holocaust in History* (Hanover, N.H.: University Press of New England, 1987), Chap. 2.

nicide have followed necessarily from the advances of technology, only that there is a material and conceptual connection between the two historical lines. The objection cited to this assertion, it will be noted, is itself a version of the more general view that inventions of any kind (moving backward from bombs to the wheel or to fire) are value-neutral, and that the user, not the maker or the process of making, is accountable for the consequences that use of the object may lead to. This general thesis, however, is itself specious, assuming a radical indeterminacy in the nature of an object's function or use that is in one sense self-contradictory (the fact that not everything is possible at any moment of history or for every object does not imply that everything is equally probable; we recall here Napoleon's quip that "you can do anything with a bayonet except sit on it"). It furthermore suggests a version of the fact-value distinction, with an implicit premise in that distinction of hard and autonomous facts—the artifacts that are value-neutral—which is also problematic.

Reference to the fact–value distinction has a special pertinence in this context, because it introduces a second, more important aspect of technology that bears on the phenomena of genocide and omnicide; namely, its own ideational or structural character and the way in which that character is then conceptually implicated in those phenomena. The issues here are complex, and the concept and practice of technology are undoubtedly open to alternative descriptions. But the evidence and precedents for the one adduced here are substantial; these center on the fact–value distinction and on the related distinction between means and ends—for both of which it can be shown that technological practice typically draws on seriously defective accounts. Those accounts (and a number of related ones) are intrinsic to the practice of technology. They are also significant features of the setting in which the presence of genocide and omnicide makes itself known, where we find the "aestheticization of politics" that Walter Benjamin identified with fascism, but which, placed against a background of which fascism is only one part, turns out to have an even longer reach.

The argument here is necessarily compressed and sketchy. If one starts with the conception of technology or "technique" suggested by Jacques Ellul in *The Technological Society*, we find, first, that technique acts to "mechanize" the world, conceiving its own role as that of a problem solver and thus acting to reduce the parts of the world—events, objects, people—to discrete and enumerable units that are then reconnected by a single "final cause" or principle that is itself more like a means—namely, efficiency.[7] Be-

---

[7] Jacques Ellul, *The Technological Society*, trans. J. Wilkinson (New York: Vintage, 1964). See also for an account that arrives at certain similar conclusions but on quite different grounds, Herbert Marcuse, *One-Dimensional Man* (Boston: Beacon Press, 1964).

cause technique is effective only as the "facts" of a situation—its problematic—are defined for it, not in the determination of purpose or justification, it soon moves from being something external to man, used by him for his purposes, into "his very substance" (6). The process thus obscures and in any event separates the role of purpose or ends from the mechanism of technology and even from the concerns of its user. The issue of means or process comes to be the central preoccupation of technology, and this in turn ensures that the issue of values is virtually excluded as nonrational or emotive; the single feature acknowledged that is at all comparable to value appears in the relation between the machine and its product—that is, in the ideal of efficiency. The effect of this conglomerate method as a "framing" device is to deny all external or contextual questions, to emphasize the mechanistic features of duplicability, interchangeability, *im*personality—shaping not only the solutions to all problems, but also the problems themselves in this image. The method and devices useful for devising solutions thus come to acquire the status of ends; the question "why?" is reduced insistently to "how?"; the status of the individual is equated with that of a part related only mechanically to a more inclusive whole.

At work here is a tacit purpose, in Max Frisch's words, "to so arrange the world that we don't have to experience it": for experience, too, is now subordinated to a dominant form, to the remoteness effected by "aestheticization," and to a goal that, if it is accessible at all, will be openly nonrational, even arbitrary, except as it conforms to the will of force or efficiency. The pattern thus defined is exactly that of the conceptual framework in which the practices of genocide and omnicide are found. The latter, too, reveals the domination of a formal purpose that initiates the identification—and then the subordination which may logically extend as well to extermination—of a group with no consideration of anything *in particular* that the individual members of that group have been or done; here, too, the claim emerges that an end as wanton as the destruction of mankind might be warranted by an (alleged) threat to one group of people *because* the mechanism for such total destruction exists. The process of action becomes so dominant in these cases, so intrinsic, so much a matter of problem "solving," that the relation of the means to the ostensive end—and then the character of the end itself—is obscured. It is predictable, even inevitable, that individual persons are reduced to means exclusively, parts of the mechanism, and thus are expendable as the work of the mechanism itself seems to require (or, even less than that, suggest) it.

The phenomena of both genocide and omnicide, then, whether viewed as ideals—and we need to remind ourselves constantly that they have been viewed as ideals, explicitly or covertly—or if only as useful means, see the act of problem solving as detachable from the issue of what the status or origin of the problem is, what it is about (much less from the more general question about the nature of problem solving as such). The phrase, the "Final Solution," must echo in the mind of anyone at all aware of the amorphous shape of history. For even beyond the perverse irony that infects the phrase, we must also recognize its literal core—that for it, as a preface to genocide and again for omnicide (which would be, after all, a still more final solution), it is the way that those possibilities are first conceived, individually and in kind, with the premise that all questions translate into problems and that for every problem there *is* a solution, that conduces also to the substance of the particular and grotesque character of a "final" solution. On the face of it, a claim that humanity may be destroyed to save humanity would seem an evident absurdity. To understand how such a claim could be accepted as the basis for a strategy of international purpose suggests an unusual pattern of conceptualization and practice—and just such a pattern, it seems, is fixed in the technological framework. The latter framework is usually directed to lesser issues and "problems," but it is naturally, intrinsically, unable to distinguish between the orders or substance of problems as such; thus, no problems—and no solutions—would be or could be ruled out by it.

Again, I do not contend that the conceptualization and practical development of technology define necessary or sufficient conditions for the phenomena of genocide and omnicide. In a period of history where such complex factors as nationalism, totalitarianism, industrialization, and class structure are all in motion, any single line of explanation will provide at most only an opening on the whole, one that is limited by the formulation of the question from which it starts. But there can be no doubt about the reality of the objects of that question, in genocide and omnicide. And if we ask then why the latter appeared when and as they did in recent history, asking here for a moral history that includes but also goes beyond the ostensively material conditions, the characteristic features of technology turn out also to be features of their structures. Formally, such a finding of recurrence (more modestly, of analogy) may be less than a historical account might hope for; it surely does not preclude the relevance of other factors (although it may be related to them as well: I should argue that the configuration outlined bears also, for example, on the apparently independent questions of why the Nazi genocide should have taken root in Germany, and why, when it did, it fixed on the Jews as its object); nor does it imply that the technological ideal itself does not have a history requiring explanation. These qualifications, however, do not affect the claim made so far of the relevance of this one element in the common background, causally tied to them, of the phenomena of genocide and omnicide.

Admittedly, the question still remains of whether genocide and omnicide are related to each other by anything more than a common genealogy and chronology. Here it seems to me important to note features of a direct connection also between the two. The most notable of these features is the likelihood that the threat of omnicide presupposes the phenomenon of genocide; that is, that omnicide itself implies genocide, is made possible at least conceptually only insofar as the phenomenon of genocide is itself taken for granted. I mean by this claim something more than the vacuous logical relation that to risk the death of everyone is also to risk the death of the "kinds" of which individuals are members as well as of the single kind to which all individual persons, taken together, belong. The point I stress is more substantive; namely, that the prospect of omnicide as it is now evident is based on the willingness of those who pose the threat to destroy a group (usually a nation), and who make no distinctions between combatants and noncombatants, between adults and children, and so forth, and who place no limits on the numbers or extent of extermination. It may be objected that this is not an inevitable feature of the threat of nuclear war; it is possible to plan a more limited "action," and it is even possible that such limitations might work in practice. But the actual planning of nuclear deterrence is invariably of a different order from this. The idea of a nuclear strike (first or counterstrike) is to prevent a response in kind, indeed, any significant response; and the most obvious way to ensure this is by preparation that, if implemented, would result in the virtual annihilation of a populace. Certainly no safeguards, not even any professions of safeguards, are offered by the nuclear planners against such an outcome. (And this says nothing, of course, about the distinct possibility of a global chain reaction that might be triggered by severe, even "limited" nuclear explosions.) The logic of such planning suggests that if a single bomb could be built that would destroy an entire populace, this technology too would be readily sought (more than one of them, of course) as part of the arsenal of preparedness. Genocide has, in fact, been so much taken for granted as a feature of nuclear war that it has not, to my knowledge, even been mentioned as one of its presuppositions.

Undoubtedly, one reason for this omission or absence is the commonplace assumption that nuclear war is like any other war, only larger and more devestating in scale. Because past wars have characteristically pursued the conquest, not the annihilation, of an enemy, this is also the ostensive purpose of nuclear war: any other outcome becomes an exceptional or chance occurrence. In any war, it could be argued along the same lines, certainly in recent, nonnuclear conflicts, attacks have occurred that, notwithstanding the generally limited goals of those wars, have blurred the traditional distinction between combatants and noncombatants; in this sense, again, nuclear war might seem no different in principle from nonnuclear war. But the response to this objection is no less obvious: that in none of these other instances, devastating as they have been, has it been imaginable that an attack would, by itself or in conjunction with the response it evoked, result in the virtual destruction of a people, thus, that such destruction might follow necessarily—not as the consequence of a separate and independent decision—from a first, designedly limited act. It may well be that had such a possibility been an option in the past, it would in fact have been chosen; but I am not asserting that individual or corporate agents in the past were more morally enlightened than they are now—only that the choices available to the latter have changed radically, that the prospect of genocide as well as that of omnicide is now entailed in the willed consideration of nuclear war.

I do not wish here to discuss whether such a decision could ever be justified, although it seems to me obvious that it could not be. That question is related to the distinction between "just" and "unjust" wars, as well as to the question of the general justification of value assigned to human life, and both those issues involve reference to a wider range of moral principles and analysis than can be undertaken here. The more limited claim made here is that genocide, newly recognized and condemned as an extraordinary crime, is implicit also in the threat of omnicide by way of nuclear war (that is, by those who prepare it). Genocide is one outcome (perhaps the only one) in fact that could prevent the omnicide they are otherwise prepared to risk, since the total destruction of an enemy nation might well be the only way of preventing the escalation and general conflagration that would almost certainly follow if enough of the enemy survived to mount a response (which would in turn evoke a further response, and so on).

This relation of implication, it should be noted, moves in the other direction as well, albeit less dramatically; for there is also a clear sense in which genocide lays the ground for, if it does not strictly imply, omnicide. This is not only a psychological reflection, although it is also that. Elias Canetti, in *Crowds and Power*, suggested that monetary inflation in the Weimar Republic had something to do with the later Nazi genocide, as it accustomed people to thinking in otherwise unimaginable numbers. It is a much shorter step from conceiving the destruction of a kind (in genocide) to an enlargement in the notion of "kind" that omnicide involves.

Such a suggestion that concepts may have a life history independent of judgments that are passed on them does not mean that someone who recognizes the phenomenon of genocide must himself somehow be contaminated by the idea, but only that concepts often escape their original or primary contexts—and more than this, because, again, the process of this combination of conceptual and practical transference does not depend only on psychological grounds. Genocide, notwithstanding the ostensively general rationale that prefaces its determination of an object, includes in that determination an intrinsically arbitrary feature; its rationale is always underdetermined. To treat an individual only as an instance of a group and thus as fully "defined" by that membership is in effect to deny the status of the individual qua individual. This, for example, is what the concept of collective guilt does when it ascribes the real (let us assume) guilt of a few members of a group to the group as a whole. Genocide passes just such judgment of collective guilt (more neutrally, of identification); omnicide does so on a still larger scale, as it wills the sacrifice of the entire group of groups; there are here, in effect, no limits or prohibitions at all. The willingness to threaten universal destruction may not mean that a judgment to this effect has been explicitly made (the wonder is, in fact, that people are willing to make such threats even in the absence of that judgment—that is, even without the semblance of a justification for the mass extermination of omnicide). Either the planners of nuclear warfare do not take account of such a possibility at all, however—in which case they are irresponsible, even in their own terms, as planners—or this judgment is accepted as a presupposition, in which case they can be judged, it seems to me, only as morally blind.

The willingness to risk omnicide is invariably accompanied by justification based on one or both of two grounds: that threats of nuclear attack are necessary to avoid the necessity of actualizing them and that certain principles justify even the chance that such threats might have to be actualized—thus, that the principles being defended would justify even the most extreme consequences of omnicide (if those should ensue). Here, too, there is a formal resemblance to the justifications provided for genocide, and not only because of their (common) questionable logic. For one thing, the justifications are both put in terms of self-defense against an enemy who is an actual or potential initiator. Moral and conceptual considerations suggesting that the means even of self-defense may at times be open to question; that the construction of an arsenal—even for self-defense—may by its own momentum alter its ostensive purpose; that there are consequences to be taken account of in killing as such (and particularly in nuclear war) that are independent of any claims of self-defense—all these are simply ignored, subordinated to an unquestioned end which might in the event be contradicted by them. The Mutually Assured Destruction (MAD) doctrine, which is a premise of all nuclear "defenses," moreover, tends to ignore or to deny its own intentions on the grounds that these intentions are only hypothetical; that is, that a counterstrike would be initiated only if someone else launched a first strike. But the history of warfare shows clearly that preemptive strikes are easily (often deliberately, but even when not) conflated with supposed counterstrikes and, more than this, that a hypothetical intention is an intention nonetheless: to agree to do something if (and/or only if) certain conditions occur is nonetheless to agree to do it (that is, to intend it). To be sure, intentions are not the only elements that matter in· moral judgment, and undoubtedly a distinction can be drawn between intentions that appear as intrinsic to an action that is indeed taken and intentions that are attached to hypothetical or contrary-to-fact actions (what so-and-so would choose to do or have chosen to do if such-and-such were to happen or had happened). But there can be no doubt, it seems to me, that the latter are indeed, and nonetheless, intentions.

It might be argued that the discussion so far ignores an obvious and large difference between genocide and omnicide; specifically, that the former is directed by an agent against someone else, whereas the latter (by definition) includes the agent himself. Do the adherents of the MAD doctrine "intend" suicide by it? And are they then only deceiving themselves and/or others by stressing the notion of deterrence? Or are they perhaps "higher-minded" in their aims because of a willingness to sacrifice themselves for whatever cause it is that motivates them? Although intentions are functions of actions that include evidence of what the agent had "in mind," they are not restricted to that evidence. I have tried to show in my comments on technology why a MAD proponent would be unlikely to anticipate or even to care very much about this suicidal intention, why he would be likely to assume that he (or the group as part of which he acted) would escape its consequences. The MAD doctrine in practice turns out not to be simply a means for deterrence; it is invoked as a justification for being a step—a decisive step—ahead of likely enemies or opponents. What motivates this is not unreasonably seen as an expectation that the MAD proponent himself will survive a nuclear holocaust, if only the technology that his strategic planning presupposes is adequate. Technology has room for obsolescence (indeed it assumes it), but it has no place for mortality, at least not as a concept. Thus the will for omnicide comes cloaked with an illusion very much like that of genocide: that its agents have a transhistorical sanction which serves at once as justification and protection.

It is conceivable, of course, that someone who is not suicidal in any conventional sense and who also recognizes the qualitatively different scale of nuclear war might be willing to destroy himself and everyone else in the name of an ostensive principle or set of principles—a latter-day Samson. It is even possible that an absolute moral judgment might at some point be warranted to the effect that it would indeed be *better* that mankind should cease to exist, that humanity collectively deserves the fate of omnicide or, less dramatically, that whether mankind exists or not, given the infinitesimal place that its existence occupies in cosmic space and time, makes no difference one way or the other. But none of these amounts to the finding that human beings, individually or as a group offering judgment on other people as well as on themselves, are likely now or ever to be in a position reasonably to render such a verdict. As justice requires wisdom as well as power, we might well grant that certain principles are so important as to warrant self-sacrifice; there might also be pacts among groups of people to the same, but now collective effect. But these possibilities are not a ground for justifying the collective killing of other people who may have no knowledge of the principle for which it is done or who may know it and reject it. Still more, a decision for collective murder (or even for risking that) would be unwarranted by any principle that is not also accompanied by an extraordinary egoism (not a principle at all) in the person or group responsible for it. Such a decision would presuppose that the persons affected by the decision who had no part in it had no right of self- or group-determination, and we have seen how this denial is the basis for the putative justification, in another context, of genocide as well.

Last: if we ask (as I have been) what it is that makes the willing of genocide and omnicide possible, one feature remains to be noted which has been mentioned only indirectly so far but which is so basic that it has dominated the view even in its absence. The goal or "final cause" that shapes genocide and omnicide in common is not distinctive because it involves the act of killing. Virtually all societies of which we have knowledge have provided an institutionalized sanction for varieties of killing, whether through capital punishment, through provision for waging war, or, less flagrantly, through significant imbalances in the distribution of economic means that then turn into verdicts on life and death for some members of the society. It might be argued, moreover, that the numbers of (actual or potential) people in each of these categories have been large in virtually every society and that at a certain point it does not matter how decisions were made concerning the people killed. To this extent, one might object, the differences between genocide and omnicide, on the one hand, and the other institutionalized forms of killing, on the other, are incidental. (Certainly pacifists would be inclined to argue along this line, although the objection would not necessarily be exclusively theirs.)

It is nonetheless important to recognize that in genocide and omnicide we encounter the distinctive notion of *generic* killing, in which the category of the *genos* is raised to a principle. This is a significant difference from other instances even of premeditated killing, as it is always arguable (although not necessarily correct) that some practical end might be served by such an act.

In genocide, the contention that an instrumental purpose is intended (as in the Nazi claim that annihilation of the Jews was identical to the cure for a disease) is quickly undermined as we see the contradictory impulse that defines the *genos* quite apart from any practical consequence (and sometimes openly opposed to it: the Nazis pursued the extermination of the Jews even when they were aware that this purpose of "self-defense" was interfering with the ability of Germany to carry on the war it was engaged in). A similar claim can be made for the threat of omnicide where, again, the pretense that it might serve a practical purpose—an ostensive end—is still more quickly discredited. In both phenomena, then, there figures a willingness, finally an intention, to raise killing to the level of a principle, the end of which turns out to be the principle itself.[8] As the notion of a kind insofar as it applies at all to human beings—a particular group or humankind as a whole—seems disconnected, substantively, even logically, from the act of killing even so far as that act at times, when directed against individuals as individuals, might be defended on instrumental grounds, by contrast when it is built into the act, as in generic killing, we recognize a demonic purpose, one that inverts the distinction between good and evil altogether. If there is even a psychological justification here, it is the justification of myth—a reversion to the cult of sacrifice or, more simply, to the search for a scapegoat.

I HAVE so far said little about the second question mentioned in the opening lines of this chapter concerning the consequences of genocide and omnicide (even as possibilities) for the social reality or culture in which they appear. The issues here are complex, not least because the concept of culture has become problematic—often being invoked honorifically (as shorthand for "high culture") or, at the other extreme, sociologically—for any set of social norms and practices, no matter how restricted the set. Whether one can speak of a world culture as now challenged by the phenomena of genocide and omnicide or even of a "Western" culture as most immediately confronted by that challenge (that is, as potential agents or victims) are also questions perhaps unanswerable except by stipulating an exclusionary

---

[8] I return to omnicide as *intended*, although the event itself has not in fact occurred. Suppose that the nuclear holocaust that must be admitted as possible does occur. At that point, the argument (by whoever is left to make it) that the nuclear arsenals had been intended to prevent such an outcome would be challenged at least by a charge of negligence. And although negligence may be understood as involving an agent who did not intend the consequences of his action, an alternative description is that what he *did* intend can be judged culpable (for not taking into account possible or likely consequences or their quality). In genocide, intention and culpability are more evident but not formally different.

definition of culture. In any event, they require more systematic attention than can be given them here. But at least two social and symbolic implications do follow from the complex of features outlined; these bear on the technological background to genocide and omnicide and then to the impulse for violation (in which violence is the most extreme but also the most patent manifestation) which that complex of factors supports.

The first of these implications is that genocide and omnicide are social phenomena in the broadest sense of that term; they are not merely geopolitical or psychological or military eruptions that are closed off (and so isolable) from the life of the society in general. This is due not only to the extent of their likely consequences, large as these must be. Enough has been written about the "mass" society or "technological man" to make the point obvious that the consequences of these phenomena are evident in every area of social existence: in legal and political institutions that seem increasingly to be detached from any sense of purpose or final cause; in social relations, where the notion of universal computation—the technological ideal—threatens the very possibility of individual communities; in the arts, where we find that their objects (when these are admitted at all) turn out to be the arts themselves (paintings as "about" painting, writing as "about" writing, etc.). There are many problems, no doubt, in speaking of "the spirit of an age," but the evidence is compelling of links among such cultural developments, and between them and the technological ideal I have claimed to stand in the background—as foreshadowing and evocation—of genocide and omnicide. In them all, the mechanism and method become the focus of concern, and this means that if the purposes or ends of the means are not simply ignored, they are shaped to serve the means, rather than the other way around. It may be too much to claim (as it would be too much for any historical phenomenon) that genocide and omnicide are inevitable outcomes of or accompaniments to the technological ideal, but they are clearly consistent with—that is, uncontested by—that ideal; in the ways I have suggested, they epitomize it.

Admittedly, it is easy to romanticize or (more neutrally) to exaggerate selected features of past history and thus to find in it invidious contrasts with the present; it is also easy, probably for the same reasons, to mistake the proportions or causal features of the present. Moreover, there is ample evidence—in contrast to his claims on behalf of the One Culture—for T. S. Eliot's claim about culture as such, that it is "the one thing we cannot deliberately aim at."[9] In this sense, our present consciousness of the form or presuppositions of our society is at least as much a symptom of the society

---

[9] T. S. Eliot, *Notes toward the Definition of a Culture* (New York: Harcourt, Brace, 1949): 17.

itself as an agent capable of working on it. But the realities of genocide and omnicide are unmistakable, and even if they did not originate with the design of intention, they are too large to be unmotivated or gratuitous, at least in retrospect. We might assume, then, even without other evidence, that they do not stand by themselves; there is ample evidence (or so I have argued) of a pattern of which they are part.

It may seem that the second implication I have referred to—the impulse for violation—is at odds with the first one, that technology presupposes a perhaps too-strong conception of normalcy, of homogeneity. But the sense of normalcy there is the result of a conflation of norms and the differences among them—a conflation that first denies them any serious role and then enlarges that denial into a rejection of the concept of purpose or value altogether. What finally emerges is the threat of violation not to any particular norm or set of norms, but to all norms, and thus even to the possibility of the concept itself. Much anthropological evidence has testified to the role played by normative distinctions (as between the sacred and the profane, the permissible and the impermissible) in the structure of all societies of which there is record. The inference is often drawn from this evidence that the pattern of division as it gives shape to social existence is the object of such rules—the line dividing social spaces rather than their particular contents; and this interpretation underscores the possibility that I take to be realized in the context of genocide and omnicide—that the pattern of social structure itself is finally the victim of the violence expressed and represented by them. So far as culture impinges on social reality at all, it does this by way of a network of norms (again, the particular ones hardly matter) that have authority for members of the culture. Such norms may be set to any possible level or object. ("Where there is dirt," Mary Douglas writes, "there is system.") The arbitrariness, the indifference to the issues of context or reason, the denial of persons and individuality, the mechanization of the social process, all of which are constant themes internal to the concepts and *a fortiori* to the practices of genocide and omnicide, consistently challenge the standing of such norms as such and thus also, we may predict, the possibility of social existence and culture even in a minimal sense. Even the concepts of truth and falsity, in addition to their epistemic status, need to be understood culturally and then as defining such norms. Thus, on one formulation: "Sociologically, a truth is whatever militates against the human capacity to express everything."[10] The closing phrase of that statement is especially significant, it seems to me, and fully exemplified in the many attempts to understand why the Nazi genocide against the Jews occurred.

---

[10] Philip Rieff, "The Impossible Culture," *Salmagundi* 58-59 (1982–1983), 413.

Those attempts, serious and reflective as they often have been, seem yet consistently to fall short of the events they are intended to account for. The reason for that may be in this: as they look for reasons and causes within a structure where the lines of what is permissible, either in reason or in practice, are clearly marked, the actions they try to understand were intended precisely to challenge the possibility of any such lines, to see how far the human will could extend when it was unfettered. There is good reason, in studying Nazism, to place emphasis on the crime of the genocide against the Jews. This emphasis, however, should not obscure the fact that there was in Nazism a broader aura of criminality as well, of the willingness to violate all accepted norms—attacks on civilian (non-Jewish, also German) populations, ignoring conventions on the treatment of prisoners of war, transgression of laws they themselves had formulated. To the extent that this is relevant to understanding in more general terms the phenomenon of genocide (and by extension, omnicide), it suggests a threat implicit in them against what otherwise serves as foundational for society or culture as such.

From a slightly different direction that converges on the same point, George Steiner notes the improbability that "one can devise a model of culture without a utopian core." Viewed in these terms, society and culture require at least the illusion of potential value—more generally, the contrast defined by the very assertion that there *are* norms. But in the presence of the menace of genocide and omnicide, mere survival becomes the "utopian core," or at least the only possible candidate for such a foundation, and it is doubtful whether that can serve as a basis for culture or society or indeed for anything more than the kind of struggle that those two varieties of murder themselves embody. No doubt many cultures have "sublimated" adversity and hardship into social dreams of a utopian future; but those dreams have been at some level compatible with the reality that fostered them, and it is difficult to foresee what transmutations would be possible for a collective experience shaped by the threats of genocide and omnicide. When Dostoyevsky predicted that "If God is dead, then everything is permitted," he had, with all his prescience, only a dim anticipation of the practices that humanity might yet devise as a means of ensuring that the distinction between what is permitted and what is not permitted should simply be discarded.

It is true that I have not taken account of the human—social, cultural, moral, psychological—capacity to block out, to forget, or to ignore, and thus perhaps to act "as if" genocide and omnicide were no more than remote or accidental possibilities. But, for one thing, thinking (even forgetting) requires something to think with, and the constitution of such instrumentalities is not entirely within the control of the thinker. And second, we might—we ought—not choose to forget that genocide and omnicide, whatever else they are, are also, even first, products of the human imagination. One danger in forgetting this is that we will be led to think that we need concern ourselves with nothing else—and that since the threatened end would radically transform the world, we must anticipate it, prevent it, with our own transformation. If we do not change everything, in other words, we change nothing (since the change we are trying to prevent would *also* change everything—into nothing). This has always been the impulse of apocalyptic thinking, and it is the impulse that has led many of the antinuclear protests and recent discussions of genocide (of the Nazi genocide or others) to lose sight of the immediate injustices and brutality in social practice that are themselves almost certainly elements in shaping just the feared future realizations of genocide and omnicide. One way to avoid thinking seriously of the end, in other words, is by thinking exclusively of the end. A second, no less urgent, danger in forgetting or denying the human origins of genocide and omnicide would be in concluding that the world in which we find them is the only possible world. It is hardly a sacrifice of the "facts" of nature and of history that the twentieth century has so strenuously celebrated to agree with Thoreau that "we always live the life we are imagining we are." Once we recognize this, it should then also be possible to imagine, as he did, a different one.

II

INTENTION AS ACT: REALIZING THE PAST

4

Intentions and the "Final Solution"

Although less attention has been paid recently to the dispute between the "Intentionalist" and "Functionalist" accounts of the nature of Nazi policy-making in respect to the "Final Solution," this does not mean that the points of disagreement between those accounts have been resolved.[1] Indeed, it seems evident that the "Historians' Conflict" that dramatized the earlier dispute in the public eye was itself no more than a postponement of the same issues that had first been raised there. When writers such as Nolte and Hillgruber proposed, for example, to broaden the framework of responsibility for Nazi policies—in effect to recast the roles of perpetrators and victims—the earlier disagreement about what the Nazis intended or whether they even *had* intentions in respect to the "Final Solution" only reappears, albeit with an enlarged and altered group of agents.[2] The claim, for example, that

[1] See on the "Intentionalist" side, e.g., Karl Dietrich Bracher, *The German Dictatorship* (London, 1979); Gerald Fleming, *Hitler and the Final Solution* (Berkeley: University of California Press, 1982); Eberhardt Jäckel, *Hitler in History* (Hanover, N.H.: University Press of New England, 1984). For "Functionalist" statements, see Martin Broszat, "Hitler and the Genesis of the Final Solution," *Yad Vashem Studies* 13 (1979): 61–98, and Hans Mommsen, "National Socialism: Continuity and Change," in Walter Laqueur, ed., *Fascism: A Reader's Guide* (Berkeley: University of California Press, 1976). A collection of statements on the dispute and its emergence into the Historikerstreit appears in James Knowlton and Truett Cates, eds., *Forever in the Shadow of Hitler?* (Atlantic Highlands, N.J.: Humanities Press, 1993). See also the exchange between Martin Broszat and Saul Friedländer, "A Controvery about the Historicization of National Socialism," *New German Critique* 44 (1988): 81–126; and Saul Friedländer, *Memory, History, and the Extermination of the Jews of Europe* (Bloomington: Indiana University Press, 1993), chaps. 4 and 5.
[2] Ernst Nolte, *Das Vergehen der Vergangenheit: Antwort an meinen Kritiken in sogenannten Historikerstreit* (Frankfurt: Ullstein, 1987); Andreas Hillgruber, *Zwierlei Untergang: Die Zerschlagung des Deutschen Reiches und das Ende des Europaischen Judentums* (Berlin: Siedler, 1986).

the Nazi genocide against the Jews was a response to the precedent—and thus to the subsequent threat—of Soviet policies of extermination is in this sense quite independent of analysis of the formal process by which Nazi policies were determined. It could be argued, admittedly, that the position advanced by Nolte and Hillgruber seems in fact to support the Functionalist view of Nazi history, by so attenuating the factors of historical causality (at least where the "Final Solution" is concerned) as to make the notion of individual or even of corporate intention implausible. But this inference would be contrary to *their* intention. For when these historians emphasize the Soviet threat as a dominant consideration in the background of Nazi policy, this implies that the Nazis realized and reacted against the Soviet threat—conditions that place that account within the Intentionalist school of explanation. What occurs here in fact is a not uncommon appeal to the notion of "mitigating circumstances" as a historical, as well as a legal or moral, category—one that is not only compatible with but also reinforces the intentional status of the action being considered. Yes, the Nazis adopted certain extreme policies, but they did so because of what they perceived as an extreme threat to their own existence. That perception, moreover (so the argument goes), had at least a plausible basis in fact and was thus a plausible basis for their intention—the decision to act on which becomes in turn, then, a "judgment call" that could reasonably have gone either way.

This argument has in its own terms been severely, and it seems to me cogently, criticized. But I am less immediately concerned here with the large, substantive issue of who intended what (and when) than with a number of seemingly rudimentary questions concerning the concept of intention—specifically as intentions are judged to have affected the sequence of causes and effects, which, in the end (whether intentionally or not) resulted in the large-scale extermination of Jews by the Nazis, a fact that in itself neither the Functionalists nor the Intentionalists have disputed. Viewed from this perspective, an odd consensus appears, not only between the historical "revisionists" and their critics, but also between the Intentionalists and the Functionalists. At least so far as the concept of intention is concerned, these two sets of historiographic opponents, whatever their disagreements, are at one. Both conceive of intentions in the same terms: as a state of mind prior to an action which the "intendor" first envisages and then "intends," that is, aims (and so acts) to realize. Intentions, in other words, are mental acts that precede and refer to a subsequent act—as in the formulaic New Year's Resolution: "I intend to turn over a new leaf." The act intended is conceived as an idea before the intention: first the act is conceptualized, and then a decision is made to "intend" it. (This is why I can intend "to go to the beach tomorrow," but even Columbus could not have *intended* to "discover" America, because if the "idea" of America had been clear enough to be intended, it would already have been "discovered.")

I have made a point of emphasizing that both the Functionalist and Intentionalist conceptions of intention assume this common definition, although the former finds intention missing in the Nazi genocide and the latter finds it present. It may seem that agreement of this rudimentary sort is hardly worth mentioning, since it is common enough that historians who disagree in the conclusions they draw from a common body of data may nonetheless agree on many of their methodological premises (it would be surprising if the latter were not the case). But so far as concerns judging the "policy" of the "Final Solution," the methodological concept of intention is arguably itself also a substantive part of this disagreement—substantive enough, in any event, so that the definition of intention itself turns out to be partly what is in dispute between the two accounts. This at least is the thesis posed here which contends, more positively, that on a second and different view of the concept of intention from that held in consensus by the Intentionalists and Fundamentalists, the ostensive disagreement between the subsequent interpretations disappears: also the Functionalists turn out to be Intentionalists.

Two competing models of intention can be distinguished among the common applications of that concept. The first of these models, what I call the External Model, is the view of intention that has been shared by the Functionalists and Intentionalists. The second, alternative view, which undermines the apparent disagreement between them, has come into prominence in the last several decades under the influence of the linguistic and the phenomenological schools of philosophy—thus, by an odd confluence of such different figures as Wittgenstein and G. E. M. Anscombe, on one side, and Sartre, joining them from the other. It will be referred to here as the Contextual Model of Intention.[3]

The External Model of intention conceives of intentions as meeting two principal conditions: first, that an intention is explicitly (and thus consciously) related to a specific object or goal which is itself independent of the intention; secondly, that the intention chronologically precedes both the realization of that goal and the acts initiated toward that realization. Intentions are thus "external" to the end intended and to the means employed in the effort to realize it. My claim here, then, is that this External Model is assumed in both the Intentionalist and Fundamentalist accounts of the "Final Solution," notwithstanding their disagreement on the presence

[3] See, e.g., Ludwig Wittgenstein, *Philosophical Investigations* (Oxford: Basil Blackwell, 1958), 159–172, and *Zettel* (Berkeley: University of California Press, 1967), 43–58; G. E. M. Anscombe, *Intentions* (Ithaca: Cornell University Press, 1957); Jean-Paul Sartre, *Being and Nothingness*, trans. Hazel Barnes (New York: Philosophical Library, 1956), "Introduction: The Pursuit of Being."

or absence of intentions in the single historical event at the focus of their discussion. The two sides have also agreed, of course, on one documentary finding in particular, namely, the absence of any specific written order by Hitler himself that might be judged to have set in motion the policy of genocide against the Jews. It is indeed the absence of this palpable evidence that underlies even the apparent disagreement between Intentionalists and Functionalists: both would conclude that *if* convincing evidence of the existence of such an order should be found, this would significantly alter the disagreement between them.[4] The Functionalist interpretation would, by their own criteria, be refuted by that discovery, and this is openly conceded by them—if only by the prominence given in Functionalist accounts to the "fact" that no such order has been shown to exist or to have existed.

The disagreement between Intentionalists and Functionalists thus revolves around the question of what can legitimately be claimed about Nazi intentions in the absence of such explicit historical evidence. On their side, the Intentionalists contend that even if palpable evidence is never found of an explicit decree authorized or signed by Hitler ordering the "Final Solution" (they offer reasons why such evidence is unlikely to be found or have existed—principally, Hitler's reluctance to "sign off" formally on such momentous decisions), the elements of what has come to be known as the "Final Solution" were at once so cohesive and of such an order of importance that, given the structure and hierarchy of the Nazi state, some such command, whether written or oral, *must* have preceded the acts themselves. So, for example, Jäckel accepts as a decisive consideration in arguing the Intentionalist case, that ". . . Given the nature of the Nazi state and its ruler, it is difficult to imagine that an act of such scope [the genocide against the Jews] with such far-reaching consequences, one so compromising, moreover, to the conduct of the war and the chances for victory, should have been initiated by subordinate agencies."[5] The "Final Solution," in other words, could not have been set in motion by anyone other than Hitler himself, and it could not, because of the combination of its complexity and consistency, have "happened" accidentally as a result of the convergence of smaller-scale and to some extent independent solutions. Again, and quite apart from the merits of the argument, it is the External Model of intention that is being applied here: for an effect of the magnitude of the "Final Solution" to have occurred, a prior and independent "intention" *must* have stood at its source. It follows, then, conversely, that if it could be demon-

---

[4] On the dispute over the existence of this written order, see the summary by Michael Marrus, *The Holocaust in History* (Hanover, N.H.: University Press of New England, 1987), chap. 3.

[5] Eberhard Jäckel, op. cit., 58.

strated that no such intention had existed, this would itself be sufficient proof that the acts constituting the Nazi genocide had not been intentional at all; if intentions are not "external" in this way, they are not intentions.

There is a legitimate sense in which the Functionalists could charge their opponents here with the fallacy of begging the question. For it is the Functionalists' contention that even large-scale policies can come into existence as the result of a series of smaller-scale steps taken by "local" agencies which thus are not envisioned—or intended—by any one person or any group as subordinate to a single or overarching goal. Such smaller-scale decisions might converge on a single point in such a way as to seem to reflect a common guiding intention; but this appearance does not itself suffice as proof: here, as elsewhere, appearances can be deceptive. What would be required in the instance of the "Final Solution" (as for intentions elsewhere) is a prior and independent statement—or at least prior and independent evidence— of intention: in this case, an edict or order issued by an authoritative source. That such an order has not been found or demonstrated to have existed is a sufficient reason on the Functionalist account for concluding that no such cause stands at the origin of the "Final Solution." The latter act, they then infer, occurred piecemeal and without overarching coordination, involving a number of individual and ad hoc decisions that resulted first in the incarceration and then the mass execution of Jews—decisions made in the context of other and often more urgent decisions and by various, often competing, bureaucratic agencies. Such decisions, Broszat argues, did not originate as part of a general design, nor were they sustained by a concerted effort intended to realize that design. They only "evolved in the end into a comprehensive 'programme.' This interpretation cannot be verified with absolute certainty, but in the light of circumstances . . . it seems more plausible than the assumption that there was a general secret order for the extermination of the Jews in the Summer of 1941."[6] (Hans Mommsen carries this thesis even farther; on his interpretation, even the Wannsee Protocol of January 20, 1942, does not constitute an overall plan of extermination.) What transpired on this account were a large number of independent decisions to persecute and in many cases to kill the Jews, but no single and overriding directive that would have been required and evident if those decisions had been part of a systematic policy.

Again: if one asks what common ground exists between these two accounts which differ so radically on the analysis of the causal background of the "Final Solution" (and thus on the related issue of the political and moral responsibility for it), at least one common element is evident—the concept

---

[6] Martin Broszat, op. cit., 93.

of intention. The differences between the two accounts concern the question of whether the Nazi genocide *was* intentional—not what is to count *as* an intention. The Intentionalists claim that the evidence points to the existence of such an (external) intention; the Functionalists dispute this. But they agree on what the nature of that intention would have been *if* it existed: an antecedent commitment which then led to—caused—the subsequent series of acts constituting the Nazi genocide.

It is at this juncture that the possibility of an alternative to the External Model of intention becomes significant, since with such a possibility the disagreement between the two positions might also be shown to change. Admittedly, the differences between the two positions in their interpretations of the "Final Solution" might be no less extreme on the second model of intention than on the first; if this were the case, it would surely be additional, perhaps conclusive, evidence of the genuine differences between them. On the other hand, an alternative conception of intention might enable one of the positions to meet the other on its own ground, that is, on its own premises, and yet to come away with its original thesis intact. This is indeed the conclusion I propose. For quite apart from the claim made by both Intentionalists and Functionalists that the issue between them can be settled in terms of the External Model of intention alone (I do not mean here either to judge between the claims on these terms or to equate them), the Contextual Model in effect enables the Intentionalists to meet the Functionalists on their own ground: it could grant the Functionalists their description of events constituting the "Final Solution" and still conclude, against them, that the policies and actions at issue were indeed intentional.

At this point, it becomes useful to shift the focus of the discussion here from the specific interpretations of the Nazi genocide at issue between the Intentionalists and the Functionalists to a framework of conceptual analysis based not in historiography but in philosophical psychology. In the latter, the analysis of the nature of intention in relation to consciousness and human agency have been central concerns. From this perspective, fundamental objections have been raised against the External Model of intention; and the alternative model, cited here under the rubric of the Contextual Model, has been presented in its stead. It is important, then, to see both how the objections raised in this nonhistorical source of analysis pertain to the historical question at issue (as that is addressed by the External Model) and how the alternative posed by the second model circumvents those objections without opening itself to others.

The objections to the External Model of intention by proponents of the Contextual Model infer from a combination of empirical and conceptual evidence two principal sets of claims. The first of these involves the criticism that intentions—even individual intentions and *a fortiori* corporate intentions—are necessarily ascribed on the basis of the acts that the intentions are claimed to be the intentions "of." Intentions, in other words, are "read off" from acts, and this means that they are read off backwards, from the present to the past, not the other way around. This assertion in part reflects the common difficulty of access to evidence. In many situations statements or other indications of prior intention on the part of an agent are meager or even nonexistent—but where it is still reasonable (and sometimes necessary) to assume, on the basis of the character of the acts in question, that they did not occur either unintentionally (involuntarily or gratuitously, that is, without *any* intention) or mistakenly (that is, where an intention to do one thing produces another and quite different result). In other words, intentions are often ascribed even when no prior, or "external," evidence is available, on the basis of the act itself and/or of other present evidence. If, for example, a fire destroys a building and an inspection shows that the fire seems to have begun simultaneously at various parts of the building, this in itself—in the present—would be evidence (not indubitable, but probable) that the fire had been "intended," even though no other external evidence existed; the process here is a matter of inference, based on the improbability of simultaneous "combustions." Furthermore and even more important, intentions often (and on some accounts, always) evolve as functions of actions—as the actions evoke a consciousness of ends (or intentions) *on the part of the agents themselves* not previously envisioned. In this sense, intentions may take shape simultaneously with the actions intended, in response to the part of the act that has immediately preceded it. In this sense, an individual or corporate agent may "discover" even his (or its) own intention during the time when the act of which it is the intention unfolds. (This seems, indeed, the most common manifestation of anything approximating corporate intentions.)

Second, even when explicit professions of prior or external intentions exist, it would be generally admitted that although such professions count as evidence of some sort, they do not conclusively settle the question of what the intentions are that characterize the action at issue. Individuals or groups sometimes lie in speaking about their intentions; they may also deceive themselves or be unaware in a number of other ways of what exactly they are doing. Even overt statements of intention are thus subject to corroboration; indeed they require it—and that corroboration comes from what is done, beyond what is said (although the saying itself is also, of course, a form of doing).

On these several grounds, then, statements of prior intention turn out to be neither necessary nor sufficient conditions for "knowledge" of intentions. Intentions are sometimes ascribed where there is no such evidence, and even when such evidence exists, it is subject to further confirmation or disconfirmation in terms of the actions that ensue, with which the statements of intention are associated. It is these acts, then, that speak the last word about intentions. This means that the basis on which intentions are ascribed is not prior to the "object" or goal of intention but contemporary with it, an aspect of its realization or failure, but in either of those events, part of the process of actualization. It is not, in any event, bound to occur prior (or as external) to that process.

This first consideration may seem to address only the question of how we determine what someone's intentions are, not how one "has" or knows one's own intentions—that is, how intentions occur in the first place. But here another objection against the External Model is raised by the Contextual Model, an objection based on certain principles in the general theory of mind. On the External Model, to "have" an intention is interpreted literally—that is, an intention is viewed as an "object" (an idea and/or feeling) located in a mind or will, which is also in some sense an object (or space that objects or impulses may then fill). To "have" something is to possess it, to be able to identify it spatially and/or temporally and to be able to distinguish it in those terms from whatever is not part of it. Thus, intentions on the External Model would be separable from both the goal "intended" and the actions taken to realize that goal (and the intention). They must then be located someplace else. But where, Anscombe asks, "is that [intention] to be found? . . . Is it formulated in words? And, if so, what guarantees that I do form the words that I intend? For the formulation of the words is itself an intentional act. . . ."[7] On the External Model, in other words, either intentions entail an infinite regress (in which case they would never get started) or they exist in a metaphysical and inaccessible limbo, a "place" that is not in any usual sense of the term a place at all. If intentions disclose themselves as the physical embodiment of a prior act—in words or as a feeling or mental image—then there is a problem in providing assurance that what was intended is in fact what is embodied; we require an independent criterion to judge that the intention has been adequately expressed. But this would require assurance that the independent criterion has itself been adequately applied—and so on. On the other hand, if intentions are prior but require no palpable embodiment, what—and where—*are* they? They seem here to be mysterious entities, able to "act" but having no substance themselves.

What emerges from this second consideration thus reinforces the implications of the first one: intentions—including even my own—exist as an aspect of what is *done*. Intentions may emerge in the process of acting—and, in fact, it is in the context of acting that corroboration of the existence and character of intentions is possible. Intentions, in other words, are not only impossible to ascertain independently, they do not *exist* independently or apart from the actions with which they are "subsequently" associated. In themselves, as "external" to the actions, intentions have no claims; not only are they not "things in themselves," they are not "things" at all.

It will be evident that at the basis of this Contextual Model is an attack on the Cartesian theory of mind according to which the mind is a substance or thing. Insofar as the mind is reified in this way, its acts—including intentions—also are reified and also become entities, since they then "originate in" or "belong to" a particular place. But, on the other hand, if this "ghost in the machine" conception of mind is rejected, then its consequences are also placed in question: intentions become aspects or functions of acts, unfolding as the acts themselves do. And this is indeed what the Contextual Model proposes.

It might be objected to these last comments that in order to settle the issue between the External and the Contextual models of intention, we are forced to choose between two competing theories of mind which underlie them—a much larger issue and one that moves far afield from the singular historical question from which the present discussion set out. Undoubtedly, at some point in following the implications of the two models of intention, such a choice might well be entailed (and it is important for the methodology of historiography to have this formal consideration made clear). But for the analysis here, it is sufficient to conceive of the two as nonexclusive alternatives—suggesting, in other words, that intentions occur or are ascribed at different times on each of these models, and thus that they each may have claims as explanatory means.

It seems evident, at any rate, that the concept of "corporate intentions" is more immediately (perhaps even only) intelligible on the Contextual Model than on the other, since unlike the External Model, the Contextual Model requires no assumption of an independent corporate "mind" or "will" but only the evidence of actions that converge on a goal, quite aside from any other, independent (external) evidence.

It is precisely the latter kind of evidence that is available and explicit in relation to the Nazi policy of genocide against the Jews and that would thus, on the thesis argued here, identify that policy as intentional even if no other "external" evidence existed or was yet to be forthcoming. (That some evidence of this type exists in respect to the Nazi genocide only adds to the force of the Contextual Model in that case.) In this sense, everything claimed by the Functionalist position in its premises could be granted (for the sake of the argument): Let it be agreed that no single determinant decree ordered the "Final Solution"; let it be granted that the idea of the "Final Solution," of the genocide against the Jews, evolved in stages, so that even seven or eight years after the Nazis came to power, it was not yet "intended," at least in the sense that that goal is not presupposed as an explicit motivating or ulterior cause in the various items of racial legislation imposed by the Nazis or even (up to that point) in the evidence of their brutal treatment of the Jews under their control—or even in their development of the network of concentration camps and ghettoes in Germany, Western Europe and Poland, all of which occurred before the date (sometime in 1941) when, by general "intentional" agreement, the design of the "Final Solution" became clear.

With the invasion of Russia, and the Barbarossa and Commissar orders that accompany it, however, any denial of the Nazi genocide as intentional in the strict sense of that term becomes increasingly difficult to maintain; and with the establishment, beginning with Belzec in October 1941, of the six "death camps," it becomes prima facie implausible insofar as the intention involved is judged by criteria at all close to the standard ones. The facts and numbers here are well-known: six camps; upwards of 2.5 million Jewish dead, who were transported to their execution from Germany itself, France, Greece, the Netherlands, Belgium, Slovakia, Croatia, Hungary, other parts of Poland, in a period extending from December 1941 to November 1944. Even without the evidence that exists of the centralized coordination of this process through Himmler's offices in the RSHA, the facts themselves here disclose the design of intention.

Assume (contrary to the evidence) that no independent statements of intention defined and conjoined the purposes of these camps; assume (again contrary to the evidence) even that the Nazis responsible for carrying out the purpose of the individual camps were unaware of the full network of camps and other institutional means of murder that were being employed. Even with these assumptions, the very fact of what was being done is sufficient to have constituted an intention, since the alternative, namely, that these acts were either natural or accidental or even that they were intentional but directed toward a different goal, become on the face of the matter impossible to credit; that is, if the concept of intention has any institutional or corporate meaning at all. The intention is *there*, in the "facts" themselves, attested to by a "Functionalist" description of small-scale or local events fully as much in evidence as would be required by Intentionalists who impose putatively stricter requirements.

The alternative account which would hold that, even at this point, what was going on was the convergence of a number of individual decisions that seemed to have been moved only by a common purpose or intention cannot be denied as a logical possibility—but even aside from the documentary evidence of coordination and design that this hypothesis contradicts, there remain the acts themselves and the implausibility of the suggestion that a pattern of this sort does not of itself represent an intention or could have ensued only as a function of intentions. Notice, for example, the formulation of Broszat: "It appears to me that there was no overall order concerning the extermination of the Jews and that the programme of extermination developed through individual actions and then *reached gradually its institutional and factual character in the spring of 1942 after the construction of the extermination camps in Poland.*"[8] Broszat's point here seems to be a causal argument: that because the "programme of extermination" developed gradually—not even preceding the construction of the extermination camps— even when the latter had been built and were in operation, the "Final Solution" was even then "institutional and factual": it was in some sense going on—but still without an overall intention (since that would properly have preceded the phenomenon, and it didn't). But this assumes that *in addition to* the facts and actions thus acknowledged, there would have to be an overarching consciousness, an explicit and cohesive articulation of policy; that is, an external intention. But on the Contextual Model, such an additional requirement is gratuitous and even if it were met would be insufficient. Since intentions reside in the acts themselves and since the ensemble of acts is not in question, neither is the intention that the acts represent.

On the Contextual Model, intentions, even when the evidence for them is overt and explicit (that is, external), are necessarily known by a form of inductive inference. From this fact, as it applies to the Nazi genocide, the Functionalists conclude that because induction does not produce the certainty of deduction, any ascription of intention can be doubted. On the Contextual Model, however, one can readily grant the validity of this general argument without crediting the conclusion as an objection, since the latter conclusion, on that model's view, would hold even if there were explicit (that is, noninferential or nonascriptive) evidence. There need not have been a central and prior decree ordering the "Final Solution," a single consciousness aware of each element of its practice or of its overall goal— and yet still there could have been, there *was* an intention in the relation joining the individual parts of that policy. To insist on the requirements cited by the Functionalists for admitting the existence of intentions would in fact ensure that not only was the "Final Solution" not "intentional," but also that virtually no corporate acts in settings as complex as those defined

---

[8] Martin Broszat, op. cit., 93 (emphasis added).

by relations among or within modern states in a technological age can be judged to be intentional: the very concept—and hence possibility—of corporate and even individual intention would be challenged. The latter implication indeed seems a constant feature of the Intentionalist position. The External Model of intention on which the Functionalist position depends presupposes for the existence of intentions a condition that is rarely met even when the presence of intentions is most flagrant and undisputable; even when the condition stipulated by them is met, furthermore, it leaves the presence of intentions in doubt.

To maintain the Functionalist account consistently then, as based on the External Model of intention, is in effect to forgo the possibility of historical explanation, at least so far as human agency and intention are at times understood to have a legitimate role in such explanation. The Functionalists might claim that the latter conclusion does not necessarily follow, that it holds only in respect to *certain* historical events or processes—of which the Nazi genocide against the Jews was one. They could claim this, however, only on the supposition that what is at issue in analyzing the history of the "Final Solution" is whether or not it occurred intentionally—when it is the question of what corporate intentions *are* that is a prior and decisive issue for the claims they make, one that they fail to address directly and thus, in the end, also mistake.

5

The Second Time? The Fifth?
The Question of Holocaust-Uniqueness

Current usage cites "*the* Holocaust" with as much assurance as Biblical allusions once did "the Flood" or "the Exodus"; for each, there could be only one referent. Yet in contrast to the other expressions, the first of these raises questions concerning the distinguishing features that justify the definite article: *the* Holocaust. Its moral enormity alone, of course, warrants unusual emphasis, but judging the Holocaust unique is not only a matter of emphasis but also something more, implying that even on the largest scale in man's moral (that is, *im*moral) history, the Holocaust still differs from other atrocities. If this claim is meant as more than a figure of speech—as hyperbole or metaphor—it clearly requires the elaboration of historical detail that would indicate the precise reference of the term *unique*, that is to say *in what respects* what is claimed to be unique is so.

This issue is at the center of Steven Katz's proposed three-volume study, which represents at once the most extensive and the most intensive effort so far undertaken to assert and defend the "Uniqueness-Claim." In the first volume of that study (the only one to have appeared so far), Katz outlines the overall design of his argument for the Holocaust's uniqueness and then begins the process of historical comparison on which that thesis depends.[1] He is thus nothing if not forthright in stating the conclusion to which his comprehensive study has led him and will also, he believes, lead his reader; namely, that the Holocaust *is* unique—dissimilar in essential and significant characteristics from any of the historical acts of group atrocity to which it

[1] Steven T. Katz, *The Holocaust in Historical Context*, vol. 1 (New York: Oxford University Press, 1994).

has been or (because of the sweep of his investigation) even can be compared. Now, of course, Katz is not the first or only scholar to hold or defend this thesis, and he is aware of this (even if at times he makes his own thesis sound unique). In one form or other, writers as various in their backgrounds and ideological dispositions as Yehuda Bauer, Eberhard Jäckel, Elie Wiesel, and Emil Fackenheim have made the same claim. More than most and arguably any of these writers, however—and quite apart from the question of whether or not the common conclusion they urge is warranted—Katz takes seriously both the methodological and the historical issues involved in the "Uniqueness-Claim," formulating them explicitly and attempting to respond to them. In this sense, his work defines the methodological status of the Uniqueness-Claim at its clearest; when that is viewed together with the historical account he then builds on it, the overall view he provides may serve as a test of the Uniqueness-Claim more generally, and it is in this role that I address it here.

Two principal assertions converge in the methodological setting from which Katz moves towards his conclusion. The first of these premises holds that the Shoah (Katz more often uses this designation although "the Holocaust" appears in the title of his work) can be analyzed in standard historical terms, at least as fully and systematically as any complex historical event can be. The second claim is that, scrutinized in this way, the Shoah is indeed distinctive—"unique": qualitatively different from any of the mass killings or atrocities to which it has been or can be compared.

These two premises are obviously not tied to each other logically: the first does not imply the second, and although the second presupposes the first, it also goes beyond it. Katz contends as a common implication of the two viewed together, however, that no account of the Shoah that defends the Uniqueness-Claim can hope to be adequate without a sustained comparison between it and other large-scale instances of mass or group murder in world history. Only by establishing this "historical context" can the specific interpretation of the Shoah as unique withstand critical examination. Indeed Katz undertakes the process of comparison more systematically than anyone who has yet written on the subject, as fully in some instances as scholars of the individual occurrences of mass murder to which the Shoah is compared; this is, I believe, *his* book's distinction. Thus, he devotes much of this first volume to considering comparable ancient and medieval atrocities, promising for volume 2 the analysis of "modern" examples from the sixteenth century to the present. (Volume 3 is to focus on the "Final Solution" and the Nazis themselves: "what they intended and why.")

Katz does not suppose that either his own Uniqueness-Claim or the grounds on which he bases it are themselves unique. As mentioned above, other scholars, quite diverse as historians or theorists, have posited the same claim, basing this on what they also take to be the standard historical forms of evidence and analysis.[2] But, Katz points out, at least some of these views of the Shoah misconstrue the evidence or the historical method (or both) and have yet remained influential; still more commonly, the Uniqueness-Claim has been based either on asserting "transcendent" properties in the Shoah's metaphysical or religious distinctiveness (and meaning), or, in a negative interpretation of the same evidence, announcing the Holocaust's "ineffability" or "incomprehensibility." Katz rejects or at least brackets both the latter conclusions, except for the fact that they typically invoke the Uniqueness-Claim at their basis. The objection he raises to these variations on the theme of uniqueness is straightforward and, in my view, compelling; namely, that just as the evidence of the Holocaust's uniqueness must be anchored in the historical detail of that event, so too, the implications of that claim need not move beyond history, indeed that historical analysis by itself could not provide the means or ground for any move to a theological or any other kind of transhistorical ground. In this respect, he asserts a stronger foundation for the claim of uniqueness than appears in many other versions of the same thesis. Along the way, he also points to a moral lesson for historiography more generally: to fail to judge the Shoah comparatively obscures its individuality as much as does the historicist attempt, at the other extreme, to reduce the Shoah to an impersonal confluence of economic or social forces. The appeal to transcendent meaning mystifies the Shoah just as, from the opposite direction, reductionism trivializes it. Both of them, in any event, end in misrepresentation.

When added to the very large body of evidence that Katz undertakes to present, his advocacy of a "plain" or normal historical methodology—commonplace as such a program may sound—achieves for his work the effect of a tour de force. He adduces evidence for what many other writers (among those who dispute the Uniqueness-Claim) deny, almost always on shakier grounds—since they do not attempt the systematic comparisons that he does. By the same token, he goes beyond what writers who agree with him in asserting the Shoah's uniqueness have by and large simply assumed. His definition of the project, then, is a valuable contribution to the historiography of the Holocaust, notably expanding its more common analysis and often illuminating of the historical examples cited. (Unfortunately, the very

---

[2] For a representative group of formulations of the Uniqueness-Claim (and some of the standard criticisms of it), see Alan Rosenbaum, ed., *Is the Holocaust Unique? Perspectives on Comparative Genocide* (Boulder, Colo.: Westview Press, 1996). See also Alan Milchman and Alan Rosenberg, "The Holocaust: The Question of Uniqueness," and Avishai Margalit and Gabriel Motzkin, "The Uniqueness of the Holocaust," *Philosophy and Public Affairs* 25 (1996): 65–83.

breadth of Katz's historical comparisons sometimes dilutes his thesis by in-
flating it; so, for instance, he considers among occurrences to be contrasted
with the Holocaust the Church's persecution of witches and heretics. But it
is difficult to take seriously the claim that such persecution is a relevant analogue, let alone a precedent of the Shoah; the contrast thus seems pointless
and excessive—overdetermined—although admittedly, even if one grants
this, without affecting his thesis itself.) In the process of comparative enu-
meration, moreover, Katz introduces a series of pertinent distinctions. He
points out, for example, that the Holocaust is not unique either in respect
to the absolute number of its victims or in the proportion of its victims to
the size of the group attacked: other historical atrocities rival or exceed the
Nazi genocide against the Jews in both those respects. If it is to be found
unique, then, that judgment must rest on grounds other than "mere" numbers or proportions.

And indeed there is, in Katz's view, a more fundamental—although still
comparatist—historical ground, a foundation, on which his thesis is based:
"Never before [did] a state set out, as a matter of intentional principle and
actualized policy, to annihilate physically every man, woman, and child be-
longing to a specific people" (28). Even here, of course, readers will recognize that this claim has precedents (for one of numerous examples, Eberhard Jäckel employs much the same language in *Hitler's Weltanschauung*[3]).
Furthermore, Katz's concise statement itself faces conceptual objections,
only some of them anticipated in his own account. The total annihilation he
refers to in the "Uniqueness Claim," for example, is in his view a necessary
condition of genocide; thus he criticizes the vagueness of the U.N. Convention on the Prevention and Punishment of Genocide (1948) according to
which the intention to destroy a group "in part" also qualifies as genocide.
And indeed the immediate difficulty in defining exactly which groups are
covered by the Genocide Convention (is such a group required to have a
minimal number of members? What is the requisite relationship among the
members?) becomes almost an impossibility if the "parts" of a group intended for destruction are also admitted as objects of genocide.

The role of intention is equally important in Katz's Uniqueness-Claim,
since on his view it is the intention to destroy the group (group destruction
as the object of intention) that distinguishes genocide—and so the Holocaust—from mass killing. The object of the latter would not be deliberate
destruction of the group qua group, but the killing (often but not necessarily intentional) of a number, even a large number, of individual persons

---

[3] Eberhard Jäckel, *Hitler's Weltanschauung: A Blueprint for Power*, trans. H. Arnold (Middletown,
Conn.: Wesleyan University Press, 1972).

who may or may not be members of a common group and who, even if they are, are not attacked *because* of that membership or as a means of destroying the group identity. Again, neither the absolute number nor the relative proportion of victims to group members when a group *is* attacked is sufficient or necessary for speaking of genocide (or the uniqueness of the Holocaust). It is generally acknowledged, for example, that other populations or groups suffered heavier losses than the Jews did in the Holocaust (e.g., the number of Russian dead in World War II, for which Katz cites the figure of 27,000,000).

Katz acknowledges that, given the modern technology of destruction, an entire *genos* might be annihilated even in the absence of an intention to destroy the group as such. But few writers claim inadvertence for the Nazi genocide against the Jews—nor does the failed realization of the intention behind that act reduce the charge of genocide or the uniqueness of that one instance (in this respect genocide differs from homicide, which must, after all, be "complete"; otherwise it is only attempted homicide). Thus, Katz claims, the Nazis' intention distinguished the crime of genocide against the Jews, insofar as it willed the annihilation of the group over and above its individual members and irrespective of where the members of the group were located geographically.

Despite this attentiveness to historical method, however, the Uniqueness-Claim as Katz presents it nonetheless slights two significant historiographic issues, the first of considerable substantive importance, and the second still more crucial to his argument and so also to the Uniqueness-Claim more generally. The first involves the concept of intention itself. The uniqueness of the Nazi genocide, Katz reiterates, appeared in the "intention" of the "Nazi state" to destroy the Jews as a people. But although intention is thus proposed as crucial for genocide and certainly for that genocide, Katz hardly considers the question of what it means for a state (or other corporate body) to "intend" to do something. Does the term in such contexts refer to the intention of a single dominant figure (e.g., a Hitler)? to the common intention of a group of policymakers? to a version of Rousseau's "General Will"—that is, representing the people's collective intention? to a common element of individual citizens' intentions—*all* of those individual citizens (as Daniel Goldhagen at times claims in his condemnation of "Hitler's Willing Executioners"), or most of them, or—only—many of them?

Such questions are not quibbles; they are at the heart of any analysis bearing on the issues of collective moral responsibility or the process of historical causality as that is governed or affected by group actions, both of which topics have been themselves subjects of a substantial literature. The differing answers given these questions, moreover, have led to corresponding differences in analyses of the Holocaust (as in the dispute between the "intentionalist" and the "functionalist" accounts of its history). Katz mentions in passing the post-Wittgensteinian philosophical discussion of individual intention, which focuses on the question how we determine or assess a single person's intentions (including our own); as I indicated in Chapter 4, nearly all the same issues addressed in that discussion recur in the consideration of group or corporate intentions, together with some additional ones related to the concept of group acts. Further analysis of the latter topic might not affect the Uniqueness-Claim, but there is no way of determining this beforehand; unless it is clear what sense of intention is being applied in analyzing the corporate act of the Holocaust, the status of the claim for its uniqueness (as dependent on the intention responsible for that act) will itself remain indeterminate.

The second problem whose neglect affects Katz's account and the Uniqueness-Claim more generally concerns their framework or "final cause." This is the question of what follows from the Uniqueness-Claim even if that thesis proved or were assumed to be true. Or to put the issue as bluntly as it can be stated: *So what* if the Holocaust is unique?

Just how much depends on the answer to this question is suggested by the use of the term *unique* in the Uniqueness-Claim rather than the more modest "singular" or the still more precise "unprecedented" which (assuming *it* could be demonstrated) would yield a quite different conclusion. For except as those two terms might be stipulated to be synonymous, common usage recognizes a difference between them. What is *unprecedented* occurs for the first time; nothing like it has occurred before. *Unique*, by contrast, points to the future as well: what is unique has not occurred previously, *and* there is sufficient reason to believe that nothing like it will occur in the future. We speak of a person's fingerprints as unique (not unprecedented, although that is also true) just because they are one of a kind, not having appeared before and (by hypothesis) not to be duplicated in the future. Katz himself acknowledges that no such hedge constrains "the" Holocaust. Quite the contrary: the Shoah's one-time occurrence assures the possibility, in historical terms, of subsequent comparable events. (He does not address the question of whether the first occurrence makes a *re*occurrence—that is, a second time—more likely, although this too seems a relevant possibility.)

Thus, if the *uniqueness* of the Nazi genocide is taken to mean only that nothing essentially like that event had occurred previously, *unprecedented* is the more precise term—and would still, after all, assert an important distinction. (Another way of putting the difference between the terms *unique* and *unprecedented* is this: if the statement that a particular event was unprecedented is true when the statement is made, that statement would remain true even if an essentially similar event should occur subsequently: the first time that something happens remains the first time no matter how many times the same thing is later repeated. On the other hand: if an event occurs that is essentially similar to an earlier one that had been pronounced unique, the Uniqueness-Claim that had at first been asserted as true is now demonstrated not only to be false, but also to have been false at the time it was made.) Katz's own methodological scruples as a historian would require that he judge the Holocaust primarily in reference to the past; his insistence on using "unique"—and again, he is far from alone both in this and in its fault—thus adds an inflationary note to what is already an ambiguity. It is a pronouncement not only about the past but also about the future— adding hyperbole to an event so extreme in character that hyperbole produces exactly the opposite effect of its intented one: it diminishes rather than enlarges.

This objection by itself, however, does not affect the substance of Katz's "Uniqueness [Unprecedented] Claim" or the most basic problem affecting that claim, which can be put in the form of a deceptively simple question: What follows if the Shoah *was* the first of its kind in the respects Katz asserts it to have? What significance would that have? Or, still more severely, as I have already proposed: *So what?* To the extent that the Uniqueness-Claim is central to his thinking about the Holocaust, as it is for the many other writers who—for his reasons or others—emphasize this same feature, readers might reasonably expect to find a discussion of what exactly turns on the Uniqueness-Claim as true or warranted. But about that question, readers will search in vain even for recognition of the issue itself. The argument proceeds here as though the effort to establish the "fact" of uniqueness were an end in itself, with any further justification for undertaking its discovery (or also, presumably, for its refutation, if that should be their conclusion) self-evident.

But the justification for either of these is *not* self-evident, indeed not evident at all. The sheer variety of possible alternative consequences, often at odds with each other, attests to this—beginning with the narrowest possibility that the status of its individuality is sought in the interest of filling out a "mere" chronicle which is then to be added to the indefinitely long chronicle of human history as such. In this appearance, the claim that the Shoah was unprecedented (in anything more than the trivial sense that the same assertion holds for every historical occurrence) would be worth mentioning only as an addendum to the historical record: the Holocaust occurred, and it was the first time that anything like it did occur, much as the "invention"— that is, the first occurrence—of the steam engine or the telephone is noted as part of the chronicle that records the dates associated with those "events."

Nothing in the register either of Katz's writing or its appearances else-where, however, suggests so modest a role for the Uniqueness-Claim. To some extent, of course, the justifications that Katz himself rules out may serve as negative guides; for example, his rejection of attempts to equate histori-cal uniqueness with metaphysical or theological "meaning." Nor does he in-fer from his version of the Uniqueness-Claim a comparative moral ranking that places the Shoah "ahead of" other atrocities. Indeed he explicitly re-jects any form of moral calculus that purports to distinguish degrees of evil or the ranking of evildoers (e.g., as based on the numbers of victims). That the Shoah is "unique" in respect to the features he cites renders it in his view no worse than other instances of atrocity that lack those features—an extension of his repeated contention that his interest in the question of uniqueness is "purely" historical.

This attenuation of the Uniqueness-Claim, however, seems to me mis-taken or, at the very least, unsubstantiated (although admittedly also logi-cally independent of the claim itself). There may be good reason for wish-ing to avoid the one-to-one relation of a straightforward moral calculus correlating the number of victims of a particular act and the measure or de-gree of evildoing ascribed to the act or its agent. But a literal connection of this sort is not the only formula by which responsibility and guilt—or evil—can be comparatively assessed; this is clear in such common (and broad) distinctions as those recognized among or between types of wrongdoing (for example, the differences between lying or stealing, on the one hand, and murder, on the other) and then in distinctions within types of killing it-self (e.g., the difference between premeditated and involuntary killing). And Katz here, perhaps to avoid the charge of special pleading for the ex-tremity of the Shoah, runs the risk from the opposite direction of throwing the baby out with the bath water; that is, of denying invidious comparisons among even the most disparate types of moral violation. That evildoing can-not be assessed only by adding up or comparing the numbers of victims does not mean that there are *no* differences in degree or quality among wrong-ful or evil acts, or even that the sheer or proportionate number of victims will not be one among other factors that bear on such judgments.

The contrary evidence on this point seems clear. The difference between manslaughter and murder, for example, is not commonly formulated in de-grees of evil, but the difference between the legal penalties respectively imposed for the two reflects the larger measure of responsibility (includ-ing the presence of intentional deliberation) ascribed in murder, with the number of victims a potential factor in making this determination. And more generally: however we define evildoing or wrongdoing, the element of deliberation—and its quantification in terms of its specific features—is invariably a factor in its assessment. To be sure, deliberation or premeditation is not the only such condition, but it is a crucial one that in any event demonstrates the possibility of distinguishing degrees of moral responsibility and thus also of wrongdoing. It is possible, then, to acknowledge differences in the extent of evil or evildoing without denying the difficulty of measuring that extent or falling into mystification. And from the opposite direction: the necessary basis for a moral or legal system that equates, for example, shoplifting and murder would be a maxim asserting that all moral and legal violations are equally culpable (that is, qua violations), a principle that, for good reason, has not been part of even the most determinedly formal or punitive codes.

Whatever force there is to this objection, however, Katz excludes it as irrelevant to the *historical* status of his Uniqueness-Claim. It is evidently not his purpose to locate the Shoah in a history of evil, certainly not in a "progressivist" history, or to consider the question of whether any such history is relevant or even possible. The question of the "final cause" of his thesis thus persists: What difference does it make if the Uniqueness-Claim is true or not? It is difficult—not impossible, but difficult—to credit the idea that amassing of evidence and argument for the Uniqueness-Claim is only "its own reward" and that nothing follows from it other than establishing one more historical datum. And this raises the suspicion that notwithstanding his explicit rejection of transcendent "meanings" attributed to the Shoah, the Uniqueness-Claim may nonetheless function in just that way, moving beyond history, although now with some delay before we discover what that function is. Again, Katz himself would no doubt deny crossing this line, but, in the absence of any proposed alternative, what seems often even in his own terms to be an equivocal view of the significance of the Uniqueness-Claim points in that direction. Certainly that claim exerts an inflationary pressure on the whole of his text, in both the presentation of his own position and his criticism of others, and in any event clashing with his plea for the straightforward historical analysis of the Shoah.

On the other hand, there is a possible rationale for the Uniqueness-Claim that would be consonant with his methodological stipulations, arguably very much in their spirit, but one that Katz himself does not mention. If we assume for the sake of argument Katz's conclusion that the Nazi genocide against the Jews was indeed unprecedented in design and scope—in the corporate and comprehensive intention responsible for it—surely the historical question would immediately follow of why this "first-time" event occurred when, where, and as it did, involving the specific agents and victims who were part of it. Viewed in these terms, the now "Unprecedented-Claim" describes a historical "novum"—following which claim, the role of histori-

cal analysis would then be enlarged from mere description to the broader
framework of historical explanation—with *this* then becoming the rationale
for the scholarly account as a whole. To be sure, such a challenge to historical analysis would not be novel either, whether as bearing specifically on
the Holocaust or on other large-scale historical events. It was, for example,
the focus of Hannah Arendt's *The Origins of Totalitarianism* (as suggested in
her title); more currently, it motivates the growing literature on the "prevention" or "early warning systems" of genocide, although here, too, the efforts are not very far advanced. But this means only that Katz's work, with its
promise of a comparative history of genocide, becomes itself a likely source.
As the human capacity for cruelty and murder has been long extant, then if
nothing had previously occurred that approximated the Nazi genocide in its
character or scope, historical reasons for that absence should be retrievable
(presumably the will for it would have been present even if the means and,
beyond that, the idea were not). The questions thus come to the fore both
of why the Nazi genocide occurred when it did—a question that might be
addressed to any historical event—and of what conditions accounted for
this, its first-time occurrence: Why did what happened happen for the first
time when it did? And these would be followed by another more speculative
but related question: What difference does its first-time appearance make
subsequently—that is, now, rounding out the more than fifty-year period of
the post-Holocaust or, casting forward, in the future?

Once again: neither Katz nor other writers who defend versions of the
Uniqueness-Claim on historical grounds point their readers in the direction of these questions.[4] Quite the contrary in fact, in most of these cases
and also for Katz himself. Insofar as Katz considers the causal origins of the
"Final Solution," he emphasizes the primary role of ideas, specifically identifying in them the Nazi turn to metaphysical, quasi-religious abstraction
that cast the Jew in the role of demon. It is thus the Nazis' conception or image of the Jew that Katz finds to have motivated the "Final Solution" in its
"uniqueness." One need not minimize the causal role of ideas or ideology
to recognize that these are by themselves incapable of explaining events as
complex as the Shoah (indeed that they cannot account for even the ideas
that *were* part of it). Of course, Katz knows and acknowledges the standard

[4] Saul Friedländer's conception of "redemptive anti-Semitism" as a distinctive motivating element in the "Final Solution" is, for example, a possible exception to this claim; he evidently
wishes to distinguish it on historical grounds—as well as others—from Goldhagen's quite *ahistorical* conception of "eliminationist antisemitism." See Saul Friedländer, *Nazi Germany and the
Jews*, vol. 1 (New York: HarperCollins, 1997). Even Friedländer's conception, however, comes
close, in my view, to circularity, insofar as it leaves the distinguishing "redemptive" feature of
Nazi antisemitism named but unexplained.

explanations of antisemitism that point to cultural, economic, or psychological causes. But these etiologies are in his view insufficient if not for understanding the more commonplace manifestations of antisemitism, then certainly for explaining the Nazi genocide in its (now) uniqueness. To account for that, Katz prefers what sounds much like the ahistorical causes and sources that he criticizes in the allegedly transcendent accounts of the Holocaust's uniqueness. The Nazis, in his view, placed the Jews outside of space and time, defying the standard patterns of causality and of evidence; with this, the explanation of how they (the Nazis) came to do what they did must be itself similarly dislocated as a historical event.

In arguing for this quantum leap from historical to ahistorical intentions as an explanation of Nazi designs, Katz criticizes Raul Hilberg in his *The Destruction of the European Jews* for assuming a determinist model of history according to which the Holocaust was inevitable. In this retelling of Hilberg by Katz, the efforts of the early Church were bent first toward conversion of the Jews and only later gave way to policies of expulsion—still later, at the hands of the Nazis, to be transformed into a policy of extermination, each of the several stages following necessarily from the preceding one. But surely Hilberg could—and on my reading of him, did—outline this progression without committing himself to historical determinism, referring rather to an evolutionary process involving a series of individual and/or group choices. Nor would Hilberg's account, understood in this way, be more likely than Katz's to obscure the distinctiveness or uniqueness of the Shoah (the spur for Katz's criticism). It remains unclear, in any event, whether Katz is here objecting to historical determinism as such or to determinism only in historical representations of the Shoah because of the novum—the interruption of history—that he identifies with it. He seems to assume that historical explanation has to choose either determinism or a radical form of indeterminacy, with no third possibility of human choice and action that might produce related historical consequences but nonetheless remain underdetermined. But surely it is this last alternative that most often applies to historical explanation and that also applies most plausibly to the Shoah itself, however we affirm its singularity.

That Katz himself speaks at times of an apparently extrahistorical pattern of causality—he refers, for example, to an "essence" of Nazism—thus requires a fuller explanation than he provides. This is the case even if we recognize in the history of historical writing about the Holocaust that no single "explanation" of its occurrence has produced a consensus, indeed that few accounts of that history claim full adequacy even for the terms they favor—and that those who venture any such perspective have also been subjected to sharp criticism on just that ground. If there has ever been an instance of historical underdetermination—with the causes cited less than the effect—the Shoah is it. None of the individual causes that, even with good reason, are cited as contributory—economic, political, cultural, religious, psychological—add up to the event itself. If anything, it is a clue to the distinctiveness of the Holocaust that it remains as unpredictable in retrospect as it so evidently was in prospect: aside from some general forecasts of catastrophe for the Jewish people in exile, no specific pronouncements anticipated the extent or the means—still less, the particular source in Germany—of the Holocaust. (Alternatively, it has to be admitted, collecting together those causes of the Nazi genocide that have been posited singly produces an extraordinary view of *over*determination: with all the contributory causes that have been alleged for it, the Holocaust should have occurred not only once but many times, and well before it in fact did.)

His emphasis on evidence and on the general standards of historical method and comparison suggests for Katz's thesis and his text a sense of limitation or skepticism. But perhaps because of the extremity of the Uniqueness-Claim itself ("unique" cannot be increased by "more" or "most"; the one term says it all), a number of Katz's substantive claims as well as his book's general tone are inflationary and, because of this, at odds with his explicit plea for straightforward—deflationary—history. Many historians, for example, have judged that the "Final Solution," if not initially part of the Nazis' design, came to be integral to it; that at least by the time the Nazis became engaged in the "World War," their war against the Jews was not simply an incidental part of that engagement. In Katz's view, however, "the Nazi state was predicated on and had as its raison d'être. . .the 'solution' to the 'Jewish question.'. . ."(315). The "Final Solution," in other words, was not one among other Nazi intentions, but *the* motivating force of the Nazi regime. Few other historians of the period, however central a place they accord the Shoah and whether they accept its uniqueness or not, agree with Katz that the Shoah stood alone not only in the annals of murder but as the primary causal agent in the history of Nazism. It does not seem to me that Katz provides—or could provide—sufficient evidence in support of this view. (To be fair, he does not attempt to, but this leaves his contention of the centrality of the Holocaust to Nazi ideology and wartime planning still more arbitrary than it would be otherwise.)

At the other extreme, when he does speculate about historical causality in relation to the Shoah, Katz is capable of such wistful banalities as "The individual and collective deportment of Jews is not the primary cause of anti-semitism" (397)—to which he attaches an equally irrelevant footnote: "This is not to deny that Jews, both individually and as a community, like all individuals and communities, have many faults." The question is not whether such statements are in some sense true, but what place they have in a serious work of scholarship, even if one recognizes the author's primary concern with methodology and description rather than with explanation.

What then of the thesis that *is* central to Katz's work? As mentioned, he is in this first volume of *The Holocaust in Historical Context* engaged with historical comparison among instances of mass murder drawn from ancient and medieval history that might be likened to the Shoah. The most immediate question, then, is whether, in those historical terms, Katz makes the case for uniqueness or even, in its more modest formulation, for the lack of precedent: Is it true that no comparable ancient and medieval atrocity has the Shoah's features of intentionality and totality aimed at group annihilation?

As based on the examples analyzed in Volume 1, the Unprecedented-Claim seems to me at least defensible. That invidious process of comparison rejects such major possible examples as the destruction of Carthage (which Rafael Lemkin had cited as an instance of genocide) and the institution of slavery in its "classical" varieties. Jumping ahead of the argument historically, Katz also excludes the Turkish massacre of the Armenians (1915–1917), probably the single most often cited instance compared to the Nazi genocide (for the denial of which *as* genocide, the historian Bernard Lewis was not long ago fined a token sum by a French court). Quite apart from the issue of truth, the drawing of such distinctions is macabre and often—perhaps always—invidiously offensive. And in an obvious sense, the distinctions are quite beside the point: so far as the victims are concerned, the way in which their deaths are classified makes no difference at all. But the lines between, for example, murder and manslaughter or among "degrees" of murder, are significant for both legal and moral judgment. It is for the same reason that the distinctions toward which Katz argues are important as well.

On the other hand, any inference as general as that asserted by Katz, based on examples covering three thousand years and diverse cultures, has to be treated gingerly—not least because of the always-present question of whether any relevant instances have escaped notice. And indeed, at least one comparison omitted by Katz comes to mind, which is the more troubling because of its own charged character. This instance appears in the Hebrew Bible as the Israelites entering Canaan are first (Deuteronomy 20:18) commanded to kill the inhabitants—"not [to] let a single person live"—and then are seen (Joshua 11:12-15) to have carried out that commandment (the commandment would later be prescribed by Maimonides as a continuing imperative; applicable, that is, also to "future" Canaanites).

Prima facie this omitted example comes closer to challenging not only the Uniqueness-Claim but also the Unprecedented-Claim than most (arguably, all) of the examples more usually cited as exceptions or refutations.

But even apart from the question of how that one, or other possible, counterexamples are judged, the general issue raised by such possible counterevidence is worth noting. Only suppose now the discovery of a set of historical circumstances and acts that (by hypothesis) *do* meet all the criteria of "uniqueness" but that also, as the evidence disclosed, antedated the Shoah: What effect would this have on the Uniqueness-Claim and the conception of the Holocaust in which that claim stands at the center? An unavoidable result of Katz's own methodological emphasis is to establish this danger as a constant presence—with his thesis comparable to, and as fragile as, any paleontological reconstruction of the "first" human. Just as for the latter case, the discovery of a single new item of evidence bearing on the former might force the withdrawal of *both* the Uniqueness- and the Unprecedented-Claims, together with all the theoretical or ideological implications (these remain in his account indeterminate) impelled by them.

This possibility underscores the importance of determining what difference the Uniqueness-Claim makes. For if, as I have proposed, the claim of the Shoah's distinctiveness were viewed not only or primarily as a matter of record but as an occasion for bringing together standard historical causes into a composite explanation, then elements of that analysis would remain pertinent even if the Uniqueness-Claim itself had to be revised. Is it not obvious that nothing in the enormity of the Nazi genocide against the Jews would change if that act should turn out to be the second—or fifth—instance of its kind? The identity and the number of victims would remain the same; the same intention and deliberation on the part of the murderers would have been responsible. Nor would such precedents diminish the importance of understanding in historical terms why the Shoah occurred when and as it did, with its specific agents and victims. We would here be seeking to explain not a first-time phenomenon, but the particular event and, beyond that, the phenomenon—the kind. And the latter, after all, would be relevant to explaining also the then first-time phenomenon (whenever that was judged to have occurred), as it would also be something that any purposeful historical account would have to consider, quite apart from the number of its occurrences or precedents.

Some of the difficulties that the Uniqueness-Claim faces derive from its own intrinsic hyperbole which, I have suggested, often carries over into the attempt at a comprehensive comparative history (of which Katz's is the most sustained example) but which does not need figurative enlargement at all—which suffers in fact from the effect; the emotive artifice then clashes with other parts of the accounts that themselves represent literal enormity. The rhetorical register of his account as a whole is thus uneven, with its central Uniqueness-Claim imposing itself on all the other parts of the narrative, including even its most straightforwardly descriptive parts. The effect of this is misleading, because if the Uniqueness-Claim holds at all, it depends first and last on the plain historical evidence—as Katz sets himself to assemble it. This rhetorical dissonance is the more unfortunate because the methodological credo of Katz's work is so notably restrained and focused on its subject. As the most impersonal and deliberately detached histories of the Holocaust have shown that the descriptions they provide, which in almost any other context would be regarded as figurative or hyperbolic, are in fact minimalist and straightforward (with Hilberg's classic account epitomizing this contrast), Katz's account, even with the emphasis it puts on the Uniqueness-Claim left unexplained, points to the same valuable lesson: that whatever other conditions or qualifications apply to representations of the Holocaust, that event can certainly be described, told, compared. And also the property of "uniqueness"—even in the restrained sense of "unprecedented"—is one among numerous other historical predicates, with its applicability also historically demonstrable (or refutable). In this sense, uniqueness is not itself unique. The recognition of this, far from diminishing the enormity or significance of the Holocaust, at once reinforces and expands its historical place, together with the connections that lead away from it—backward to the past and forward to the future.

6

The Third Reich and the
Breakdown of Professional Ethics

The enormity of the Nazi genocide—its combination of systematic calcula-
tion and horrific consequence—encourages a view of the framework of
German history within which it took place as so remote in moral space and
time that observers may be tempted to assume that the framework and its
elements bear little resemblance to their own circumstances. The event itself thus becomes at once more remote and less explicable in standard historical terms, a process that reaches extremes in the recurrent references
one finds to the Holocaust as incomprehensible or ineffable or in the concerted, only slightly more moderate efforts to assert its uniqueness. Earlier
in this volume I argued against the view of the twelve-year Nazi rule as a conceptual or practical aberration which, because of that special status, would
also escape the standard categories of historical analysis. Indeed some of the
most penetrating and telling accounts of Nazism are those that pay closest
attention to its commonplace and day-to-day processes which, in their individual causal patterns, hardly appear as extraordinary at all. Admittedly, this
tactic, which finds reasons and causes in the piecemeal parts of the phenomenon that eventually presented itself as the "Final Solution," is itself a
potentially dangerous tactic, recalling the adage that "to understand all is to
forgive all." And it may well be that in psychological terms a fuller understanding of historical circumstance often has the effect of gradually diminishing the role of moral judgment under the weight of historical detail and
plausibility. But there seems to me no systematic alternative to searching for
the origins of even the enormity of the Nazi genocide in the commonplace
background from which it emerged, only then hoping to understand (as
much as is possible for any complex historical pattern) how individual and
group processes of judgment shaped the social and political policies of the

Third Reich, specifically as they ensued in the war against the Jews. And to do this without ignoring the moral contingencies and decisions without which the general historical process itself becomes quite inexplicable.

This "alltäglich" emphasis turns in the present discussion toward what I shall describe as the breakdown in professional ethics under the Nazi regime, as that breakdown occurred in a number of the central professions. The term, *breakdown*, as applied in this context, may seem too impersonal or neutral a designation for a development that was in large measure intentional not only in its means but also in the ends toward which those means were directed. No doubt, the power and general brutality of Nazi rule, often directed against the German populace itself, was a cause and not only a consequence of this collective lapse; to this extent it might be argued that the professions were themselves also victims of that rule. But it is sufficient for my account if the breakdown can be shown to have been one among other contributors to the implementation of Nazi·policy and (more important) that it reflected in its "professional" agents both a sense of purpose and an awareness of the differences between the new norms of professional conduct they advocated and the older norms that these displaced.

This last claim seems to me crucial. It alleges more specifically that for the professions considered (medicine, law, the academy), certain professional standards that held before 1933 were then systematically violated and reformulated (these two steps virtually as one) in accordance with Nazi political policy. Furthermore, this process was sustained by influential groups within the several professions that were conscious of the changes effected and that, at times, participated in initiating them; even when their roles were less active, they accepted and endorsed and acted on the changes once they were initiated. This is also to say that the professions as corporate groups could not have been unaware of the departures from previous standards and codes of conduct asserted in the new ones. The pertinent questions then arise of how and why and what this tells us about the status of professional ethics during the time at issue—and perhaps about professional ethics more generally.

The thesis posited does not, I believe, designate the standards of conduct displaced in the Nazi period anachronistically. For all their variations, certain accepted standards of professional ethics in Germany immediately before the end of January 1933, when Hitler became chancellor, differed markedly from those which came to be introduced after that date. Furthermore, the earlier standards were in general close to the norms and codes adhered to then in cognate, non-German professional societies.[1] The latter

[1] On the general status of the codes of professional societies in pre-Nazi and Nazi Germany, see Charles E. McClelland, *The German Experience of Professionalization: Modern Learned Professions and*

fact seems to me to leave the breakdown of professional ethics in the Third Reich more disturbing than if it had occurred in a context that was already exceptional in professional terms. The *un*exceptional professional context underscores the possibility of similar breakdowns elsewhere, now or in the future; it also suggests that in the absence of an explanation of what led to this one extensive collapse of professional ethics, we can hardly feel secure about the apparent adherence to such norms in other contexts: how firm or basic a commitment is represented there? To comprehend the practice of professional ethical conduct requires an account, in other words, also of the pathologies to which that conduct is subject.

To be sure, codes of professional conduct, like any other moral codes, are more likely to fail or to change under the pressure of external coercion than without it. But this near-tautology has the additional defect, with respect to the example at issue here, of placing responsibility for the breakdown in professional ethics in the Nazi era outside the professions themselves. And although there is evidence of such external pressure and its effect, the evidence is no less strong that the professions themselves abetted and contributed actively to the changes constituting the breakdown. It is this process—the initiative and/or complicity of the professions in the violation of their own codes of ethics—that in terms of moral analysis seems the most significant aspect of this example.

I refer, then, to the standards of three professional groups under the Third Reich and the systemic changes in the standards of those groups, specifically, medicine, the law, and the academy. The prior history in Germany of these professions varied (most important, in respect to the role of government regulation). I cannot in this context say very much about these histories or about the evolving internal organization of the professions—their *professionalization*; what is crucial, in any event, is the common pattern of breakdown at one terminus of that history (that is, under the Nazis), and I shall cite examples related to each profession indicative of that pattern.

Medical Ethics. This area of professional ethics in the Third Reich has been more extensively discussed than any other.[2] Of the violations in medical pro-

---

Their Organization from the Early 19th Century to the Hitler Era (Cambridge: Cambridge University Press, 1991).

[2] Cf., e.g., Robert Jay Lifton, *The Nazi Doctors: Medical Killing and the Psychology of Genocide* (New York: Basic Books, 1986); Michael Burleigh, *Death and Deliverance: Euthanasia in Germany c. 1900–1945* (Cambridge: Cambridge University Press, 1994), and *Ethics and Extermination: Reflections on Nazi Genocide* (Cambridge: Cambridge University Press, 1997). See also Götz Aly, Peter Chroust, and Christian Pross, *Cleansing the Fatherland: Nazi Medicine and Medical Hygiene*, trans. Belinda Cooper (Baltimore: Johns Hopkins University Press, 1994); and on Nazi medical "experiments" in the concentration camps, James M. Glass, *Life Unworthy of Life* (New York: Basic Books, 1997), 91–98.

fessional norms, I mention two. The first of these involves the program of so-called euthanasia (known as "T-4" after the Berlin address of its headquarters) carried on principally from 1939 to 1941 in the course of which—as a campaign against "life unworthy of life [Lebensunwertes Leben]"—between 50,000 and 70,000 people (mainly non-Jewish Germans) were killed by injection or by gassing and, near the end of the period, also by shooting. The second example is that of the medical experiments performed on human subjects after 1941 at certain of the death and concentration camps. In each of these programs, physicians who had been formally certified to practice medicine (virtually all of them prior to the Third Reich, although in the twelve years between 1933 and 1945 newly certified doctors were added) supervised the process. In the "Gnadenstod" or "mercy killing" of the "T-4," physicians were required to perform the killing by injection or gassing; some were involved in the planning of the program itself. In the same T-4 program, physicians were also required to, and did, fill out false certificates concerning the cause of death for the victims; these were then typically sent to surviving relatives.

In each of the programs cited, an ostensible justification was provided: for the euthanasia of "incurables" (this included the senile or insane or retarded as well as patients outside these categories who were severely handicapped), they were claimed to be a drain on needed resources, an impediment to the ideal of eugenics, and/or incapable of a minimal quality of life. For the experiments on human subjects conducted in the death or concentration camps, the justifications emphasized their potential military application (as in the Dachau experiments that exposed human subjects to high altitudes and to freezing temperatures) or the ideal of general biological knowledge (as in Mengele's "twin studies" at Auschwitz).

In both of these programs, the physicians involved took part in their roles *as* physicians and were identified as such. Furthermore, no evidence shows that they would have faced danger had they declined to participate; indeed, the available records show that they were almost always volunteers. In both projects, moreover, the doctors involved were aware—they could not have been unaware—that the practices they were engaging in departed sharply from previous medical norms and the practices that held at the time of their training when "euthanasia" even in its noneuphemistic sense was proscribed, as were human medical experiments likely to ensue in death or serious harm to their subjects. To be sure, professional norms are neither intrinsically nor have been historically static; but the rationales given by the participating Nazi physicians, as these were recorded, so emphasize the *new* values being acted on in the procedures cited that there can be no question that the physicians were both aware of the break with the past code of their profession and conscious that what they were doing would, even then, be a matter of dispute on professional grounds certainly outside and even within Germany, among both professional and nonprofessional groups.

Obviously, new social and technological developments may warrant additions to current professional norms or alterations in old ones. Why then speak here of a breakdown at all, rather than, more neutrally, of a change? It seems to me that four conditions, taken together, justify applying the former term—conditions met here both in the examples cited from Nazi medicine and in the other examples that follow from law and the academy: (1) The new practice departed in significant ways from previous practice and interpretation of the professional norms. (2) The new practice conflicted (and was known to conflict) with the norms of cognate professional societies in countries with which German professional societies previously— and to some extent, contemporaneously—had contact and compared themselves. (3) The physicians involved in effecting the changes were almost invariably associated with the Nazi movement (in the medical experiments, almost always as SS members);[3] political ideology thus was an apparently constant and strong factor in setting medical norms. [The order for the T-4 program was signed by Hitler himself—a particularly notable example because Hitler typically distanced himself from taking open responsibility for such radical steps, as well as because of the acceptance it entailed of nonmedical (in this case, political) authority over professional practice.] (4) The radical shift in norms and practice was implemented without open discussion inside or outside the profession, and no attempt was made to reach a professional consensus. Indeed, a constant effort was made to conceal these two programs both inside and outside the profession. And the physicians involved in the programs agreed to and abetted enforcement of that code of silence as well.

Judged by any standard of formal conditions for a code of professional ethics, these actions amount to a breakdown in its full pejorative sense. Such formal conditions are not typically part of professional codes themselves, but they are in effect presupposed by them, conditions of the concept of a professional code and what makes such codes possible.[4] Drawing on the violations noted above, these conditions may be summarized as: (1) that the

---

[3] It is estimated that between 40 and 50 percent of German doctors joined the Nazi party, a larger proportion than of any other profession and much larger than the proportion of the general population, which was less than 10 percent. (This figure excludes the 20 percent of the profession as of 1933 who were Jewish.) See McClelland, 225.

[4] There is considerable disagreement, and vagueness, in the literature about the common principles of professional codes of conduct. See, e.g., Daryl Kroehn, *The Ground of Professional Ethics* (New York: Routledge, 1994).

standards or criteria of professional conduct must be publicly stated and disseminated by the professionals involved, as individuals and/or through their societies; (2) that these standards should represent, if not a consensus, then a substantial measure of agreement within the body of professional opinion and practice; and (3) that the norms, or any changes proposed or made in them, should be shown to have a basis in the goals of the profession and in accordance with its standard methods. (The latter are of course also subject to change, but the issue then is even more radical.)

Admittedly, it might be argued that the violation of even these conditions need not imply a *breakdown* in professional conduct. Perhaps even radical changes may sometimes be warranted even if they do not meet one or more of the conditions cited—with the question then left open, perhaps depending on the perspective of the person judging it, of whether such changes represent a breakdown or an advance. This challenge expresses an agnosticism that governs at least one account of paradigm shifts in the history of science—which might now be applied by analogy also to the history (past or present) of ethical practice. I shall return to this putative defense, but for the moment I propose only one summary point and a related question. The summary point is that the conditions cited for codes of professional ethics— what makes the codes possible—are by any measure fundamental. The question is this: If the violation of those conditions, as exemplified in Nazi medicine and the other professions to be discussed, do not constitute a breakdown in professional norms, what *would*?

Legal Ethics. Legal positivism has historically exerted a strong influence on German jurisprudence, in both legal theory and practice. On this conception, legal judgments set out from the law as it is articulated within the constituted legislative framework, with no reference to "external" considerations (such as moral issues) or even, at an extreme, to quasihistorical issues such as original intent.[5] In these same terms, the post–World War II analysis of legal structures and practices under the Nazi regime has been dominated within Germany itself by the argument that judges and courts were applying the laws as they had been independently—that is, legislatively, and therefore legally—formulated. In point of fact, however, the status of the courts and the standing of jurists were much more complicated and equivocal than this, since the Nazi regime fundamentally altered the status of the laws that the juridical system was supposed to apply as well as the juridical process itself.

---

[5] See here especially, Ingo Müller, *Hitler's Justice: The Courts of the Third Reich*, trans. Deborah Lucas Schneider (Cambridge: Harvard University Press, 1991); see also Michael Stollers, *The Law under the Swastika* (Chicago: University of Chicago Press, 1997).

One basic change that epitomized the others occurred in respect to the oath of office required of judges (through the German Civil Service Law; June 26, 1937), in which the judges were required to declare their loyalty to the Führer and not, as had previously been the case, to the law (and/or constitution). Even earlier, with the "Enabling Act" of March 23, 1933, which authorized the chancellor to formulate laws without the consent of the Reichstag and which "might deviate from the Constitution," moreover, there could be no doubt of the commitment that jurists were making in uttering their then still-traditional oath of office. It is hardly irrelevant that in the first year of Nazi rule the number of jurists who were members of the Nazi Party rose from 1500 to 80,000, or that in that same year the Civil Service Law of April 7 initiated the exclusion from the profession of their Jewish colleagues, a substantial proportion of the profession. (The common pragmatic defense of participation in or acquiescence to such changes on the grounds of professional survival is not irrelevant, but it also underscores the question of how deep the commitment to a specific professional code went.) In these several ways, the conception of the law and the norms that had previously bound magistrates and jurists were altered at their foundations. The contention that after these changes judges and magistrates were only administering the law as it was "given" to them by normal legal means seems problematic and even specious on the face of it. (The immediate issue is not what the jurists should have done in response to such changes or pressures—although that surely is an issue—but the hollowness of the justifications they accepted for administering the "new" laws.)

Although the status and reactions of individual lawyers or judges pose a fundamental issue for legal professional ethics under the Nazi regime, it is not the only or the most flagrant one. That title might well be reserved for the formation of the "People's Court" ("Volksgerichtshof") which, in the aftermath of the Reichstag fire (and its "unsatisfactory" legal conclusion— unsatisfactory because the responsibility alleged remained in dispute), was established by Hitler to replace the Supreme Court specifically in trying cases of treason. The five-person panels of this court were to include two judges; the other three members were to be drawn from the Nazi party, the SS, and the armed forces. There was no appeal from the verdicts of the People's Court; its sessions were typically held in camera. Defendants were rarely able to present witnesses; counsel for the defense had to be qualified ("Nazi") attorneys. There was nothing secret about either the practice or the verdicts of the People's Court: the existence of the court and its functioning were known, certainly within the legal community. To be sure, in terms of the Enabling Act, both the role of the court and its functioning were "legal"; it is also true that a relatively small proportion of qualified judges or magistrates participated in the "deliberations" of the People's Court over the course of its ten-year history. But the records of its decisions (and of its sentences as well as of the judges presiding) were made known at the time; the charges brought in these courts were largely directed against non-Jewish German citizens. German jurists, whether members of the Nazi party or not (many of them also sitting on other courts), concurred or participated in the People's Court, carrying on their own other work apart from *its* work as though the latter extraordinary institution had no bearing on the legal system or process more generally. (Another branch of the juridical system devised by the Nazi government was the system of "Special Courts" which were given jurisdiction over non-German citizens in occupied countries and territories, again with indifference to standard legal procedures. Even by comparison with the latter courts, however, the role of the People's Court within Germany itself sets it apart.)[6]

Academic Ethics. The best known and most widely discussed instance of violation in academic ethics appears in the thought and practice of a single figure, the philosopher Martin Heidegger, who served as rector of the University of Freiburg from April 1933 to April 1934. Beyond the limits of this extent, however, Heidegger's career embodies many of what became general practices or features of university life in Germany under the Third Reich. These can be described, furthermore, quite apart from Heidegger's personal dispositions (e.g., his antisemitism) and even apart from his membership in the Nazi party. Furthermore, they replicate the pattern of violations in the other professions previously referred to—here in respect to the tradition for which the German terms "Lernfreiheit" and "Lehrfreiheit" are still often used. What those ideals had entailed as academic norms in the pre-Nazi period was open access to the sources and products of inquiry for faculty and students; admission, retention, and advancement in the university on the basis of academic ("professional") judgment; and the assessment of ideas apart from reference to the status or history of the investigators.

Heidegger became rector of the University of Freiburg at a time when the Nazi exclusion of non-Aryan faculty and students from the University had begun; he presided over part of that process during his year's tenure as rector, and he remained on the faculty of the university (as well as a member of the Nazi party) until the war's end. Features of the academy—not only at Freiburg, but throughout Germany—included, beyond the racial exclusion of students and faculty, such changes as the political appointment of the

[6] How troublesome this issue remains is evident in the fact that it took some forty years for postwar Germany to nullify the verdicts of the People's Courts—and that even now some of the verdicts of the SS courts still stand.

"Führer-Rektor" at each of the universities; the censorship in libraries and university curricula of topics and texts (this included, in May 1933, official ceremonies of bookburning at many of the universities); the politicization of the natural sciences (especially biology and physics) as well as of the social sciences and the humanities; the advancement of academic careers in inverse relation to the disappearance of a significant number of faculty members (Jews and others associated with them) beginning in 1933 and almost completed by 1935—and directly linked to the "race" or to the political views of the individuals concerned. Some academic figures might have escaped harm if they agreed to remain silent, but they refused to accept these terms and emigrated. (Paul Tillich was a prominent example of this group's members.) Others whose views were opposed to the Nazis' remained nonetheless, maintained silence, and survived. But a much larger group than either of these actively supported the "academic" policies mentioned (and often Nazi political aims more generally); they became in effect "Hitler's Professors," in the phrase used by Weinreich as the title to his early book on the subject.[7] With this, they altered the shape of the universities, in terms of limiting the research undertaken there, censorship of the sources that could be drawn on in the research that was undertaken and in the classroom itself, and restricting the composition and advancement of both the teaching faculty and the student body on the basis not of intellectual ability but of social identity or political commitment.

THE factors I cited earlier as breaches in the conditions governing professional norms recur in all these examples, with the exception in certain cases of the imposition of rules of secrecy, although also that criterion applies frequently and sometimes in still more exaggerated form. The breaches in medical ethics, for example, were not only secret in planning but were also kept secret as practiced. The other shifts in professional standards, however, were also decided initially in secret and by a small group within the profession who achieved and maintained power by means that were not substantively (i.e., nonideologically) related to the work or standards of the profession itself.

How to explain this recurrent pattern of the violation of prior and supposedly well-established professional norms is more difficult than to de-

---

[7] Max Weinreich, *Hitler's Professors: The Part of Scholarship in Germany's Crimes against the Jewish People* (New York: YIVO, 1946). See also Konrad Jarausch, "The Perils of Professionalization: Lawyers, Teachers and Engineers in Nazi Germany," *German Studies Review*, 1986; Alan D. Beyerchen, *Scientists under Hitler: Politics and the Physics Community in the Third Reich* (New Haven: Yale University Press, 1977); Monika Rennenberg and Mark Walker, eds., *Science, Technology, and National Socialism* (Cambridge: Cambridge University Press, 1994)

scribe it. The problem is compounded by the fact that in considering such violations, there is no way to separate professional issues from those of personal interest or simple opportunism—although it is quite unlikely that changes as dramatic as those cited could be fully explained by the latter, which are presumably social constants that cross the lines of classes and types of work. Ideally, analysis of the pattern would start from a representative number of individual cases, tracing specific careers and conduct within the professions. Some scholarly analysis has in fact moved in this direction, but much more remains to be done, and I can here offer only a general view of the issues that will affect any such explanation.

One inference that might be drawn from the pattern of the alleged breakdown is that professional codes of conduct are themselves ideological, at least as much as any set of moral norms. Since there is nothing surprising in the conflict between one ideology and another, the acceptance or furthering of Nazi practice or ideals in the professions under the Nazi regime is but another instance of this. On this account, the term *breakdown*, characterized neutrally, could be viewed once again as only the displacement of one set of norms by another, a version of a *moral* paradigm shift with its entailment of cultural relativism.

There seems to me no reason, however, to concede this view, if only because even a history based on paradigm shifts need not imply a value-neutral conceptual frame. But this contention requires broader discussion than is possible here and seems to me in any event unnecessary since the question of evaluation can be confronted more concretely and directly. A likelier account in these terms would be that the distance between professional and general rules of conduct is less specialized, and less insulated, than it is often assumed to be. Certainly it seems clear that the *resemblance* between professional and nonprofessional conduct in the Third Reich was stronger than the *differences* between them. It may be too much to infer as a general conclusion that there is no difference between professional ethical norms and other nonprofessional or commonplace ones. But it is clear that in the context of Nazi Germany, with whatever special circumstances pertain to it, the professional and more commonplace norms, on their two sides, did not diverge widely; if anything, professional norms departed more sharply from their traditional expression than the general, nonprofessional norms did from theirs. At the very least and most important, professional norms posed either no or very little hindrance to the obtrusion of values from outside the professions.

I began this discussion by suggesting that I did not mean to present the example of Nazi Germany as a mere symbol which would then have the effect of distancing it from assessments of professional ethics much closer to home. I do not wish to imply by this that what happened in the professions in Nazi Germany could have occurred or could yet occur with the same measure of probability in any other country at any other time; certain quite specific material conditions were features of the German context as it turned toward Nazism—as well, of course, as the single acts of presumably responsible individuals that sustained the collective policies. By the same token, however, there is no reason for assuming the uniqueness of this occurrence; even if the specific causal background remains (as it must) underdetermined, it would be misguided to avoid inquiring about more general implications of the breakdown.

One crucial element is the active role of the professions themselves in bringing about the breakdown: whatever else may be unclear in their histories, it is indisputable that they were not simply victims of an external force that compelled them to think and to act as they did. For many of them, substantial evidence indicates a link between their professional roles and the Nazi ideology—a link that proved irresistible to them. Whether this was due mainly to a commitment to the one or the allure of the other hardly matters; the conjunction between the two did the work. If it is impossible to distinguish the motives for such commitments among the principal alternatives—the ideology itself, ambitions for personal advancement and power, "peer-pressure"—it seems reasonable to conclude that a strong voluntary element helped shape the course of such professional conduct. Whatever other effects the professional norms had, they did not deter the radical alteration in them. Is it possible to conclude from the active participation of German professionals in the process of the "Final Solution" that the changes in the codes of conduct they espoused during that time encouraged the process itself? It is difficult to see how this could not have been the case, or how the professionals who were involved could not have recognized this as having been the case.

To be sure, neither the responsibility nor the culpability of "professionals" ends where the profession itself does. So, for example, physicians and judges and professors of literature or philosophy also faced substantial moral decisions outside their professional roles. When the German resident of a city was suddenly given the opportunity to move into a well-furnished apartment for a minimal payment (in effect, a windfall), the decision to act on that opportunity was obviously voluntary (no penalty would be exacted for *not* moving in) and no different for the professional than for anybody else. This too would involve the decision not to ask about the previous residents, not to want to know about them, and then to take advantage of this ignorance: all these are part of the moral context. It would be interesting to know how various social or economic groups (and the various professions) responded to such opportunities, and whether there were significant (or any) differences among them. I know of no statistics bearing on this question, but an implication of what has been suggested here is that there is unlikely to have been significant differences between the response of "professionals" on such occasions and the response of other groups. (This implication would serve in fact as a test of that view.)

What emerges from these comments as a moral for professional ethics might be summarized in the maxim that E. M. Forster reiterates as an epigraph for his novel, *Howards End*: "Only connect." A constant danger in the process of professionalization (and so also for professional ethics in its assumptions) is that the individual professions and their codes will come to be viewed as conceptually and substantively distinct from any more general or overriding rules of conduct. One can, of course, understand the impulse within the professions to find special privileges or immunities for the roles of their members, and it is also clear that professionals often have special responsibilities defined by the charges and tasks of their professions. But far from preempting or overruling more general nonprofessional ethical codes, the individual professional codes may also (and, I argue, much better) be viewed as instantiations or implications of those more general ones—a connection that is important for both professionals and their "clients" to keep constantly in sight. If the breakdown in professional ethics in the Third Reich is not necessarily due to what had been the privileging or separation of professional from general norms, it is obvious that their codes did not enable the professors or the profession to resist the general turn; in some ways, the status of the norms seems to have made the professions even more vulnerable to changes such as those mentioned than did the more general and nonprofessional norms in their domains.

Julien Benda is remembered more often for the title of his book *La Trahison des Clercs* than for the thesis he presented in that work itself. The betrayal that he attacked therein was the willingness of the intellectual, of the cleric (for the present discussion, the professional), to shed his role as a disinterested seeker of truth to assume the role of partisan. I do not mean, in objecting here to Benda's account as related to both practice and principle, to dismiss the ideal of professional disinterest; in *some* form—in scientific, legal, scholarly judgments—that ideal is undeniable so long as anything more than power or force is to be accorded a place in the court of judgment. But it is also important to recognize the conditions that qualify that condition—to understand disinterest as itself expressing an interest, of which, therefore, we ought also to become as self-conscious and self-critical. This is what I understand Forster's "Only connect" to mean in this context: the effort to see one's own immediate actions in relation to other ones, certainly to the larger moral frameworks on which they depend. If such frameworks include at an intermediate level the strictures of professional norms, at their outer boundaries they reflect the larger moral principles that assert at once the value of life and justice and the wrongfulness of gratuitous repression and harm. Where the failure to see the connections among these several levels occurs, the potential consequences of human actions become progressively both larger in scope and more damaging. And if professional failure in Nazi Germany's Third Reich was neither the first nor (almost certainly) the last example of such systemic violation, it remains a clear instance, one that we now ought to recall and also to connect with.

7

Heidegger Recalled

Snowblindness

Starting with his own several memoirs, Martin Heidegger's biography has been inscribed in a large number of unreliable texts—fitting, it might be suggested, for his objections to what he claimed was the obsolete "foundational" conception of truth. Elzbieta Ettinger now adds to these accounts of his life and work her elusive rehearsal of the affair between Heidegger and Hannah Arendt[1]—a relationship generally known as having occurred but with its features heavily veiled and now, even with the correspondence between the two that Ettinger brings to light, not much clearer in detail or less perplexing in character.

The ingredients for high drama in that relationship are unmistakable, with passion and intellect joined in and between the leading figures, the couple themselves traversing a half century of unusual historical crisis. They would later die only months apart (1975 and 1976), but it is the beginning of the relationship that has been more difficult to get at and that Ettinger's account sets out to relate—when the renowned thinkers-to-be first met (fall 1924) and then consummated at the University of Marburg: Heidegger the rising star of German philosophy, only a few years away from succeeding to the chair of his mentor, Husserl, at Freiburg and with that prospect very much in mind (35, married, two children, philosophy having displaced his earlier studies for the priesthood); Arendt, first-year student (18, Jewish,

---

[1] Elzbieta Ettinger, *Hannah Arendt.Martin Heidegger* (New Haven: Yale University Press, 1995).

unmarried). At the time, the probability of anyone's challenging an affair between professor and student was as remote as the distance then conventionally honored between the two ranks—even more remote, evidently, since the professor and student themselves seem quickly to have bridged that gap, spurred on by Heidegger's opening letter to "Miss Arendt" in which he asks only, Ettinger reports, "that she let him help her to remain faithful to herself."

Arendt evidently "let him" (she "did not need coaxing," Ettinger claims to know), and Ettinger places the "beginning of physical intimacy" at the end of February 1925. How much or little of the banality of Heidegger's line Arendt recognized—even after she herself turned banality into a distinct moral category—remains something of a puzzle. She would subsequently describe Heidegger, in letters that Ettinger cites, as "ly[ing] notoriously always and everywhere, and whenever he can" (1950); "He certainly believed that . . . he could buy off the whole world at the lowest possible price and cheat his way out of everything that is embarrassing to him"(1950). But her devotion to Heidegger withstood this awareness, as it had already and would continue to withstand humiliation after humiliation. The times and places of their meetings—at one point, even the occasions when they could write to each other—were set by him not only in Arendt's student days but also after the seventeen years of silence between them ended, the silence that began in 1933. With their postwar renewal of communication, Heidegger's wife, Elfriede, also learned from him of the earlier affair, and Heidegger was not above using *her* (all too willing) as a combination of excuse, buffer, and bludgeon to underscore Arendt's awkward position in the role now as "friend" in place of the earlier lover.

Arendt's commitment to Heidegger, as it overrode her recognition of his character—he had *no* character, she once concluded—was so notably deep and constant that even the traditional blindness of love hardly explains it. It persisted through her own two marriages, the second of which (to Heinrich Bluecher) evidently involved great depth and feeling; it lasted through separation and silence (most remarkably the seventeen-year period that combined both) and rebuff, as well as the "gofer" role she accepted even late in their lives (as when Heidegger asked Arendt to take charge of marketing the manuscript of *Sein und Zeit*). Arendt's willingness to subordinate—it would not be misleading to say abase—herself in the relationship did not seem to diminish even when her own success and prominence increased. Indeed these were matched step for step by Heidegger's resentment, which he expressed by refusing to applaud or indeed even to acknowledge her accomplishments. (Her reaction to this? "I am quite ready to behave toward

Heidegger as though I have never written a word and will never write one" [1955].)

And, of course, hovering over the whole of the fifty-year span was the specter of Nazism and the shadow it might have been expected to cast on each member of the couple for the other: Heidegger, Nazi party member from 1933 to the war's end, who would use his bully-pulpit as rector of the University at Freiburg for pronouncements of a new vision for Germany, which included his discovery (November 1933) that "the Führer and he alone is the present and future German reality and law"; and who then, after 1945 and the Third Reich's demise, would pass thirty prolific years of metaphysical authorship (and professional rehabilitation) without a public word condemning that regime or, more to the immediate instance of his lover, its implementation of the "Final Solution." On the other side— Arendt, who, also in 1933, left Germany for exile in France, saw from inside the internment camp at Gurs even before the Vichy government took it over and, reaching the United States in 1941, embarked soon afterward on the searching account of fascist power and antisemitism elaborated in *The Origins of Totalitarianism*; she supported herself almost throughout the twelve years of Nazi power by employment with various Jewish organizations dealing with the consequences of that power.

Admittedly, history that we read backward with assurance would be viewed much more tentatively when projected looking forward. Thus the specter of Nazism might well have seemed remote and unthreatening indeed in 1924 for the young student from a household in enlightened Koenigsberg, a household so at ease with its social and cultural surroundings that "the word 'Jew' was never mentioned"(Arendt, interview, 1964). But the specter was more distinct by 1928 when, Ettinger declares, the affair between Heidegger and Arendt (more accurately, this phase of the affair) ended; when, not coincidentally, Heidegger learned of his appointment to the professorship at Freiburg and—coincidentally or not—turned to another woman "waiting in the wings" (Elisabeth Blochmann) *and* when the Nazis had built up, in rhetoric and membership, a noticeable head of steam, including clear soundings of various völkisch themes by Heidegger himself. On the way to that terminus, Heidegger had begun to encourage Arendt to leave Marburg (and, presumably, him), suggesting to her, in Ettinger's paraphrase of a Heidegger letter to Arendt, that "She had failed to establish herself and did not fit in": a "Dear Joan" letter of classic formula and, one might guess, practice. By 1933, although the "Final Solution" had not been defined in detail, its foundation was being laid, together with the popular support it would require and eventually get. Three months after Hitler became chancellor at the end of January, and soon after the beginning of the exclusion of Jewish students and faculty from the state-sponsored universities (all the major ones in the country), Heidegger maneuvered himself into the rectorship (soon to be designated the Führer-ship) of Freiburg; Arendt, a bit later in 1933 and after receiving a last response from Heidegger in which he angrily assured her of how much he was doing for the Jews at his University, crossed the border of exile. No word would then be exchanged between the lovers for the next seventeen years.

During that period, the "Final Solution" had been posed as an answer to the "Jewish Question"—an outcome known, of course, to both Heidegger and Arendt in 1950 when contact between them was revived. They were both also aware that Heidegger himself stood condemned at the time of complicity in advancing the cause of Nazism in the academy and that, because of his activities, he had been banned from the university of which he was once rector (the ban lasted four years, from soon after the war's end until 1950). What effect did such events (and the long hiatus itself) have on the relationship between Heidegger and Arendt? Leaving aside the physical intimacy that Ettinger's reader does not hear about after its first moment, virtually nothing. In 1950 Heidegger needed the support of all the friends who might respond; and Arendt, presumably for the same reasons that moved her earlier, was again willing to come forward, straining to interpret her own reservations about him and his Nazi misadventure partly as faults in those who for other reasons incited criticism of Heidegger, partly as a "pathology" or "professional deformation" afflicting Heidegger (as it were, beyond his control), partly as the baneful influence of Elfriede, whose anti-semitism antedated her awareness of the Arendt affair and who was decid-edly *not* willing (as Martin himself was) to reinvent or even to accept the cliché "Some of my best students were Jews."

There seems in fact to have been only one juncture at which Arendt's mis-givings about Heidegger seriously threatened her commitment; this was in reaction to her discovery of the letter she at first believed Heidegger had personally sent to the retired Husserl forbidding him access to the uni-versity. When Karl Jaspers pointed out to her that this was not a personal let-ter, but a circular letter sent to all (former) Jewish faculty, she persisted and, regarding Husserl's subsequent illness and death which were ignored by Heidegger (at least until after Husserl's death), referred to his role then as that of a "potential murderer." Strong words, but evidently not strong enough to overcome her attachment.

It is difficult to identify love from the inside, let alone from the outside— but if ever judgment can be made from appearances, there seems no doubt and almost no limits on Arendt's love for Heidegger, its emotional and intellectual aspects joined and flourishing side by side in the early years of their relationship, and then enduring or at the very least revived even in the aftermath of a gap of large proportions in both world history and their personal histories. By the same standards, there is little doubt about the hedges and trimming on Heidegger's side in relation to her—unless, perhaps, the beloved who "offers the cheek" has some invisible means of catching up with the lover "who kisses." Arendt herself continued to believe even in her later years that no other woman had meant as much to Heidegger as she had, but the evidence suggests that Arendt was probably not the best or even a good judge of this. Admittedly, the imbalance and the misconception that Ettinger describes are not implausible—or more puzzling—in this relationship or in their common occurrences elsewhere. But not many other such instances personify history's encounter by the combination of intellect and passion that this relationship did, and so its perplexing character emerged and persists with special force.

I have cited the account Ettinger provides, based on the Heidegger-Arendt correspondence to which she had access, as an addition to the numerous unreliable texts of the Heidegger Bildungsroman. (Arendt's history, however full and contentious, has not been similarly affected.) This criticism is not directed at the failure of the Heidegger-Arendt correspondence or of other records to solve the more general "Heidegger question" (how to understand the political and personal venality of the world-renowned philosopher of Being) to account for Arendt's postwar reconciliation with Heidegger, or to show what consequences their relationship had, early or late, on their respective thinking. Ettinger, like other recent commentators, could have said more than she does about these matters, but her purpose was more narrowly to bring to light the newly disclosed material from their correspondence. Nor, unlike much writing about Heidegger, is her book tendentious in charting his biography aside from his relationship with Arendt (she leaves the more general and deeper question of the connection between his life and his thinking untouched). If Ettinger has any ideological ax to grind, it is a mildly feminist one that shows Arendt as a victim—a conclusion Ettinger only glancingly joins to the other evidence she presents of Arendt as a collaborator in that victimization.

Two errant aspects of Ettinger's design undermine her account, however—the first of these, where she as writer purports to know more than she has given evidence for (or, in some instances, could give evidence for); the second an elementary issue of method. So, as an instance of the former: Ettinger asks and then replies to the question of what it was that drew Arendt to Heidegger: "What truly mattered to her was not erotic attraction, which may or may not have existed—she was sensual without being strongly sexual—but the special role that she played in his life"(87). How much, the question might here be posed, would one person have to know about another person—about *any*body, let alone as complex and traveled a figure as Arendt—to demonstrate this nest of claims? Certainly none of the slight biographical evidence that Ettinger provides, indeed none that her most intensive biographers, such as Elizabeth Young-Bruehl, have provided, would yield this conclusion any more than it would a number of alternatives. Ettinger hardly does much better than this in what might otherwise seem a more straightforward description of Heidegger at the beginning of the affair with Arendt: "Strict, rigid, hard-working, the son of devout Catholic peasants—[he] seems to have [previously] known little of genuine passion, of a physical and spiritual bond"(3). Perhaps, as Ettinger evidently means to suggest, his new relationship with Arendt changed all that in Heidegger's life. It is not obvious, however, that the qualities contrasted between Heidegger's pre- and post-Arendt character do in fact exclude each other; it is not even clear, and there is some contrary evidence for this, that Heidegger had been idly waiting for Arendt to come along before undergoing the transformation that Ettinger claims then occurred in him. Just when or how Heidegger's reputation as a womanizer arose are questions that Ettinger does not broach, although after taking the major step of choosing her book's subject, it is difficult to understand why discretion should have hindered this second, much smaller one.

Does any of this matter, other than as prurience on the part of readers more interested in reading between than along the lines of a text? Perhaps not for the larger interests of history, and perhaps not for the interests of metaphysics or the life of the mind either, but surely it matters for a narrative in which a relationship between two figures, each with a passion for life and for work, is the thing. The ideal of history as a seamless web, after all, was never intended or understood to exclude the seamy.

What Ettinger glides over here in her leaps of inference also reflects the second problem referred to: her indifference to the rudimentary questions of scholarship about the sources of her account. That Heidegger and Arendt had an affair that began at Marburg has been generally known, as has the fact that their relationship was in some form revived following World War II. What has produced varieties of speculation are the questions of how the relationship evolved, what its importance was for them (early or late), and the ways in which it did or did not impinge on their thinking. One large obstacle in the way of answering such questions has been the restrictions placed around the Heidegger-Arendt correspondence and around the Heidegger archives more generally. The latter are held under severe restraints by Heidegger's literary executors in the Deutsches Literaturachiv at Marbach (access is permitted, as the rules have been explained to me, only to those manuscripts that have been published, which in turn depends on the executors' permission). The bulk of the Arendt papers are partly at Marbach, partly in the Library of Congress; these include, at Marbach, about a hundred letters to Arendt by Heidegger (1925–1975) and about thirty letters from Arendt to Heidegger (1928–1975). (Ettinger notes that Arendt made copies of all the post-1950 letters she sent to Heidegger and some of the earlier ones. Is it these (pre-Xerox) copies that Ettinger is working from? Were the letters of which Arendt made copies indeed received by Heidegger? Were the letters sent and received identical to the copies now held? etc., etc.) I understand that there are, in the Heidegger archives, seventeen letters from Arendt to Heidegger that remain out of public reach. Ettinger does not explicitly identify these or anything else in the Heidegger holdings that might bear on the relationship, although, according to an account in the *New York Times Book Review* (September 21, 1995), Ettinger was allowed by the Heidegger executors to read the letters in that holding. She does not mention, though, let alone elaborate on these complexities; nor does she, in citing the letters from the Arendt collection, say anything about the extent of the holdings, what letters she did or did not make use of, what restrictions she accepted even in relation to the Arendt collection, and what significance the answers to these questions could have for the story she tells. I mention the matter of restrictions because Ettinger herself hints at them, although again without explanation: she acknowledges the permission of the Hannah Arendt Literary Trust to "use" Arendt's own letters to Heidegger and his wife (Are these the copies Arendt made, or are they the originals?) and then acknowledges the permission of the Trust to "peruse" Heidegger's letters to Arendt (these are presumably the real thing). The difference between "use" and "peruse" is obviously fraught; but exactly what it, or anything else in the background of the "novelties" in this volume, amounts to is left for the reader to find out. Perhaps nothing yet to be found or brought to the public eye in any of the still sequestered archival material would substantially change the outline of the relationship between Heidegger and Arendt that emerges in Ettinger's account. But at this point neither her readers nor perhaps Ettinger herself knows this—and there is at least a chance that some of the answers to such questions would make a difference.[2]

There is by now ample evidence that, among their other great abilities, both Heidegger and Arendt knew how to wait; whatever more venturesome moral we learn from the story of their relationship, it can certainly add some-

[2] Almost all the questions noted still remain after the recent publication of *part* of the Arendt-Heidegger correspondence, in Ursula Ludz, ed., *Hannah Arendt and Martin Heidegger: Briefe, 1925–1975* (Frankfurt: Klostermann, 1998): What portion of the correspondence does this represent? How was it selected? Etc.

thing about this to currently impatient scholarship for which patience is a defect as well as a risk. It is the more notable, then, that in a study that is intended to recover history, questions of method should be so slighted that the results delay and even hinder. But so it is: the representation of a flight of extraordinary intellect and undoubted passion stumbles over an only too visible—historical—obtrusion, although it may not stretch this representation too far to see in it also a portrait of the relationship between the two lives.

"Nur noch ein Gott kann uns retten" ["Only A(nother) God Can Save Us"]: Heidegger's Last Words

[A Cautionary Tale:

The setting is a Bierstube in a small German town. The five friends have been meeting here in late afternoon, after work, for more than twenty years, watching each other's hair turn gray and their bodies thicken. Only their opinions have remained unchanged—that and the cameraderie. The tone this afternoon, however, is somber. Johannes has learned that he must have "exploratory" surgery, Dieter has been downsized from his job as a machinist, and Ulrich's younger son has been arrested for selling drugs. The talk is desultory, lapsing for comfort into other, vicarious tales of misfortune. Klaus, the optimist of the group, finally becomes impatient and tries to distract the others. Gesturing at the empty beer mugs on the table, he bangs his own down beside them and says with mock seriousness: "Nur noch ein Bier kann uns retten."]

HEIDEGGER's controversial *Spiegel* interview—controversial both for the silence it broke and for what he left unsaid in breaking it—was published in the May 31, 1976, issue of the *Spiegel*, the first issue to appear after his death.[3] The interview had taken place on September 23, 1966. Choosing the unlikely medium of a mass-circulation weekly for his first public accounting of his relation to Nazism, Heidegger agreed to the interview on condition that it not be published until he had died and apparently with an understanding that even its existence would be kept secret (although in fact a number of people outside the *Spiegel* learned about the interview at the time it was conducted or later became aware of it).[4] Thus, frozen in a ten-

---

[3] *Der Spiegel* 23 (1976). The unrelated lead story in the same issue was featured under the title "Schul Angst."

[4] Heidegger himself mentioned the interview to Richard Wisser during the conversation in preparation for a television interview that was then broadcast on September 24, 1969. See Richard Wisser, "Afterthoughts and Gratitude," in Gunther Neske and Emil Kettering, *Martin Heidegger and National Socialism*, trans. Lisa Harries (New York: Paragon House, 1990), 89–124.

year interval during which he evidently had no second thoughts about what
he said or did not say in the interview, Heidegger's first public accounting
of his 1933–1934 rectorship at the University of Freiburg and his Nazi associations leading up to it and afterward turned out also to be his last words
on those dangerous topics.[5]

The interview, conducted for the *Spiegel* by Rudolf Augstein and Georg
Wolff, was transcribed and then returned—twice—to Heidegger for edit-
ing. (A photograph of one page of the transcription as edited by him, with
extensive handwritten deletions and interpolations—including what seems
to be one correction of a question *addressed to him*—is included in the same
issue of the *Spiegel*.) After Heidegger had returned the edited transcript,
and without consulting him, the *Spiegel* editors made a number of changes
in the wording and even in the sequence of what became the interview's
published version.[6] (Evidence of these changes is apparent in the difference
between the photographed page of Heidegger's revisions and its published
counterpart.) No one has claimed that these changes substantively altered
anything Heidegger had said, although this silence remains inconclusive as
long as neither the original nor revised transcriptions are available. (Victor
Farias reports having requested and being denied access by the *Spiegel* to
them—on "ethical" grounds.)[7]

The *Spiegel* published the edited interview under the title "'Nur noch ein
Gott kann uns retten,'" thus highlighting a statement by Heidegger re-
ported in the conversation itself. This title, subsequently used also in three
of the four English translations of the interview that have been published
and repeated in numerous other references (the latter based sometimes on
the German text, sometimes on translations),[8] seems to have been chosen

---

[5] Heidegger had addressed the question in his "de-Nazification" hearing in 1945, a formulation that was not, however, directed to the public; he also left a statement, written in 1945 probably in conjunction with the hearing, with his son, Hermann Heidegger, for publication as the
latter might see fit. "Das Rektorat: 1933/34: Tatsachen und Gedanken," in M. Heidegger, *Die
Selbstbehauptung der deutschen Universitat/Das Rektorat 1933/34* (Frankfurt: Vittorio Klassman,
1983), trans. Karsten Harries in the *Review of Metaphysics* 38 (1985). The Wisser interview, although intended as a public statement, carefully, and evidently by agreement, avoids the question of Heidegger's relation to Nazism.

[6] On the sequence of editorial changes, see Hermann Heidegger's comments in an appendix
to Neske and Kettering (233–236). The version of the *Spiegel* interview included in the Neske
and Kettering volume is the final version that *was* approved by Heidegger and differs from the
version published in the *Spiegel* itself.

[7] See Victor Farias, *Heidegger and Nazism*, trans. Paul Burrel (Philadelphia: Temple University
Press, 1989), 297.

[8] The translations are by David Schendler, "Only a God Can Save Us Now," *Graduate Faculty Phi-
losophy Journal* 6 (1977); Maria Alter and John D. Caputo, "Only a God Can Save Us," *Philosophy
Today* 20 (Winter, 1976): 267–284; and William J. Richardson, "Only a God Can Save Us," in
Thomas Sheehan, ed., *Heidegger: The Man and the Thinker* (Chicago: Precedent, 1981). (Lisa

by the *Spiegel*, not by Heidegger himself. It is, in any event, the interpretation of that title—more basically, of Heidegger's *statement*—that I ask about
here. What is at stake in this matter perhaps amounts to no more than a difference in nuance—but perhaps not; it is in any event a difference that the
interview's translators and those who cite them have passed over without
notice, and since it is a difference of the sort that Heidegger often made a
great deal of in reading other authors, it may be well to "interrogate" it in
respect to his own thinking.

"Nur noch ein Gott kann uns retten": Thus Heidegger caps his response
to a question in the interview of whether philosophers or anyone else can
repair the condition of the contemporary world ("Weltzustand") that Heidegger had begun grimly to describe—at a stage in the interview when, to
the evident relief of everyone present, it moved on from the issue of his Nazi
associations to the less threatening question of the present state of the
world. And Heidegger then becomes more severely judgmental—and in his
interviewers' view, more openly gloomy, "pessimistic"—than he had been
before in reviewing his own past ("Technology tears people away and up-
roots them from the earth more and more," "We don't need an atom bomb
at all . . . [since] the uprooting of human beings is already taking place," etc.).
On the usual translation of the title, Heidegger doubts all possibility of
recovery, assessing the world situation as so imperiled and difficult that no
human agents—not the politicians, not the philosophers, not Heidegger
himself—can effect the changes required to reverse or undo the process
that had led to the condition; thus, "*Only* a God can save us."

Now this reading of Heidegger's statement is certainly plausible on linguistic and contextual grounds. In it, the semantic unit "nur noch" adds emphasis beyond what "nur" would mean appearing by itself (as it could have,
and with the same denotation); understood in this sense, the phrase underscores the enormity of the task of reversal or rescue and in effect places
it beyond human means, within the capacity of *only* a God. And Heidegger
might indeed have meant no more than this. But it is also possible that he
did intend something different which comes out in a variant reading of the
same brief exclamation. Here it is not "nur noch" that is the semantic unit,

---

Harries, who does not use the statement as the title for her translation [Neske and Kettering,
pp. 41–66], renders the statement in the interview as "Only a God can still save us"—sending
the "noch" (improbably) further forward in the sentence. For references that repeat the "standard" formulation, see, e.g., Richard Bernstein, *The New Constellation* (Cambridge: MIT Press,
1992), 137, 139; Jacques Derrida, *Of Spirit: Heidegger and the Question*, trans. Geoffrey Benning-
ton and Rachel Bowlby (Chicago: University of Chicago Press, 1987), 125; Tom Rockmore, *On
Heidegger's Nazism and Philosophy* (Berkeley: University of California Press, 1992), 307; Richard
Wolin, *The Politics of Being: The Political Thought of Martin Heidegger* (New York: Columbia University Press, 1990), 174.

but "noch ein" (that is, "another"). To be sure, also in this reading, "nur" remains part of the statement (and perhaps then too also a—or even *the*—point of emphasis within it). But with the shift in phrasing that separates "nur" from "noch ein," the statement as a whole also takes on an altered meaning: Thus, "Only *another* (i.e., "noch ein") God can save us."

As I have suggested, this alternative reading goes unmentioned by Heidegger's translators—an omission that might be due only to the slight difference it might be supposed to make (more of this below). A substantive reason is also possible, however, and this is the fact of Heidegger's startling appeal to a "God" at all—with the mingling of irony and despair in that appeal at once severe and unmistakable and thus the more likely to draw attention away from other issues. For the Heidegger who here turns to a God for help, we remind ourselves, is the same figure who had consistently held up "thinking," *human* thinking, as at once the need and means for the recovery of Being—what man required and presumably was capable of even in his much-diminished state; who had himself at one time entered the public arena with the expectation of heralding and leading a cultural transformation in the German university; and who at that same time had assured his audience that, on a larger scale, still another man was then leading the way back through history to Being ("The Führer himself and alone is the present and future German reality and law"). Confronted by his interviewers (gently, to be sure, and hopefully) with reminders of these past commitments, that same Heidegger now denies that philosophy or thinking (the distinction between them remains invidious for him) or any other "merely" human effort has a chance of realizing this goal—a possibility that at one time (that is, over a *period* of time) he had taken for granted:

> . . . Die Philosophie wird keine unmittelbare veranderung des jetztigen Weltzustandes bewirken konnen. Dies gilt nicht nur von der Philosophie, sondern von allem bloss menschlichen Sinnen und Trachten. Nur noch ein Gott kann uns retten.

> . . . Philosophy will not be able to bring about an immediate transformation of the world's present condition. This holds not only for philosophy but for all merely human tendencies and endeavors. Only [a, another] God can save us.

What could here understandably strike the reader first, then—also, evidently, the *Spiegel* editors—is Heidegger's concession of the defeat of thinking and philosophy. If, as he had earlier announced, traditional philosophy ended with Nietzsche, now also its successor appears permanently incapacitated—even with Heidegger's own and best efforts in its behalf. But a no less sharply edged issue also surfaces here in his appeal to a *God*, provoking the questions first of what or who this God is and then what consequences such an appeal for salvation has for the status of individual (presumably including his own) responsibility that Heidegger had also stressed, indeed, that on one reading, is central to his central work, *Being and Time*. Is Heidegger resurrecting here the God of Western religion who, first as Creator, continues to intervene in history? It would require a more extreme overcoming of the past than mere skepticism to find *that* God restored: Whatever else has been contested in Heidegger's view of Nietzsche, no one doubts that he added his own certification to the latter's pronouncement of the death of God, at least of the god Nietzsche had in mind. And since nothing else in the *Spiegel* interview suggests changes in Heidegger's view of *that*, his reference to God remains counterfactual, indeed a reductio ad absurdum. Only a God like the God once supposed to exist can save us—but that God, if he ever existed, certainly does not, *cannot*, exist now; thus, the invocation of another such God amounts to an expression of hopelessness. The God who could save us if he existed is no more able to do so than the earlier one who—by acclaim, as it were—no longer exists. Only if such a God intervened, would the situation (and we) be saved, but that will not happen and therefore. . . .

The bleak prospect thus depicted by Heidegger is noted by his interviewers in the questions they raise both before and after his concise exclamation, as they react to the impotence he ascribes to philosophy for rescuing mankind, and then to the broader improbability of any help whatever. This assessment of the world's "condition" would be sobering if it came from any source that warranted serious attention; proposed by a figure for whom the power of human thinking had before this hardly even been doubted, and for whom a version of thinking as a means of restoration, almost of redemption, had always been understood to be *possible*, its unsettling effect is intensified.

But that there may be reasons for overlooking a distinction does not, of course, establish the distinction, and we come back then to my starting point: What difference *does* it make if we read, "Only another God can save us" rather than "Only a God can save us"? But now an answer appears, I believe, in the nature of the God who could save us if he existed, but who doesn't exist. Is that God one among many? Or is he One as *the* God had been? The English translations refer here in common to "God," not to "god," thus presuming on the text since the German "Gott" would begin with an upper-case letter whether in the service of monotheism or polytheism. The latter ambiguity between uniqueness and plurality is preserved, it should be noted, even in reading the statement as "Only a God can save us," because the reference to "a" God leaves open the question of whether that

God might be one among many or an exclusive one. Elsewhere, it will be re-called, Heidegger, speaking in his own voice, does invoke Gods (or gods) in the plural. (So, for example, "Poetry is . . . a pointing, an indicating in which the G(g?)ods are revealed not as intended and substantial but in the ges-ture."[9]) It may well be that part of his motivation in this usage is to under-score the difference between the status of the Gods he might indeed credit and the (one) God of traditional philosophical proofs and religious belief whom he would not. When he refers then to "a" ("ein") God, he could mean either one of many or—more restrictively—One.

In this sense, then, there *is* a difference between the statements "Only a God can save us" and "Only another God can save us"—since in contrast to the former reading, which leaves the ambiguity quite open, the latter ver-sion limits, if it does not quite eliminate it. "*Another* God?" Well, that implies a predecessor: first there was one, and then—now—there may be another, and not—anticipating another possible ambiguity—"another" in the sense of one quite different from its predecessor. Here German usage is more precise than its English counterpart: the difference between "noch ein" and "ein ander" that is conflated in the English "another" is in German quite ex-plicit (as we might embarrassedly find out if we asked our host at dinner for a different ["ein ander"] serving when we meant a *second* ["noch ein"] one). "Noch ein" implies an additional one like or identical to the first. And in the case of God, there is, of course, an obvious first to which "another" might be added as a second: another God much like the now-discredited One who, if He ever existed, no longer does, but the equivalent of whose powers would be required if we (as Heidegger speaks plurally—"uns") are to be saved.

Admittedly, this interpretation is also possible for the reading of "Only a God can save us," and to this extent neither the translation, "Only another God can save us," nor my interpretation of that translation is assured. Which of the two formulations one settles on thus depends on how one under-stands the statement's context apart from the statement itself—that is, how much weight one gives to the renunciation that will unavoidably figure in any account of Heidegger's words. Insofar as "Only a God can save us" leaves open the possibility of one God among many as a potential rescuer, despair is mitigated by a glimmering of hope: the possibility of many Gods presum-ably makes more likely (or at least more possible) the actuality of one of them. By contrast, to say that "Only another God can save us"—another God like the earlier One who was its (literal) predecessor—seems immedi-ately to close the door that might otherwise be opened. It is *the* God who is

---

[9] "Uber das Wesen der Dichtung," *Gesamtausgabe*, vol. 39 (Frankfurt: Vittorio Klassman, 1989), 174.

needed—and with whose appearance or occurrence we have, in Heidegger's own estimate, no "causal connection." Heidegger himself supports this rendering in both the structure and substance of the sentence immediately following the one that first mentions "a" God: "The only possibility we have is by thinking and poetry to prepare the way, for the appearance of the God or for the absence of the God in decline." We have no reason (and Heidegger suggests none) to attribute any stronger likelihood to this "another" One than to the One who we have learned (on Heidegger's own account) by harsh experience and against millennia of hope does not exist.

Does the distinction suggested here make a difference? Well, some difference. Not as much, surely, as does the fact of Heidegger's appeal for rescue to *any* kind or number of God(s), where before it had been Sein and Dasein that provided at once an end and a means—an appeal made, moreover, in a conversation intended on both sides to join the world of thinking to the immanence of history and the concrete world of contingency, choice, and practical need. But as matters of small detail may also express or measure despair, so this slight distinction may affect our understanding of Heidegger more generally. We know from it—as we read "only another God" rather than "only a God"—that our need is for an impossible God and that even if we accept everything Heidegger himself had otherwise proposed for the recovery of Being and Truth, his words and his thinking will not provide that. We learn this, after all, from Heidegger himself. And if he persistently refuses in the *Spiegel* interview to concede fault in any of his earlier intellectual and political commitments or acts about which his interlocutors gently inquire—as if enacting Nietzsche's Eternal Recurrence, Heidegger would do *nothing* differently the next time round[10]—his invocation of "only another" God who can't possibly do what is required of him remains a concession of human limitation (including his own) hardly found elsewhere in his writings. Admittedly, it requires the comparison with "another *God*" to elicit this concession, but then, it should not be a surprise to find that even in his last words (albeit written ten years before his end), Heidegger claims a place in cosmic and not merely human history.

---

[10] With the single exception of the "human failing" ("menschliches Versagen") that Heidegger admits to in acknowledging his refusal to visit his dying teacher, Husserl, or to pay his respects to the family after Husserl's death. And even these, he implies, he had "made good" on by writing to Husserl's widow subsequently (a letter that she denied having received).

8

Contra the "Righteous Gentiles"

"Righteous Gentiles" is the common translation of the Hebrew "Hasidei Umoth Ha'olam" (literally, "Righteous among the Nations of the World"), an honorific title now known mainly through its conferral by Yad Vashem in Jerusalem on non-Jews who acted during the Holocaust to save Jewish lives at the risk of their own. This use of the traditional phrase, however, seems to me to misrepresent not only the conduct it is meant to honor but also a number of other related and even more fundamental issues. The basis on which it draws its moral distinctions between Jews and non-Jews and then between "righteous" and other non-Jews, moreover, is invidious and offensive. As the language of the Holocaust itself was an expressive factor in the unfolding of that event, so the language of *post*-Holocaust reflection ought to be considered—and questioned—in its consequences for the shape of this history.

The fault in the "Righteous Gentiles" is obviously not in the rescuers themselves or their actions or in the decision to honor them. It is rather in the concept of "*Righteous*" Gentiles, the norm by which they are judged and which, by implication, the much larger number of other, "*non*righteous" gentiles failed to meet. This criterion produces a twofold distortion—at once of diminishing and exaggerating. It diminishes the acts of the gentile rescuers of Jews, since the responses by which they risked their lives to save others were clearly more than only "righteous"; at the same time it exaggerates what the other, "nonrighteous" gentiles were morally obligated to do, insofar as it implies that *they* ought to have risked their lives as the rescuers did. The effect of this twofold distortion, furthermore, is to obscure the actual responsibility of much the largest number of non-Jews touched by the Holocaust—responsibility that was more fundamental and in the end more consequential than anything turned up by their invidious comparison with the heroic rescuers.

Again: the "Righteous Gentiles" cited by Yad Vashem are individuals or groups who in the Nazi-occupied countries of Europe risked their lives to save Jews and who, after passing an examination of the evidence by a Committee at Yad Vashem, are then formally recognized. (As of September, 1998, a total of 15,670 people had been so designated.) The issue that emerges here is not with the probative process but with its conclusion—that is, in the status and implications of the term *righteous* itself.

To judge someone as righteous ordinarily implies that that person has acted "rightly," as he ought to have—presumably meeting his or her obligations more fully than is usually the case in the "crooked timber of mankind" (otherwise there would be no point in mentioning it at all) but not doing more than is required of them or anyone else. To act righteously, after all, is just to do what one ought to. This connection between righteousness and the fulfillment of obligations, furthermore, is part of the connotation of the corresponding Hebrew phrase in its traditional usage. The phrase's earliest (slightly different) appearance (Tosefta Sanhedrin, xiii, 2) refers to "*Tsadikei* Umot Ha'olam" rather than to "Hasidei"—"Tsadikei" being more narrowly "righteous" than "Hasidei," with its nuance of "pietist" or "loyalist." Subsequently (in Maimonides' *Mishneh Torah*), "Hasidei Umot Ha'olam" designates any non-Jew who observes the seven Noachide laws; it has otherwise been applied more generally to non-Jews "who stood by Jews in an hour of adversity."[1]

A common feature of these diverse contexts is their lack of any stipulation that the "Righteous among the Nations of the World" must go beyond the expectations of normal—rightful—moral conduct. The title thus applies to non-Jews who reacted as they should have in the circumstances indicated, making allowance for the limitation (the condescension here is undeniable) suggested by their identity as non-Jews; that is, by their place among the "Umoth Ha'olam." Accordingly, when "righteous" is applied as a moral standard in the aftermath of the Holocaust only to gentiles who risked their lives to save Jews, this implies that they did in those circumstances what they should have done: no less, but also no more. To be sure, their recognition as "righteous" points by contrast to the response of others among the "nations" who did less than they did, but this does not mean that the "Right-

---

[1] E. E. Urbach, *The Sages, Their Concepts and Beliefs*, vol. 1, trans. Israel Abrahams (Cambridge: Harvard University Press, 1979), 544; see also Michael Zevi Nehorai, "Righteous Gentiles Have a Share in the World To Come," *Tarbiz* LXI (1992), 465–487.

eous" Gentiles did more than *they* (and presumably the others as well) ought to have. To do what one should do, after all, is only right. This implication then joins the fact that the number of "Righteous Gentiles" is relatively small (and unlikely to grow much larger), indicating the further conclusion that the then "Nonrighteous" gentiles (in terms of the Holocaust, the approximately 300,000,000 other non-Jewish inhabitants of Nazi-occupied Europe) were remiss in not doing what *they* ought to have done. In sum, then, the "Righteous Gentiles" did only what they should have, and what the larger majority of their fellow Gentiles were guilty of not doing.

The principal issue involved in judging the "Righteous Gentiles" thus occurs in the related questions, on the one hand, of what the gentiles (viewed as a single group) did or did not do and, on the other hand, of what they should have done. But this is not the only issue raised by the application of that moral standard. In addition to its invidious distinction between the Righteous and the Nonrighteous Gentiles, it implies a similarly invidious distinction between the gentiles (as a group) and the Jews. Why, after all, single out for recognition the quality of righteousness only among gentiles, unless that characteristic could simply be taken for granted among the nongentiles, that is, among the Jews? To be sure, the commemorative institutions of the Holocaust sometimes link the memory of that event's destructiveness with a celebration of heroism (the official Israeli "Holocaust Day"—intended to coincide, as closely as it could, with the beginning of the 1943 uprising in the Warsaw Ghetto—is formally the "Day of the Holocaust and of [the] Heroism"). But relatively little has been said or written more directly about heroism in Jewish reactions or conduct; certainly there has been no formal effort in the context of the "Holocaust Day" or any of the memorial museums to assemble the names of Jews who conducted themselves heroically, as has been done for the non-Jewish rescuers.

One likely reason for the latter omission has nothing to do with the question of whether some Jews acted more or less "righteously" than others did during the Holocaust. It remains a harsh truth that among the millions of Jewish victims, all of them, including those who could be shown to have conducted themselves badly or wrongly in the face of the Nazi threat, paid in the end with their lives, and that the primary reason for this was not because of their characters—whether in their failings or their virtues—but because of their identification as Jews. As honorific titles are nullified by death, so too, it seems, moral distinctions, drawn in retrospect among the Jewish victims who had only that identity in common, would be out of place.

The consequences of the invidious implication of the "Righteous" Gentile do not stop here, however. What I have suggested to be the trivializing effect of this tribute to the non-Jewish rescuers also suggests—inversely—a misleading exaggeration in the status of the Jewish victims. For if the Gentiles who risked their lives are "righteous," then the Jews, for whom death was mandated—a certainty—ought by that additional burden to warrant a stronger term of approbation. At least, it is reasoning along this line that seems required to explain the use of words like "holy" or "heroic" or "martyred" in religious or commemorative references to the Jewish victims, in contrast to those terms' more usual application to individuals who in some measure chose their fates. It was, after all, the persecutors who determined in the Holocaust who would or would not count as a Jew, with the Jews identified in this process including some who denied that identity as well as others who affirmed it, and with similar indifference to their characters or to the still more general moral qualities of their lives. As imposed identity differs essentially from identity freely chosen, we see again the consequences of an invidious distinction—this one as applied to the Jews in the Holocaust—but with its origins in the restricted application of "Righteous" to certain gentiles alone.

Even without reference to these other implications, however, the standard of "righteousness" remains an inadequate measure—first, of the non-Jewish rescuers of Jews during the Holocaust, but then also and more significantly of the non-Jewish *non*rescuers. The criteria applied by Yad Vashem in judging "Righteous Gentiles" include no requirement that they observe the seven Noachide commandments (let alone, as Maimonides stipulates, that the observance of those commandments must follow from belief in the divine authority behind them). And if, on the other hand, the rescuers surely meet the criterion of "standing by Jews in an hour of adversity," it is also clear that they go beyond it to such an extent that to describe them *only* as having met that condition becomes an understatement that crosses the line into misrepresentation.

The stringent criteria applied by Yad Vashem's examining committee to nominations for the title of "Righteous Gentile" are explicit. The designation is reserved for gentiles (1) who aided Jews in danger of being killed or being sent to concentration camps; (2) who were aware that they were risking their lives in providing that aid; (3) who acted without requiring or expecting material reward; and (4) whose aid was active, not passive (as when "rescuers" only refrained from turning someone over to the Nazis).

The second of these requirements clearly exceeds any criterion historically associated with the concept of the "Righteous Gentile." Of course, great value is attached in the Jewish tradition to the saving of human life; thus, the frequently cited Talmudic line that "He who saves a single life, it is as if he saves the world." But nothing stated in defining this value or in the conditions traditionally set for the Righteous Gentiles obligates anyone (Jew or non-Jew) to risk their own or their family's lives in behalf of other people, not even in the extreme situation in which those other peoples' lives are at risk. Indeed one has to look far in any legal or moral code, irrespective of culture and time, to find legislation or practice that makes it mandatory (not just praiseworthy but mandatory) for a person to put his or his family's lives at risk to save the lives of other people, even when the failure to take such risks makes it probable that other people will lose their lives. Perhaps there should be such a legal or moral standard, but there isn't. The few states in the United States that have "Good Samaritan" laws that require extending aid to others in circumstances in which the latters' lives may be in danger specifically exclude those situations in which the rescuers themselves would be endangered by doing so. And certainly the requirement in Jewish law that a person ought himself to suffer death rather than commit murder is not a positive commandment for self-sacrifice in the cause of saving other people's lives, surely not in situations in which the threat to life originates and ends elsewhere. When that is the case—that is, when someone else's life is at risk through no doing of your own, with the risk of your life the price of (possibly) saving his—Jewish law, although with some dissenting opinion, has generally followed Rabbi Akiba's dictum, "Thy [own] life comes first."

These considerations do not mean that the people confirmed by Yad Vashem's scrutiny are not "Righteous Gentiles" in some sense of that phrase's traditional meaning; surely they are. The designation by itself, however, does them less than full justice because their actions show them to be more than righteous in either that traditional or its current more general application. What they did went well "above and beyond the call of duty," certainly beyond what is in any usual sense obligatory for decisions of the sort that confronted them. Their deeds, in other words, were supererogatory, meritorious but meritorious *because* they were not required: precisely what distinguishes heroism from ordinary acts and obligations. No one has a duty to be heroic; to claim that is a self-contradiction. The rescuers now called "Righteous" were by common standards not only righteous but, beyond that, heroic. (Indeed, it requires something more than only being righteous to be heroic. . . .)

There can be no doubt that the "Righteous" Gentiles—anyone who voluntarily took the risks they did—should be honored. But again, the measure of honor due them for this is not because they did what was incumbent on them, but precisely because it was not. Their acts, as they came to know afterward and as could have been predicted beforehand, placed them in a precarious minority, inviting threats to themselves and their families that neither social nor religious standards required of them. Those who doubt the extraordinary quality of this conduct would do well to consider— quite apart from the absence of any such expectations or requirements by our formal legal and moral principles—who among the members of their own community they could rely on to act in the way that the only "Right-eous" non-Jewish citizens of Nazi-occupied countries did under the circum-stances they faced. More immediately, each of us might ask ourselves what and how much and for whom we would be willing to risk what those rescuers risked.

It is true that in the Nazi-occupied countries of Western Europe, non-Jewish rescuers of Jews did not, if caught, face the automatic death penalty imposed in Poland; those arrested for helping to shelter the family of Anne Frank in Amsterdam, for example, were "only" sent to concentration camps. But of course the threat of death was present there as well, and also "West-ern" rescuers were killed as a consequence of that selflessness. In choosing to act as they did, they could not have been unaware of this possibility.

Typically, the autobiographical accounts provided by "Righteous Gentiles" in answer to requests to "explain" their reactions are low-keyed and self-effacing; they describe the help they extended as "only right" or as based on the teaching of moral or religious (specifically, Christian) principles.[2] There is no reason to doubt the explanations stated in these modest self-descriptions as their authors understood and acted on them, but neither are the authors' own accounts of their motives decisive for judging what they did. Some authentic heroes in this or other situations might respond quite differently, perhaps even boasting about their heroism. But just as state-ments of that sort would not substantiate and would certainly not add to the quality of the actions they refer to, neither should a disclaimer of heroism diminish or nullify that achievement. Even the views sometimes expressed by the rescuers that what they did was a "natural" human response or that it fulfilled a universal moral obligation do not prove either of those claims. Again: the occurrence of self-sacrifice as an instance of altruism is evident; almost always when it becomes known, it is recorded and honored—but it has been not been established as a moral imperative or norm. And although the formulation of ethical ideals should not be determined only by past practices or beliefs, it seems reasonable to regard the fact that no instance of a proposed requirement appears in this long history as prima facie evi-dence against accepting it as one.

Applying moral judgment in hindsight to conditions in which life and death weighed in the balance is always fraught, turning easily to cant. To contrast the small number of "Righteous Gentiles" with the hundreds of millions of other gentiles who by implication would then be judged to have failed morally is an example of such cant, not because of the difference in

---

[2] See, e.g., M. Paldiel, *The Path of the Righteous: Gentile Rescuers of the Jews during the Holocaust* (Hoboken, N.J.: KTAV, 1993)

numbers but because of the basis claimed for the distinction. The contrast thus drawn at once understates the magnitude of what the "More-Than-Righteous" Gentiles did and exaggerates what was obligatory for those who were not. An even more serious moral consequence follows from the latter implication. The reduction of heroic acts to (only) righteous ones diverts attention from a larger group of "*un*righteous" (rather than non- or extra-righteous) acts which had far more significant consequences in the history of the Holocaust. I refer here to the decisions and acts by non-Jews which were also voluntary, not obligatory, but which contributed (and would have been known beforehand to do this) to the weight intended to crush the Jewish people—and which, if they had not been done, would have incurred no risk for those who avoided them.

Not to volunteer for the voluntary organizations of the Nazi apparatus: the SS, the Einsatzgruppen, the teams of "mercy killers," the Nazi party itself; *not* to take advantage of the opportunistic "windfalls" that occurred as Jews were deported—to take over their businesses or apartments or belongings, to assume their professional positions or practices; *not*, at a farther extreme, to brutalize or to torture—all these varieties of voluntary action could have been avoided without serious risk, almost all of them with no risk whatever. At each of the junctures named, the agents had before them an option of deciding to act by declining to act; that is, to act by inaction. And insofar as the decision for inaction would at these points have required no heroism, would have required only not doing what should not have been done—that was also, we may conclude, what they ought to have done and what could reasonably have been expected of them.

It is at this more mundane and commonplace level that righteousness became and should now remain central to retrospective moral judgment in relation to the Holocaust—of what could and should, or could not or should not, have been done. Here the balances of the scale held on one side murder and, on the other side, the temptations of material comfort or professional advancement or "saving face" or perhaps only the expression of what had been before then repressed or displaced anger moved by a variety of related or unrelated sources. Thus, to honor the heroic and "More-than-Righteous" gentiles would not, should not, diminish the responsibility—or our judgment about it—of the much larger number of others who were less than heroic, as they then, and we too now, might be. Quite the contrary. To honor those who are heroic means that the burden of being "righteous" goes back where it belongs, in the day-to-day life of ordinary people who are not and perhaps cannot be heroes, but who are nonetheless responsible for knowing and acting on the principles of common humanity. That is, for being righteous.

III

FORGIVENESS AND REVENGE: AS IN THE PRESENT

9

Reliving or Revoking the Past:
Two Views of Forgiveness

Philosophers from the Greeks on have written at length about the concept of justice; they have also extensively analyzed wrongdoing and the justifications for punishment. By contrast, and despite its relation to those other issues, they have virtually ignored the topic of forgiveness—an omission that is notable in figures who loom as large in the history of ethics as Plato, Spinoza, and Kant. If the much-needed psychology or sociology of philosophy is ever written, this demonstrative silence will undoubtedly figure as an item of evidence in attesting to philosophy's ideological origins.[1] In the discussion here, however, I propose to consider not this or other failures in the history of the history of philosophy, but the idea of forgiveness, both conceptually, as an idea, and then in the specific application of that idea to the aftermath of the Holocaust. I propose then to outline the principal features of this moral concept and of the issues that beset it—and to do this by (and because of) two views of forgiveness that come into view against the background of certain events that occurred in the setting of the Holocaust.

This reference to the Holocaust may appear both unlikely and unsettling, since to look for the defining features of forgiveness in relation to the

---

[1] I would not mean to overstate this claim. There *have* been philosophical accounts of forgiveness, but few of them in comparison with writings on most other moral concepts. See, for example, Martin Golding, "Forgiveness and Regret," *Philosophical Forum* 16 (1984): 121–137; Joram Graf Haber, *Forgiveness* (Savage, Md.: Roman and Littlefield, 1991); Jeffrie G. Murphy and Jean Hampton, *Forgiveness and Mercy* (New York: Cambridge University Press, 1988). An essay of my own, related to the present one, is "Forgiveness," *American Philosophical Quarterly*, 31 (1994):105–117.

Holocaust—an instance, if ever there was one, of the *un*forgivable—may seem strained at best, and at worst perverse. It might be objected, furthermore, that just as hard cases make bad law, so too we ought to examine ethical distinctions and principles not through examples of moral extremity but among the commonplace acts and decisions of everyday life; certainly there is no shortage of evidence in the latter of the details or complexity of moral judgment. A strong argument can also be made in the other direction, however, as occasions of moral extremity bring to light aspects of ethical questions (and even the questions themselves) that in less fraught moments may be less evident or perhaps not evident at all.

Admittedly, the danger exists that accounts taken from the setting of moral extremity may leave their audience behind, unable to see themselves in the extraordinary situations described. This danger is, however, constant for ethical discourse, whatever its emphasis or focus (in this sense, serious ethical decisions are always "extraordinary"); and so I argue to the contrary: that morally extreme situations are revealing in ways that lesser situations, however significant their ethical implications are when once we find them, may fail to disclose. A pertinent analogy here is with the "stress" tests routinely applied in medicine or engineering: To observe moral concepts under pressure is to see the elements that make them up—their capacity— quite differently from observing them when what is at stake is less weighty or severe. Certainly this analogy serves usefully in respect to concepts such as forgiveness, about which the question has often been raised of whether, given the more pressing occasions of ethical judgments, it qualifies as a moral concept at all.

Let me begin the account of two views of forgiveness with someone else's story. In 1976, a small book with the innocent title of *The Sunflower* was published in the United States, in translation from the German and French. (It has since, in 1997, been reissued in an expanded version which does not, however, alter its basic theme or structure.) The surprising author of this book was Simon Wiesenthal, already known at the time as a "Nazi-hunter"— a Jewish survivor of the concentration camps who committed himself at the end of World War II to tracking down, exposing, and (as he hoped) bringing to trial Nazi war criminals.[2] The book itself is as modest in tone and composure as its title. In it Wiesenthal recounts an episode from his wartime experience that, although less extreme than others he could have chosen, epitomizes for him the character of the Nazi genocide against the Jews. He was at the time of the episode (in late 1943) doing forced labor from a concentration camp in Lemberg in Poland; there, he found himself one day

---

[2] Simon Wiesenthal, *The Sunflower*, trans. H. A. Piehler and Carol Pimental Pinto. (New York: Schocken, 1976; revised edition, 1997).

among a group of men assigned to haul boxes of medical waste from a German military hospital. At a moment when he stood apart from his group, a nun who was working as a nurse in the hospital approached him and told him—he was evidently hers to "tell"—to follow her. She led him into a darkened room in the hospital and left him standing there. In the room, he made out a heavily bandaged figure lying on a bed; a weak voice asked him to come closer, and then began to tell its story. Karl, an SS man, knew that he was dying. He had asked the nurse to bring to him in secret one of the Jewish laborers—for (as he recounted it to Wiesenthal) he had on his conscience an atrocity committed by his unit on the Russian front. After capturing a town there, members of the unit (Karl among them) had herded a number of Jews into a house which was then locked. Some of the Jews driven into the house had been forced to carry cans of gasoline with them; the soldiers then threw grenades into the house—and the carnage that resulted was what would have been predicted (and what, indeed, had been intended). Karl, tormented by this act, had asked the nun to bring him one of the Jewish laborers so that he could now, before he died, ask forgiveness. Wiesenthal, who had been selected for this role by chance—except, of course, for the fact that he was a Jew—listened to Karl, heard him out, and reflected for a few moments. Then he stood up (he had been sitting on Karl's bed) and left the hospital room in silence.

Wiesenthal's book does not end here. Indeed, the book as a whole is more about his rejection of Karl's plea for forgiveness than it is about Karl himself. For almost immediately after making his decision, Wiesenthal began to have doubts about that response, as with it he rejected the last, and so far as he could judge, the honest request of someone in great suffering—physical and spiritual—and with little time to live. After the war's end, Wiesenthal traced and visited Karl's family (only his mother was still alive), telling her about Karl's death but not about the atrocity Karl had described or the request for forgiveness (or, of course, about his own refusal). Years later, still troubled by the same doubts, Wiesenthal sent a description of his encounter with Karl to some thirty writers and thinkers known for their considerations of moral issues—theologians, members of the clergy, philosophers. He asked each of them what they would have done if they had been in his place, confronted by Karl on his deathbed. Their responses to this question make up the second part of *The Sunflower*, and surely the question they address is one that every person might ask himself or herself. But I wish here not to review those responses (at least, not directly) but to look again at Wiesenthal's reaction, since it is there, reinforced by the divided opinions of the writers from whom he solicited responses, that the "two views of forgiveness" and the differences between them begin to emerge.

It becomes clear from Wiesenthal's account that his refusal to grant Karl the forgiveness he sought was not, at least in his own self-understanding, due to anger or to a desire for revenge, however understandable such emotions might have been if he had indeed felt them. Wiesenthal does not cite even the harsh fact—already disclosed to the reader of his book—that he was himself at the time under the threat of death, with reason to doubt that he would survive the constant and arbitrary attacks around him. Wiesenthal emphasizes, furthermore, that he believed from what the SS man said (I have condensed the description of his history) that Karl's repentance was genuine; his was not, in Wiesenthal's view, a "deathbed conversion" or an attempt to find easy comfort. Nor does it seem, from Wiesenthal's words, that his rebuff of Karl was due to the character of Karl's act, either to its own enormity or to the larger ongoing atrocity of which that act was but a small part. The reason for Wiesenthal's reaction of silence is simpler than any of these; it is at its roots related to the phenomenon of forgiveness in general, not only to its role in respect to the Holocaust. How, Wiesenthal asked himself, could *he* forgive someone for harm that a person had done to someone *else*—which was exactly what the SS man was requesting (since he had not been directly responsible for anything that Wiesenthal himself had suffered)? Is it not only the injured person who may decide whether to grant or to withhold forgiveness? What would have been the moral value of Wiesenthal's words even if he did tell Karl that he forgave him for the terrible act he had taken part in against other people, people who, because of that act, could not now or ever speak for themselves?

Wiesenthal's reasoning on this point seems to me clear—and compelling. But in moving from this assessment to reflect further on the concept of forgiveness, reinforced by Wiesenthal's own doubts, it becomes clear that a counterargument to Wiesenthal's denial of Karl's request also emerges clearly and with some force. Still more troubling than this alternative itself is the sense accompanying it that, whatever one's combination of reasons and intuitions about the differences between the now two conflicting responses to Karl's request, there seems to be no systematic or conclusive way of settling this conflict, of reaching a decision in favor of one or the other on the basis of premises that the two positions—or those who would defend one or the other—hold in common.

This conflict is in part due to the fact that the second view of forgiveness, which is opposed to Wiesenthal's—a different conception, yet one that he himself recognizes and asks about—confronts his own view on at least some of its own grounds. Should it not be sufficient for forgiveness that the person who does wrong fully acknowledges his responsibility and is willing to do what he can (even if this power is limited) to turn the wrong around, to make good on it? Is it necessary—or warranted—to require more than this? And if that is indeed the crucial condition for being forgiven, and if the condition has been met, then could not, should not, someone other than the injured person or group be able to ascertain this and then grant forgiveness, especially when the person or persons who have been wronged cannot speak for themselves (and when the wrongdoer is unlikely to be able to plead his case again, in any other setting)? Cannot someone other than the person who has been harmed serve as a judge here—perhaps even more fairly than the victim?

I think here of a related example that underscores the point. When a person who has been wronged is asked by the wrongdoer to forgive him but refuses that request, something in the way of a consequent moral issue emerges—perhaps not as large as the initial one, but still. So, for example, Maimonides proposes on just this point that at times the refusal to grant forgiveness may itself become a moral wrong—if indeed the request for forgiveness has been made in good faith about a forgivable act of injustice. Maimonides himself offers a formula for testing these conditions: the wrongdoer is obliged to repeat his plea for forgiveness (and so his acknowledgment of wrongdoing) three times before witnesses; after that, he is forgiven even if the person who has been wronged and who has been asked for forgiveness rejects those pleas.[3] At that point, too, the person who has been wronged initially becomes himself guilty of a wrong, which might be characterized in conventional terms as being "unforgiving." In this setting, the community in effect assumes the role of a "third party," empowered to accord forgiveness to the wrongdoer when that has been denied him by his victim.

The references to forgiveness so far, evidently, have been to its human, not divine, occasions; we are considering here Karl and Wiesenthal—and, through them, ourselves. Obviously, in the Christian and Jewish traditions alike, God has the power to forgive wrongs that a person or group does to other human beings, even when these are not (at least not directly) wrongs done to or against God himself: both the Hebrew and the Christian Bibles provide examples of this.[4] But the capacity—and authority—for forgiveness may be quite different where only human beings are involved, and how different that is, is the subject at issue here.

The implications (and problems) of this second view of forgiveness as it conflicts with Wiesenthal's initial response, however, extend beyond the one point of difference indicated so far. It is evident that the possibility of grant-

---

[3] *Mishneh Torah*, Laws of Repentance 2:11.
[4] With only a few exceptions (e.g., where David "forgives" those of his followers who did not accompany him to the desert [2 Samuel 19]), explicit references to forgiveness in the Hebrew Bible represent God acting in relation to man, rather than forgiveness among persons. I am indebted to Moshe Greenberg for bringing this reference to my attention

ing forgiveness to Karl (and, by implication, to the Nazis more generally) was for Wiesenthal closely tied to the fact that Karl *asked* for forgiveness and that in doing this, Karl also acknowledged responsibility for a wrongful act—meaning that he acknowledged both that he had been responsible for the act and that he now recognized, as he did not at the time (at least not sufficiently to avoid doing it), that it was wrong. Without this twofold acknowledgment, it is unlikely that Wiesenthal, either when he heard Karl's request or later, would have taken that request seriously or considered the possibility of forgiveness at all.

But this feature of Wiesenthal's encounter with Karl suggests still another feature of the second view of forgiveness as it differs from his own. Is it indeed necessary that a wrong be admitted and regretted—repented—to warrant forgiveness? Does the person who harms someone else even have to be aware of that injury, let alone acknowledge it and explicitly ask to be forgiven? These questions are motivated, although perhaps not entailed, by the first objection to Wiesenthal's position mentioned above. For if a third party can grant forgiveness on behalf of someone else who has been a victim, then it may also be possible to detach the wrongdoer still further from his act—with forgiveness then separated from anything the wrongdoer later says or doesn't say, even if he or she remains unaware (or unconvinced) of the harm that has been done.

Also this feature of the second view attaches the wrong that has been committed to the act, not to the agent. And indeed certain familiar examples of forgiveness seem to follow just this pattern. We sometimes speak of forgiving people who we believe wronged us but who have died and thus cannot ask for forgiveness; children (often adult children) are heard to say that they forgive parents for acts that the parents never recognized as wrongs, let alone apologized or asked to be forgiven for; we may forgive loved ones whether they ask us to or not, just because of the value we attach to them (we might not even tell them that we had been injured or hurt by what they did, and then of course we could not meaningfully tell them that we had forgiven them).

Admittedly, often in such cases, we are responding not from moral considerations or principles at all, but from self-interest; we hope to clear our minds and feelings of anger or resentment that we would prefer to be without because of their disturbing effects, even if we believe that the anger or resentment is in some sense still justified. But also when this occurs, our act of forgiving is genuinely directed toward someone else. However the act affects the person who does the forgiving, it also and necessarily involves the person(s) forgiven (whether they have sought forgiveness or are aware of being forgiven or not); and whatever the act of forgiving does for its agent, it also has the effect of releasing or redeeming the wrongdoer as well. Probably the most widely cited instance of such an act is Jesus' plea on behalf of his crucifiers: "Forgive them, Father, for they know not what they do" (Luke 23:34). Here it is, at least in part, just *because* those persecuting him continued to be unaware of their wrongdoing that the claim they should be forgiven is based. It is as though their ignorance of what they were doing and, consequently, the impossibility that they could ask forgiveness were themselves additional grounds for forgiving them.

Now, to be sure, one can anticipate other objections to this expanded second view of forgiveness. To have wrongs or evildoing forgiven when the person responsible has not acknowledged responsibility or remorse for those acts, it might be argued, gives carte blanche to wrongdoing. If people can be forgiven without first being held to account for their actions, would not any distinction between wrong and right, evil and good, become simply an empty and groundless exercise, with no sharper moral point to it than counting the number of falling stars? On this analysis, all conduct would seem to have the same moral status—since wrongful acts are automatically or instantaneously made good, forgiven. Ethical judgments and decisions seem entirely trivialized by such a resolution: there would be very little left *to* judge, and there would be nothing at stake in judging whatever was left.

Consider another, extreme but not uncommon possibility—where forgiveness is extended to someone who may not ask or, more strongly, *wish* to be forgiven, because (for example) he does not admit to having done something that warrants or requires forgiveness. Charles Dickens' character Uriah Heep, in *David Copperfield*, has left his distinctive mark on this disposition. Unwilling to admit that insults or rejections he suffered might have been intended, let alone deserved, Uriah *would* forgive those responsible for them, whether they wanted this or not: "But I forgive you . . . I do," Uriah insists to one of *his* victims, "And you can't help yourself" [that is, you can't *not* be forgiven]. Forgiveness itself here becomes a means of inflicting injury by denying someone else's moral freedom.

These several objections, it seems to me, are compelling—but we might still conclude that the second view of forgiveness has sufficient force to balance or even to override them. Genuine regret and atonement surely ought to count for something, and the refusal to forgive where these expressions are present would in effect deny them much—or any—weight. But if this is itself a disadvantage—or even a wrong—how can it be repaired without also denying the objections posed by the first view of forgiveness (Wiesenthal's)? What seems to emerge here, I believe, as we place the two positions side by side, are two conceptions of forgiveness that not only differ from each other but are incompatible: the one—Wiesenthal's—in which forgiveness must be sought by the wrongdoer and in which only the person or group harmed can grant it; the second, in which forgiveness can be granted without any acknowledgment of wrongdoing or request for forgiveness and where forgiveness can be granted by someone other than the person who has been wronged.

These two views differ so fundamentally that I do not see a way either of reconciling them or of finding a third alternative that could mediate between them: if you hold the first, you cannot hold the other; if you hold the second, you cannot hold the first. Their differences, moreover, are substantive, not semantic, certainly more than a proprietary quarrel over the term *forgiveness*: each of them leads to (and originates from) a context in which forgiveness reflects something of its common usage. Do the two views and the evident conflict between them also represent two distinct ethical or religious traditions? I doubt that a clear distinction is possible even on these grounds—not because such comparisons must be invidious but because there are at least elements within the respective major traditions themselves that anticipate or advocate both views (another indication, if any more were needed, that consistency is not itself a consistent feature of those traditions).

How, then, is one to choose between the two views? Because the fact remains that if they are inconsistent, a choice will have to be made between them wherever forgiveness becomes an issue. To be sure, there are instances where the two are in agreement—where they overlap and thus entail the same conclusion, although, even here, almost always for different reasons. So, for example, granting forgiveness where the requirements of the first view have been met would ensure forgiveness also on the second view (in the sense that to forgive someone without his acknowledgment of wrongdoing would surely require forgiveness when such acknowledgment *has been* forthcoming). It seems evident, however, that in some cases fundamental differences will remain between the two views, that even after all the possible means of reconciliation have been exhausted, the two positions will still result in contradictory judgments (that is, in disagreement about whether or not to grant forgiveness)—as might well be the case in judging Wiesenthal's refusal to forgive Karl. If Wiesenthal was wrong in this response, it is not because Karl did not ask for forgiveness or because Wiesenthal was unaware of that.

It is here, it seems to me, that a point is reached in moral reasoning and religious vision where our choice between the two views outlined must be based rather on what one hopes from the future than on evidence drawn from the past or from only moral reasoning and argument based on general principles. At stake here is the question of what kind of human relationships we envisage for ourselves, beginning with our relation to ourselves: the moral character that we hope to realize in our consideration of other people, with the alternative possibilities to which that future is open striving for place among themselves.

There is a network of other issues and differences between the two views that extends well beyond the single issue of forgiveness: in the first (Wiesenthal's), as it stresses individual responsibility and moral discrimination—at the price of severity, of sometimes being and remaining unforgiving; of concluding in effect that certain acts or types of act are simply unforgivable, and thus that the person who committed them must live—and also die—with his responsibility for them, also his guilt, undiminished. The second view, in contrast, emphasizes the value of clearing the moral slate, removing the sting of wrongdoing and resentment—at the possible cost of being too generous or easy in its requirements, arguably of eschewing moral accountability altogether. The terms of the choice, then, seem clear—and even clearer is the fact that the choice itself is unavoidable. At least it is unavoidable if we wish to maintain a place for the idea and practice of forgiveness at all.

And here some comments about that matter—since the question of whether forgiveness is indeed a moral concept (more simply, of whether forgiveness is to be acknowledged as a good, and if so, why) is not one whose answer is self-evident or perhaps evident at all. Important thinkers, with Nietzsche only the most emphatic among them, have represented forgiveness as harmful, even morally wrong, because it is psychologically damaging or because it impedes the process of justice (Nietzsche's sweeping indictment of justice and of morality in general precludes forgiveness as well). Or again, we might here recall Spinoza's words in the *Ethics*, "He who repents what he did is twice miserable"—taking this as a clue also to the still greater misery of someone who extends forgiveness: in the one as in the other, for Spinoza, there would be nothing more than wasted, and finally also, misleading effort. Thus we face the issue of what positive justification there is for the practice of forgiveness, asking in effect why forgiveness should be considered a moral value or ideal at all. This question involves considerations in systematic ethics that cannot be addressed here, but certain rudiments of a response can be mentioned, beginning (on both utilitarian and nonutilitarian grounds) with a number of practical considerations. In terms of consequences—both for the person who has wronged someone else and for the person who has suffered the wrong—forgiveness offers the possibility of renewing the relationship between them that was damaged by the wrongdoing. The value of this renewal will be obvious where, before the breach, there had been genuine friendship—but it holds also for acquaintances who had not been close friends or even, as members of a common humanity, for people not otherwise known to each other. The more basic goods to which forgiveness contributes, then, are the goods of love and friendship or, less intimately, of sociability. That these are not the only moral goods, and that other goods may conflict or at times override them, does not impugn their status as goods.

In addition to such practical consequences, forgiveness also represents a general principle marking an important, although rarely acknowledged point of contact between ethics and religion. This is the recognition of a common finitude in both the person who asks forgiveness and the person who grants it. From the perspective of the person who has harmed someone else, the acknowledgment of having done wrong also represents a confession of limitation: he or she has not only suffered finitude, they have also recognized it—an awareness that, in human terms, remains an essential element of self-knowledge.

On the other hand, from the perspective of the person who forgives—and does so notwithstanding the harm he has suffered—he or she acknowledges that also suffering a wrong does not entail an absolute judgment, that at least some wrongs are finite for the agent as they prove to be for his object, that at least certain wrongs can indeed be made good. The meaning or significance of wrongdoing, in other words, can be changed. Involved here is a sense that the person who is at one time the victim of wrongdoing may also, at another time, be the agent or source of similar wrongs. If, as experience constantly informs us, it is beyond our capacity never to be guilty of wrongdoing, then we also pretend to be better than we are if we forget the possibility of such failure even on occasions when we otherwise seem farthest away from it; that is, when we are ourselves the victims of wrongdoing.

Admittedly, it is possible to imagine a world from which forgiveness is absent. But that world, it seems, would have to be either more than human (one in which no wrongs are committed or suffered) or less than human—a world in which resentment and vengeance would not only have their day, but would continue to have it, day after day after day. Neither of these, as it happens, is the world we inhabit—the one because it is beyond our reach, the other because we would never wish it to be and can, to some extent, make that world—our world—exclude it. The issue, then, is not whether forgiveness should have a place in our life, but only what place it should have. This confronts us with an uncomfortable but also unavoidable decision, exemplified in an extreme form as Wiesenthal faced Karl in the darkened hospital room in Lemberg. What, he asks—as we do well to ask ourselves in turn—is to be done?

THAT forgiveness ought to have a place in our moral universe, Wiesenthal gives no sign of doubting. Yet it is also clear that in the unavoidable choice between the two views of forgiveness—unavoidable if there is to be forgiveness at all—some people who would on one view have the benefit of forgiving or of being forgiven (it is important to keep in mind that the consequences of forgiveness move in both directions) would be excluded on the other, required to live and then to die without it. And on Wiesenthal's judgment, this applied to Karl—not because he was an SS man and a member of the Nazi party, certainly not because he was German, and not even, as we have seen, because Wiesenthal doubted the sincerity or depth of his remorse. It was because some acts are irretrievable by the human will or capacity for action alone, and because forgiveness, insofar as it is a relation between or among human beings, presupposes that in their lives they themselves and no others have responsibility for what they do: no one can assume it for them, any more than another person can take on other essential features of their identity.

It might be inferred from the terms of this analysis that any act that results in the death of a person, including those that would usually be judged less harshly than Karl's (for example, an act of criminal negligence, like drunken driving, that led to a bystander's death), would also be unforgivable, since it can never be the case that a person who has been harmed is able, if dead, to respond to a plea for forgiveness or indeed to any other human gesture. It seems possible in this connection, however, to draw a further distinction between acts that are unforgivable in principle and others that are unforgivable only in fact (that is, where material circumstances alone prevent the asking or granting of forgiveness). The need for such a distinction is underscored by the occurrence of acts that are arguably "unforgivable," but where the person injured remains alive and where the consequences of the injury itself are comparable or even lesser than others that might indeed be forgiven. Consider, for example, a person who has information that would exonerate someone who has been found guilty of a crime and sentenced to a prison term: each day of that imprisonment might be considered another wrongful act (or reaffirmation of the first act) on the part of the person who continues to withhold the information that would ensure the prisoner's release. On the criterion of deliberation, this act or series of acts seems more unforgivable than a one-time incident of criminal negligence, arguably even one that ended with the death of a victim.

By contrast, on the second view of forgiveness, inasmuch as it sets no condition of acknowledging responsibility and since forgiveness may be granted by someone who had not been touched by the initial wrongdoing, so also there seem to be no limits of degree on the acts to which forgiveness may be extended. Nothing is unforgivable, whether in fact or in principle. And indeed, for any act, whatever its nature or consequence, forgiveness may in the end be assumed. Certainly, any request for forgiveness ensures—by the fact of the request and even perhaps in its absence—that forgiveness will be granted. Also their differences on the line that divides the forgivable from the unforgivable, then, separate the two views.

It will probably be evident by this point that my own inclination, between the two views, is to defend Wiesenthal's choice of silence and the rationale for that choice—thus, once again, here, to deny Karl the words of forgiveness he had sought. Not because I judge the alternative (second) view to be "wrong" and Wiesenthal's "right," but because in the choice that must be made in the face of these alternatives, we decide finally also on the future that our choice would bring with it. And here it seems to me that the difference is large enough between the two views to make that choice clear. In imagining the life we may yet lead, we find in Wiesenthal's denial of Karl's request a future in which the actions of individuals or groups will be known beforehand to live on with them—except for those actions that by aspects of design (and often by elements of moral luck as well) allow them at some point and in some sense to be reversed, to be made good where before, there had been wrongdoing or even evil. Forgiveness is then a moral bonus, a gratuity—something that cannot be assumed beforehand but that by a combination of conscience and circumstance may, if we are fortunate in what we do (perhaps also in what we don't do), become part of the moral setting in which we act.

The alternate view, again, is not rejected here because it is "wrong." Nor do I find it wanting because it diminishes the drama of human agency and its consequences (although it does this). That it leaves human decisions and acts less open to judgment—easier—is surely not in itself a count against it. The objection to it seems to me simpler but also more fundamental than these other apparent disadvantages. To forgive all is not only not to understand all, it is—by itself, at any rate—to understand very little: about justice and the good, on the one hand, and about wrongdoing and evil, on the other. It is not only or mainly that to offer a blanket response to wrongdoing—extending forgiveness whether sought or not and whether wrongdoing is acknowledged or not, and extending it indifferently on behalf of oneself or of others—seems to make the knowledge of good and evil irrelevant, at best a matter of idle speculation and in that sense an indulgence; it turns even the *existence* of good and evil into an open question.

Admittedly, even when the latter view of forgiveness predominates, the occurrence and migrations of wrongdoing may nonetheless be scrutinized closely, with serious distinctions drawn among the kinds and extents of such acts (this has been the case in the applications and migrations of Christian doctrine, although with the consequence, it seems, of diminishing its blanket claims for forgiveness). But more often on this account, the ground of moral knowledge—the forced choice between evil and good—gives way to the impression of a world of general harmony where that choice is not unavoidable and indeed where it may not even be possible. When forgiveness is immediate and without limit, there is no consistent reason why moral categories as such—either condemnation or approval on moral grounds—should be sustained at all. In thinkers as important as Spinoza and Nietzsche, exactly this claim is made: that moral judgments of any sort (thus including also the possibility of forgiveness) are fictions, not only human, all too human in their construction, but because of the tendencies to falsification that they nourish and that are psychologically harmful or dangerous as well. I confess that I can—at times wistfully—imagine this view of moral judgment as true. It is just that I cannot imagine it as true in the world we live in, a world in which the Holocaust is now a historical fact and where genocide—intended evil, as deliberate as any social act can be—remains for the future a constant "moral" possibility.

Is this an argument against the second view of forgiveness? It is, I have suggested, less an argument than a representation or portrait of the moral setting in which what first appears as a single and limited choice between two views of forgiveness also alters and then reflects on the moral context as a whole. In ethics, more than elsewhere in philosophical discourse, the principles and the issues judged and finally acted on are unavoidably interrelated, forming networks or patterns—of commitments, ideals, practices. It is the differing systematic connections among these aspects of our moral life that set out from and in their conclusions return to the two different conceptions of forgiveness that I have outlined. It was the recognition of those differences that led Wiesenthal first to choose silence as his answer to Karl's request for forgiveness, and then to raise questions about his own response; and it is from that same moral juncture, in our own reactions to wrongs suffered by others or ourselves, that we also, always, set out.

Reprinted from Tikkun Magazine, A Bi-monthly Jewish Critique Of Politics, Culture, And Society. Information and subscriptions are available from Tikkun, 26 Fell Street, San Francisco, CA 94102.

10

Holocaust-Memory and -Revenge:
The Presence of the Past

Oh son of death, we do not wish you death.
May you live longer than anyone ever lived.
May you live sleepless five million nights,
And may you be visited each night by the
    suffering of everyone who saw,
Shutting behind him, the door that blocked the way back,
Saw it grow dark around him, the air filled
    with death.
    —Primo Levi, "For Adolf Eichmann"

The most notable aspect of the place of revenge in the aftermath of the Holocaust seems to be its absence—both as a topic of discussion and before that in its occurrence. Certainly in proportion to other aspects of the Nazi genocide, little has been recorded, asserted, or even disputed about revenge in the manifold Jewish response to that event; still less has been said about this absence itself. To be sure, pointing to an omission in this way implies that something different—a presence—was to be expected; that "normally"(that is, in the particularly abnormal circumstances of the "Final Solution"), the role of revenge should have been, *be*, more in evidence. To put this claim in harsher terms: testaments to the Shoah designed to incorporate that event in Jewish history or memory are plentiful and varied; they appear in all the standard forms of historical writing, artistic representation, and cultural and religious conventions. Neither the phenomenon nor the topic of revenge, however, although they mark the past as alive and subject to judgment in the present, figures largely among these. And this, although the fact of the Nazi genocide was widely known by the war's end; notwithstanding the expectation among the German populace that with the Nazi defeat, a fearsome revenge *would* be exacted; notwithstanding an atmosphere suffused by the past that has attended the diplomatic and economic relations between postwar Germany and other nations, to say nothing about the relations between Germany and Jewish communities around the world. It is as though historical recall and analysis, imaginative identification, and mourning were admissible means of relating the past to the present, but the prospect of intervening in that past as revenge does, or even speaking *about* that prospect, was not.

There are, it seems to me, two specific and one more general explanation for this lacuna in the discourse now shaping the history and memory of the Holocaust. The first of the specific explanations suggests that revenge has rarely been mentioned in relation to that event because, quite simply, there is little to talk about. The evidence of overt acts of revenge is so sparse (this response goes) that it is not surprising that what did occur should pass relatively unnoticed individually and that the phenomenon as a whole should be ignored.

But there are two objections to this explanation. The first is that even if there is little evidence of Jewish revenge in the aftermath of the Nazi genocide, there is *some*—but even that has not been much discussed, and presumably there would be a reason for this. (Even among well-informed and concerned groups, for example, I have found little awareness of the most extreme instance of Holocaust-revenge that I discuss here; this seems to me also evidence that something active is working against recognition of the issue itself.)

And second, from the other direction, suppose that there were indeed few overt attempts or acts of revenge: does this absence itself not warrant discussion? It is possible, for one thing, that the reason no more evidence has been found is that nobody has looked for it (this, too, would require explanation). And then, if in fact few attempts were made at revenge, that in itself would, should, warrant consideration: how could it be that revenge was *not* an element in the reaction to the Holocaust?

An analogy that comes to mind here is substantively connected to the phenomenon of revenge; this is the question of Jewish resistance. There, too, in the early postwar accounts, little attention was paid to the matter, with the evidence that was noted (principally, the Warsaw uprising and the revolts in Sobibor, Treblinka, Auschwitz) often introduced to highlight (by contrast) the general *lack* of resistance. As a phenomenon, then, resistance was ignored—whether because of the belief that there was little to write about or because to mention this fact would reflect harshly on people who had after all died perhaps because of such failure; or its absence was briefly noted and then—also with little analysis or argument—attributed to a debilitating flaw in European Jewish life and character. (The most widely known exposition of this view was that of Hannah Arendt, but it also appears, among many other places, in Hilberg's authoritative history, retained in the latter's two revised versions.[1]) Among a number of recent writers, however, the assessment of Jewish resistance has turned out to be a more complex historical issue, not only on the basis of a broader examination of the evidence, but also because of two methodological considerations: first, their insistence on the comparative question that asked how *other* civilian populations in occupied territories or in the camps reacted and, second, in the conceptual question of whether the definition of resistance should be limited to overt acts or, in this context, extended to other forms of conduct as well.[2]

Both these considerations also apply, I believe, to the phenomenon of revenge, with the second of special importance because of what I refer to as the "Displacement Effect"—the appearance of revenge in other guises. To be sure, the history of revenge *need* not follow the same course as that of resistance, but the latter sounds a cautionary note—in part because for revenge, too, the fact that its role has gone unacknowledged has had the consequence (circularly) that little effort has been made to determine to what extent incidents (private or public, individual or collective) did take place and in part because, from the suspicion that its presence might be found in unlikely places or forms, we come closer to recognizing the possibility of its displaced or covert occurrences.

The latter possibility—which I discuss in greater detail later—is the second of the two specific explanations for what I have characterized as the lack of explicit reference to the phenomenon of revenge. The line of reasoning here should be clear since, filtered through the Displacement Effect, revenge *would* have been silent, deliberately *not* announcing itself. And indeed I suggest that when we take this possibility into account, revenge turns out to have had a more substantial influence in shaping collective memory of the Holocaust than has so far been recognized. Perhaps for the same reasons that invited the use of displacement in the first place, however, also *its* instances have resisted interpretation; we know also that any interpretive principle of covert or displaced meaning justifiably evokes suspicion (and resistance) because of its potential circularity. Nonetheless, certain instances of displacement reveal the motif of revenge so clearly that they pro-

---

[1] Cf. Hannah Arendt, *Eichmann in Jerusalem* (New York: Viking, 1963); Raul Hilberg, *The Destruction of the European Jews* (Chicago: Quadrangle, 1961); second edition (three volumes) (New York: Holmes & Meier, 1985); French edition, trans. Marie-France Palombera and Andre Charpentier (Paris: Gallimard, 1991).

[2] See, e.g., *Jewish Resistance during the Holocaust* (Jerusalem: Yad Vashem, 1972); Lucien Steinberg, *Not as a Lamb* (London: Saxon House, 1974); Dov Levin, *Fighting Back*, trans. Moshe Kohn and Dina Cohn (New York: Holmes & Meier, 1985); Harold Werner, *Fighting Back* (New York: Columbia University Press, 1992); Israel Gutman, *Resistance* (New York: Houghton Mifflin, 1994).

vide a baseline for analyzing more problematic examples; the silence or absence referred to, then, emerges as apparent rather than actual.

WE MAY well ask, of course, what effect on its object the Displacement Effect itself has had, since indirection makes an assertion—and pays a price—of its own. I return to this question in relation to others about the nature and moral status of revenge (for example, in the contrast between revenge and the concepts of justice and forgiveness) and then go on to discuss what I take to be a basic link between revenge and the faculty of memory. These are, I understand, large promissory notes, but let me begin to work at them by summarizing the evidence for the two specific explanations I have proposed for the apparent silence about revenge. The first of those, again, acknowledged at least some (even if only a few) acts of overt revenge, and for the purposes of this "anatomy" of revenge, it is worth examining these acts—beginning with the extreme instance I alluded to earlier.

Largely because of that extremity and the secrecy it provoked, many of the details of this episode are and probably will remain in dispute; but its general outline has now, I believe, been reliably determined.[3] In February 1945, a number of Jewish partisans who had fought in the ghettoes or among units in the forests of the Baltic states and Poland came together in Lublin, which had by then been liberated. For these partisans—all of them young, still mainly in their twenties, the backbone of Jewish resistance in Lithuania and Poland—the disorienting question now presented itself of what they should do. From their immediate point of view, the war was over; its outcome was certain, and the battles still going on were in the hands of the Allied armies. Thus after three or four years of struggle which followed their original decision to constitute a force of resistance—almost always in the face of considerable opposition within the Jewish communities—the partisans suddenly found themselves in a vacuum. Virtually all members of the group that gathered in Lublin (they never numbered more than sixty) had

---

[3] The fullest account yet to appear in print, although still partial both in detail and in the author's perspective, is that of Levi Arieh Sarid, "Irgun Ha-Nakam" ["The Revenge Group"], *Yalkut Moreshet* 52 (1992): 35–106. An earlier journalistic and impressionistic account appears in Michael Bar-Zohar, *The Avengers* (New York: Hawthorn, 1967), 40–52, and a fictionalized version appears in Michael Elkins, *Forged in Fury* (New York: Ballantine Books, 1971). I have drawn on information provided by Binyamin Harshav in personal conversations, although he is not responsible for the interpretation given here. Tom Segev, in *The Seventh Million: The Israelis and the Holocaust*, trans. Haim Watzman (New York: Farrar, Straus and Giroux, 1993) provides an account—on a number of points, skeptically—of the group. There is no entry for the Revenge Group in the *Encyclopedia of the Holocaust*, ed. Israel Gutman (New York: Macmillan, 1990), although a brief and vague reference appears in the entry on Abba Kovner (823). See also the reference in Yitzhak Zuckerman, *A Surplus of Memory*, trans. Barbara Harshav (Berkeley: University of California Press, 1993), 629–635.

before the war belonged to Zionist youth organizations of varied political leanings (from the Revisionists to B'nai Akiba to HaShomer Hatzair); in the aftermath of the Nazi genocide, they were more than ever committed to the ideal of Aliyah.

But the same reaction in the group that had first led them to resistance now caused them to defer leaving Europe for Palestine (as they could have, through the Breichah). Even as ghetto fighters or partisans, they had viewed resistance as a form of revenge—for both their personal losses and for the losses of the Jews as a people; several of the partisan units had included "Nekamah" ("Revenge") in the names they took. Thus the group in Lublin— later in Bucharest, their second staging area—proposed the continuation of resistance through the form of revenge, recognizing also that if they were to be effective, they would have to carry out their plans during the period of political disruption near the end of the war and before the reestablishment of effective legal institutions in the new Germany. The group organized itself under the leadership of Abba Kovner, who had been a leader of the Vilna Partisans. Usually referred to as the "Revenge Organization" or "Group," it more formally adopted the acronym DIN ("Judgment"), based on the first letters of "Dam Yisrael Noter" ("the blood of Israel avenges").

The specific direction the group would take was agreed on from its beginning. They conceived of revenge not as the pursuit and punishment of individual Nazis, however warranted that was. What weighed on the group more heavily than individual atrocities was the collective murder of the Jews—made possible, in the Revenge Group's view, by the collaboration of the German people as a people. As the Jews had thus been victimized by the Germans collectively, so the vengeance called for would also be collective.

Thus the group's plan—or rather, two plans—evolved, the first of them of such enormity that although preliminary steps were taken toward implementing it, reservations within the group itself and external pressure against it appeared almost from the beginning; there is no evidence, however, that the group's failure to implement this plan was due to a lack of resolve. This plan A proposed to place members of the group among the sewage and water plant workers in four German cities: Hamburg, Frankfurt, Munich, and Nuremberg—and that was in fact accomplished in two of them. The action proposed was to have these workers poison the water supply of the four cities. Again, although preparatory steps were taken toward implementing this plan, it did not go beyond that stage. Plan B was designed to strike at prisoner of war camps set up by the Allies for German soldiers, particularly those designated for SS men. A number of such camps were targeted for attack; in the event, one attack was carried out—on April 13, 1946, at a prisoner of war camp near Nuremberg that held about 16,000 former SS men.

The Revenge Group had placed several members as employees in the camp bakery who then smeared arsenic on the bread distributed in the camp (a similar attempt which had been scheduled for the same day at Dachau was called off at the last minute). Estimates have ranged from 10,000 hospitalized and 2,200 dead to much smaller numbers in both categories; the official American version (since this occurred in the American zone of occupation) as it appeared in the *Suddeutsche Zeitung* (April 24, 1946) refers to 207 prisoners as having been hospitalized but mentions no fatalities. (The latter is one disputed matter of fact that may yet be resolved—with the truth probably close to the middle of the two accounts cited.)

Even against its somber background, the story of how the plans of the Revenge Group developed sounds like an implausible melodrama. Included in this history is a trip to Palestine by Abba Kovner, intended to obtain both material support and the endorsement of the Yishuv. The endorsement was not forthcoming, then or ever, certainly not in any formal sense (it seems likely that Kovner did not even mention plan A to the people he spoke to from the Hagganah and the Jewish Agency). But Kovner did obtain a meeting with Chaim Weizmann, then President of the World Zionist Organization and the Jewish Agency, who arranged introductions for him to the chemist Ernst Bergmann (who made arrangements for a supply of poison; this has been independently attested to by Bergmann's then-assistant, Ephraim Katzir) and to a wealthy businessman who provided him with funds. On the voyage back to France on a British destroyer—the day before landing in Toulouse—Kovner was taken into custody by the British crew; he was then returned to Alexandria where he was imprisoned for two months before being sent back to Palestine. He had managed before being arrested to throw or to have thrown the poison overboard, and the Revenge Group in Europe then was forced to rely on their own resources for the arsenic eventually used in the Nuremberg attack. The evidence suggests that Kovner had been betrayed to the British, almost certainly by someone or some group in the Yishuv and probably on political grounds not directly related to the Revenge Group's goals.

The story, of course, goes on, with all the members of the Revenge Group eventually arriving in Israel, Kovner and a number of others becoming members of Kibbutz Ein HaChoresh. Only in the last years before Kovner's death (beginning around 1985) did he begin to speak for the record about the episode, and there exist a number of tapes with his account of it; with time now running out, other members of the group (or around it) have also begun to speak, although as might be expected with such retrospective efforts to "set the record straight," the results are likely to remain unsettled in detail.

My concern here, in any event, is with the *principle* of revenge on the scale conceived by the Revenge Group; some of the intensity underlying their plans is evident in the last will of a member of the partisans—Zipporah Berman, a member of D'ror in Bialystok—who was killed before the Revenge Group began its work but whose words anticipate the theme they asserted:

> With this I turn to you, comrades. . . . On you rests the absolute obligation to carry out our revenge. Let no one of you sleep at night or during the day: as we are in the shadow of death, let it also be so for you in revenging the blood that has been spilt. Cursed be whoever reads these words for whom it suffices to sigh and to return to their daily chores; cursed be he for whom cheap tears suffice, who in his crying would bewail our souls. We call you to revenge—revenge without pity, without feeling, without words about "good" Germans. For the good German—an easy death. Let him die last, as they promised their own good Jew: "You, they will shoot last." This is our demand. The scattered ashes from the ovens will not rest easy until this vengeance is exacted. Remember and fulfill our wish and your obligation.[4]

The words as written are not bound temporally—a characteristic of curses and calls for revenge. If they make us uncomfortable today, read in our own present—in a context Berman hardly could have imagined—one can believe that she would not have changed any part of what she said. Certainly it is this conception of revenge that would lead to—would *necessarily* lead to—the detail of something like plan A.

That plan by the Revenge Group is the most dramatic of any initiated in the aftermath of the Holocaust with the explicit intention of seeking revenge, but it is not the only one. It is known that a unit of the Jewish Brigade stationed in northern Italy at the end of the war (including among its members the future Israeli chief of staff, Haim Laskov) undertook an authorized initiative against former SS officers living across the border in Austria; the numbers are uncertain, but something between 50 and 150 assassinations which followed a systematic search are attributed to this group. From another of the postwar fronts, evidence has emerged that as the USSR established its hegemony in Eastern European countries, at the end of the war, a deliberate effort was made (notably in Poland and Hungary) to place Jewish members of the communist secret police (who sometimes sought out the opportunity) in charge of German prisoner of war camps or of internal

---

[4] Cited in Sarid, 36.

campaigns of "*epuration*"—with results that, again, although still uncertain in their details, almost certainly included the motivation of revenge.[5]

About what might be called "private" revenge—acts carried out by individuals returning to hometowns where their families had been destroyed or even in less calculated settings as the opportunity presented itself—I have been able to learn unsystematically of only individual acts.[6] It is certain that such acts did occur (and quite implausible that they should *not* have occurred), but so far as I know, nobody has attempted to collect or assess evidence about these. The combination of death and aging in the generation of survivors and the reticence that inquiry about such acts is likely to encounter make the prospect of recovering such information increasingly remote.[7]

The so-called Nazi hunters—figures such as Simon Wiesenthal, Tuvya Friedman, and the Klarsfelds—have in their own terms been motivated by the impulse not for revenge but for justice, tracing Nazis with the purpose of exposing them and having them brought to trial. There is an obvious difference between this goal and the act of revenge which itself judges and punishes, although something of the latter also appears here in the assumption that if the criminals sought can only be brought to trial, they will be punished. That has not always been the outcome, of course, but without this premise, the Nazi hunters would probably have given their project a different form if they undertook it at all. (It might be argued that even where the Nazi hunters have failed—in locating the Nazis they have sought or, once they were found, in having them tried or punished—they have forced them to live underground, and that this is itself a form of revenge. Perhaps

---

[5] Cf. John Sack, *An Eye for an Eye* (New York: Basic Books, 1993) (see also the sharply critical review of that book by Daniel Goldhagen in *The New Republic*, December 27, 1993); and Viktor Karady, "Some Social Aspects of Jewish Assimilation in Socialist Hungary 1945–1956," in Randolph Braham, ed., *The Tragedy of Hungarian Jewry* (New York: Columbia University Press, 1986), 73–131. See also a brief reference in I. F. Stone, *Underground to Palestine* (New York: Pantheon, 1978), 101. Charges of murder and brutality by former inmates of one postwar camp in Poland (Swietochlowice) have been brought in Germany against Solomon Morel, who recently left Poland for Israel and who had been in charge of the camp (See *New York Times*, Jan 11,1994, A3; and *Yedioth Aharonoth*, Dec 13,1994; *Ha-Aretz*, Feb 10, 1995, 31.

[6] Some of the partisan groups engaged in such actions, even during the war itself. See, e.g., Harold Werner, op. cit., 98–99, 179.

[7] As part of a video archives project in Philadelphia, consisting of interviews with Holocaust survivors under the auspices of the Jewish Family Service, the interviewers began (December 1994) to ask the survivors interviewed a standard question—if they had "heard about" instances of private revenge. The question was initiated when approximately half the planned interviews had already been completed (thus providing a control group); there has been a significant response to this question, although the interviews are still not completed.

that in turn was balanced for fugitives such as Martin Bormann or Mengele, who were never caught and who might have viewed their escape as a form of victory.)

In August 1950 Israel enacted the "Nazi and Nazi Collaborators (Punishment) Law," which was later interpreted in one Supreme Court decision (*Honigman vs. The Legal Advisor to the Israeli Government*, March 23, 1952) as intended "to 'seek revenge' on the enemies and haters of Israel." The latter phrasing seems quite consciously to conflate revenge and the institution of justice; it is worth noting in any event that with the exception of the Eichmann and Demjanjuk trials, the other, approximately twenty-five trials conducted under this law (all except the Demjanjuk trial took place in the 1950s and 1960s) were brought against Jews living in Israel who were accused of wartime collaboration. If the law was indeed intended as a form of revenge, the very limitation of its reach, confined aside from the two exceptional cases cited to the boundaries of Israel, obviously constrained the intention.

The latter point returns us to my earlier claim that few explicit instances of revenge have come to light—with whatever might be inferred about that either in respect to the failure to search for such evidence or in interpreting that conclusion itself. I would emphasize that the substantive question—"Why *not* revenge?"—is not directed especially to Shoah survivors. The partisans forming the Revenge Group had been exceptional before organizing the group; whatever hardships they endured, moreover, they had not suffered the grinding erosion that inmates of the concentration or death camps continuously experienced. For survivors of the latter, almost always weakened physically and psychologically, revenge would have been an unlikely decision at the time of their liberation, although even for them the question cannot quite be avoided. It is more obviously pertinent, however, for the rest of the Jewish community. The explanation from Zionist organizations and state institutions in Palestine and then Israel that competing political priorities and/or reasons of state left little place and scanty resources for acts of revenge goes only so far before it begs the question. And although objections to the problematic moral status of revenge do not beg the question, they surely need to be scrutinized closely before they can be judged to preclude acts of revenge.

One formulation of the question "Why *not* revenge?" appears effectively if nastily in an observation by Philip Roth on the Demjanjuk trial in his book *Operation Shylock*. Roth (or one of the two characters named Roth in that quasifictional volume) wonders about the great incongruity he finds in the process of the trial, with Demjanjuk's son (and his attorneys) moving about

Jerusalem—inside and outside the court—as freely as they might if the trial had involved a much more conventional legal issue. So Roth writes:

> Did no survivor in all of Israel think of killing John Demjanjuk, Jr., of taking revenge on the guilty father through the perfectly innocent son? Was there no one whose family had been exterminated at Treblinka who had thought of kidnapping him and of then mutilating him, gradually, piecemeal, an inch at a go, until Demjanjuk could take no more and admitted to the court who he was? Was there no survivor, driven insane with rage by this defendant's carefree yawning . . . enraged enough to envisage in the torturing of the one the means of extracting a confession from the other, to perceive in the outright murder of the next in line a perfectly just and fitting requital? [8]

The historical answer to Roth's questions obviously was no; in the event, it was Demjanjuk's Israeli and Jewish attorney, Yoram Sheftel, who had acid thrown in his eyes, not Demjanjuk's son, still less Demjanjuk himself.

IN ALL the instances cited, however one judges them, the moral question of their status is never far off (this is an obvious difference between revenge and the phenomenon of resistance or self-defense, which even in less extreme contexts than the Shoah would rarely be disputed on moral grounds).[9] This moral ambiguity is undoubtedly one factor among others behind the Displacement Effect of revenge. In any event, wherever displacement occurs, there will be reasons for it, and we need to consider in the particular case what these might be. At least one feature of revenge itself openly invites the Displacement Effect; namely, its distinctive temporal structure. Virtually any reaction in the present against an act in the past can also be interpreted as directed against a future recurrence of the same act. And under *that* description, the reaction would not count as revenge, but more simply as prudence or foresight—hardly a morally relevant motive at all. Under the rubric of deterrence, this is—notwithstanding the considerable evidence that argues against it—the principal justification for capital punishment apart from that of retribution (that is, of revenge).

When I speak about the expression of revenge in relation to the Shoah

---

[8] Philip Roth, *Operation Shylock*, p. 66.

[9] See on this issue Martin Buber's letter to Gandhi, responding to Gandhi's statement in *Harijan* (November 26, 1938) recommending a policy of nonviolent resistance by the Jews against the Nazis (*The Letters of Martin Buber*, ed. Nahum N. Glatzer and Paul Mendes-Flohr [New York: Schocken, 1991], 476–486).

by a "Displacement Effect," I borrow the concept of displacement from Freud's famous Chapter 6 of *The Interpretation of Dreams* (although without a commitment to his explanatory theory). Displacement in these terms transposes the intensity of certain central ideas to other, less highly charged ones related to the former "eccentrically" or by association; the effect, then, is of "disfiguration" or disguise—a concession, in Freud's phrase, to the "psychic censor." If one considers the appearance of revenge in the aftermath of the Shoah in terms of displacement, the number of its recognizable instances increases substantially, and not only because of the quick multiplication that any interpretive theory of covert meaning encourages. At least some of those instances, moreover, have every feature of revenge except for the designation itself.

So, for example, the Morgenthau Plan—proposed before the end of World War II by Roosevelt's Secretary of the Treasury—called for turning Germany into a pastoral country, not only demilitarized but deindustrialized and partitioned. Again, the explicit rationale for this proposal—its manifest content—was pointed toward the future (the formal title of the plan was Program to Prevent Germany from Starting a World War III), and no doubt that was a genuine concern; [10] what had been displaced in it—the latent content—seems equally clear, however, with its object squarely in Germany's past and expressing a form of international revenge. This plan, of course, never went beyond the proposal stage—although by an odd historical twist, something close to it in spirit *did* ensue; namely, the division between East and West Germany. To be sure, that division had not been originally intended; it came about when the four zones of occupation established at the war's end were reduced to two, as the USSR balked at the prospect of a single German government (and national elections). Partly because of this "accidental" background, partly for diplomatic reasons, the muted reservations expressed internationally in 1990 at the reunification of Germany were ostensibly pointed at the future: the fear of renewed German hegemony in Europe.

But those reservations, together with some notable silences, also included an element of regret that is explicable only if the divided Germany *had been* viewed as a punishment (whether intended or not). The division served in effect as a mark of Cain among nations of the world, given that the most

---

[10] See Henry Morgenthau Jr., *Germany Is Our Problem* (New York: Harper & Bros., 1945). There is no reason to doubt that Morgenthau was thinking in part of the future (however naively): "When the majority of the German people are small farmers, they will be a bit less susceptible to militarism. The owners of land, especially the owners who work it themselves, are likely to have little time for other occupations. . . ." (146); but neither is there reason to believe that he was thinking *only* of that.

rudimentary condition for any nation is its identity or unity. (In some ways, the accidental origin of the punishment served the function of revenge more aptly than if it had been calculated—since there was no one in particular to blame for it). Certainly many Germans, looking outward from the inside, saw the divided Germany as a form of punishment and, against the background of World War II, of revenge; this came into the open most explicitly in the conclusion popularly drawn that with the 1990 reunification of East and West Germany, the past had been settled and Germany, now once again whole, could resume its place as an equal among nations (I address this topic more fully in the next chapter). But the *general* public discourse, inside or outside Germany, spoke no more at the time than it had before of the divided Germany as a form of punishment. Among the few such statements openly expressed was one attributed variously to de Gaulle or Malraux: "I *like* Germany"; the one or the other is supposed to have said, "I like it so much I want there to be two of them."

Other examples of the Displacement Effect are more plentiful on a smaller scale—smaller perhaps because of the will to conceal even displaced expressions. Certainly no interpretation of Jewish response in the aftermath of the Shoah can ignore the phenomenon of revenge in such displaced forms, however slight or inconsistent or even perverse they have sometimes been. Numbers of Jews—perhaps also non-Jews, although I have not heard of this—refuse to this day to buy German goods or to travel in Germany. Most of these people are aware that something like three quarters of the present German populace were born after World War II; none of them, so far as I know, has urged a general boycott of German goods, a ban which if successfully implemented could cause serious harm. In this sense, their response—whatever its other emotional features, including repugnance or even hatred—also appears as an instance of personal revenge, a wish to return injury for injury, albeit deliberately small in scale. (It has been suggested to me that this response might be just as plausibly understood as commemorative—but if it is this, it is commemorative of the perpetrators as well as the victims, which is an alternative formulation of what revenge is.) Or again: The Israel Philharmonic has only in the last several years included the music of Strauss (who personally served as a censor of music under the Nazi regime) in its repertoire; the music of Wagner, more potent symbolically (both the music and the person), is still excluded. Again, the intention of any boycott undoubtedly reflects a more general impulse for social unification, and the ostensive reason given for the ban has been respect for the feelings of survivors. But boycotts, whatever other function they serve, are also aggressive acts, meant to punish often within the law but even then going beyond what the law mandates; here, too, we see in the form of displacement—it is not Wagner, after all, who is meant or made to suffer—the will to punish that is characteristic of revenge.

A theological version of such displacement appears in a number of formulations, epitomized in Emil Fackenheim's "614th Commandment" that I alluded to earlier: "The authentic Jew of today is forbidden to hand Hitler yet another, posthumous victory" (that is, in addition to Hitler's "victory" in the extermination of six million Jews).[11] Revenge in its displaced form here expresses itself in the continuity of Jewish identity—the obligation of Jews now to remain Jews, presumably to inflict harm on Hitler and the principles he espoused (although it can certainly be questioned whether this answers to the requirement for revenge that injury should be returned for injury).

Again, these instances are slight in proportion to the provocation to which they respond, although the mechanism of displacement is conducive to such a reduction in scale as overt revenge is not. For although overt revenge has no intrinsic upward limit—an essential difference from punishment based on justice—it surely has a minimal limit. To write an insulting letter to the murderer of a relative or friend would hardly qualify as an instance of revenge; with displaced or symbolic meaning, however, there is evidently no minimal limit either. On the other hand, also larger examples of displaced revenge are to be found in the aftermath of the Holocaust for the Jewish community. Viewed from the perspective of revenge, the bitter struggle over the acceptance of German reparations in Israel in 1952 affords a perspective on the more general relation between Israel and the world Jewish community, on the one hand, and postwar Germany, on the other. The principal objection to accepting the initial offer of German reparations was against "blood money"—that on its acceptance, Germany would feel, and perhaps be entitled to feel, that even if the "Wiedergutmachung" did not (as it could not) repair the harm inflicted by the old Germany, the new Germany would have done as much as could reasonably be expected even in the eyes of the victims. And opposed to this was the sense not only that this was not true, but also that nothing Germany could do would make it true; that notwithstanding the formal difference between the Third Reich and the new Germany, the latter had a continuing and virtually limitless responsibility for the actions of its predecessor and so also a continuing and indefinite moral obligation to Israel and the Jewish community. And indeed the latter view has seemed to prevail,[12] notwithstanding the acceptance of

---

[11] Emil Fackenheim, *The Jewish Return into History* (New York: Schocken, 1978), 22; see also *To Mend the World* (New York: Schocken, 1982), 299–300.

[12] I refer here, for one example, to a motion introduced in the Knesset which, in response to ethnic and racist outbreaks of violence in Germany against "foreigners" in 1993, would have initiated an economic boycott against Germany. The motion did not get very far and perhaps

reparations (in this sense, Menachem Begin and the other opponents of the reparations agreement were unduly concerned). One way of describing the view of constant liability, however, is as a form of displaced revenge by means of the continued (potentially limitless) ascription of guilt: a tried and effective means of punishment—even, evidently, at the level of nations.

The capture, trial, and then execution of Adolf Eichmann which occupied a large place in shaping Israeli consciousness of the Nazi genocide seems to me less clearly and in any event less exclusively an example of revenge than the other instances cited—less so, for example, than if Eichmann had been assassinated in Argentina (as he no doubt could have been by the members of the Mossad who kidnaped him). That he was given his day in court after being kidnaped (by definition, illegally) would for most people only pose the question of whether it would not have been a greater injustice for Eichmann not to have been tried at all—but this again is a question of justice rather than a matter of revenge. Even the judicial decision that Eichmann was to be executed and the execution itself (the vengeful conclusion of the process if there was one at all) seemed a relatively small component of the trial which was intended to serve many other purposes, thus in effect proportionately reducing the role of revenge. Certainly retrospective accounts of the trial rarely construe its immediate practical outcome—that is, Eichmann's execution—as a principal issue.

It is impossible to avoid at least mentioning displacement at one farther remove from those cited so far—a remove that not only translates revenge into a different act but also displaces its ostensible object, that is, the Nazis or Germans. As Israeli relations with Arabs—with Arab states or groups and Arabs individually—have also become issues for non-Israeli Jews, so also the phenomenon of "Holocaust" displacement has entered the discourse in both domains. I am not speaking here of the more general use of the Shoah in political and religious rhetoric, objectionable as that displacement is in using the Shoah as a metonymy for the prospect of the disappearance of the Jews—directed then against virtually every problem affecting Jewish identity: secularization and intermarriage, for example, as well as against more general and theoretical questions of theodicy and martyrdom. I refer rather to a form of demonization and aggression that does not seem accounted for even by the real threats Israel has faced. This is obviously a point where the grounds of interpretation are unavoidably political: if the intensity of political discourse (and action) in or outside Israel vis-à-vis Arabs are judged to have been sufficiently determined by the historical reality, then this pro-

---

was not intended to, but it is unlikely that it would have been proposed at all in respect to any other country.

posal would be undercut. At least in degree, however, certain disfigured representations of Arab character and rights—and the expression of self-assertion and force directed against those representations—reflect an emergence from powerlessness that was in recent Jewish history epitomized in the Shoah and that has since found the Arabs an available target for compensation (that is, for revenge).[13] Proposals, for example, for the "transfer" of the Arab population out of Israel recall both substantively and in its perversion of language that earlier precedent. A more superficial but equally clear manifestation of this tendency appears in the slogan "Never again," with the "again" an obvious invocation of the Holocaust, directed now, however, not against Nazis but their successors. (A notable application of this slogan was Menachem Begin's justification to the Israeli cabinet on the eve of the Israeli invasion of Lebanon in June 1982: "The alternative is Treblinka, and we have decided there will be no more Treblinkas."[14])

IN discussing the silence surrounding the topic of revenge in the aftermath of the Holocaust, I have so far alluded only to the morally problematic status of the concept or act of revenge. There can be no doubt, however, that this consideration has been a generalized factor in that silence and that it has also influenced the two specific explanations outlined above. I can here mention only some of the systematic ethical issues that bear on the phenomenon of revenge, specifically in its relation to two other moral concepts, justice and forgiveness. In respect to both of these, revenge is discomforting, deviant—the more so, when its occasion is an extreme situation which would be the more likely to evoke an extreme reaction. The most obvious source for this dissonance is the feature of revenge that has the victims of a perceived injury themselves acting on their own (or their group's) behalf; that is, with their own (or their agent's) hands—a feature that violates a primary condition of justice. The implication in revenge of the victim's role in both judging and punishing is the antithesis of the figure of justice who is characteristically portrayed as blindfolded to prevent her from seeing those whom she judges and, as a consequence, taking their identities or sta-

---

[13] Peter Novick (in a private communication) has suggested to me that a factor more direct than displaced in this attitude has been an impulse for revenge for Arab—and particularly the Grand Mufti of Jerusalem's—associations with the Nazis during World War II. Certainly those associations were at the time a recognized source of hostility, but it is difficult to know how much of a role they have had in the post-1067 "demonization" of the Arabs. Few explicit references to the Mufti's role or attempts to generalize from it to Nazi connections among the Arab populace at large have figured in the popular discourse.

[14] Arieh Naor, *Government at War: How the Israeli Government Functioned during the Lebanon War, 1982* (Tel Aviv: Yedioth Aharonot, 1986), 47.

tus into account in her judgment. In contrast to justice as "blind" and dis-interested, revenge is sighted and partial. It is not an *offense* by itself that evokes revenge; it is rather the fact that I or someone (or group) with whom I associate myself has been the victim of the offense. (In this respect, even if a legally constituted court should punish a malfactor, the person harmed might still claim that he did not have *his* revenge.)

To be sure, certain instances of revenge seem also morally warranted—notably, in cases where there otherwise seems to be no chance of obtaining justice.[15] In certain of these instances, moreover (surely Zipporah Berman thinks in these terms), revenge may appear not only warranted but obliga-tory. And what we speak of as "poetic justice" typically refers to an instance of accidental or natural revenge. But even if we recognize incremental dif-ferences in the relation between revenge and justice, reflecting historical differences in intention and consequence, in the relation between revenge and justice (so, for example, one might assess quite differently the revenge exacted respectively in the Book of Esther from Haman, his sons, and the general populace), the point remains that revenge *can* at any moment di-verge sharply from justice and thus challenges justice in principle.[16] Cer-tainly, revenge acknowledges no intrinsic limits, whereas it is precisely the recognition of such limits—that the punishment should *fit* the crime—that marks the domain of justice. Revenge may be cruel, but it is never exces-sive—at least not as revenge; to speak of it in that way seems a category mis-take that conflates revenge with justice.

---

[15] So Francis Bacon writes in his essay, "Of Revenge": "The most tolerable sort of revenge, is for those wrongs which there is no law to remedy; but then let a man take heed, the revenge be such as there is no law to punish; else a man's enemy is still before hand, and it is two for one."

[16] I have avoided reference to the place of revenge in the Hebrew Bible or in the medieval Jew-ish tradition, partly because of the scope of those topics but also because I have not found evi-dence of connections between those sources and the contemporary reactions considered here. In any event, it seems clear that divine revenge—and Biblical revenge *is* God's—would *neces-sarily* be just; both the Biblical and medieval accounts of revenge in relation to the Jewish com-munity evidently insist on just this point. Certain instances of human revenge are recorded in the Bible without being designated as revenge—for example, the revenge taken by her broth-ers for the rape of Dinah—but it is unclear exactly what the ethical status of that revenge is. (On the Biblical conception of God's revenge as "just recompense" and "not simply brutal," see Wayne T. Pitard, "Amarma *ekemus* and Hebrew *naqam*," (*Maarav*, III, 1982, 17), who argues there against the discussion of revenge in George E. Mendenhall, *The Tenth Generation* (Balti-more: Johns Hopkins University Press, 1973); a more comprehensive account than either of these appears in H. G. L. Peels, *The Vengeance of God* (Leiden: E. J. Brill, 1994). On the medieval Jewish conception of revenge as divine (and just) retribution, see Yisrael Yuval, "Vengeance and Damnation, Blood and Defamation," (Hebrew), *Zion*, LVIII (1993), 37ff.) The letters Heh-Yod-Dalet attached to a deceased person's name ("HaShem Yikkom Damo"—"May God avenge his blood") have come to be used where the deceased was murdered (almost always in a political or social context and where the murder was committed by non-Jews).

Furthermore, if revenge in practice diverges only at certain points from justice, revenge seems in principle contradictory of forgiveness. Unlike forgiveness which erases the past, revenge preserves it; rather than seeing individual acts as (at least sometimes) finite and redeemable, revenge sounds an indefinite echo. What has made the English expression "forgive and forget" a cliché is not only its linguistic chime; forgiving brings a release from the past, a deliberate forgetting, as opposed to the impulse for revenge which reinscribes the past, entering it into a potentially endless chain.[17] Even when someone has "had" what he believes to be his revenge, he cannot assume that the person with whom (from his own point of view) he has evened the score will agree that the score is even or, if he does, agree to settle for that. Quite the contrary, in fact—since to have the last word (which is surely a goal of revenge and which only one person can have) implies more than only getting "even." Thus also, to speak of having "avenged" a particular injury, with the sense this conveys of completion, is perspectival—expressed from the point of view of the avenger at a particular moment and thus in a setting that may thereafter become part of a longer, and incomplete, chain.

This dissonance between revenge and the principles of justice and forgiveness provides an additional, albeit nonhistorical reason for the silence concerning the phenomenon of revenge in reference to the Shoah. Even with the insulation of history and the ritualization of violence that separates the appearance of revenge in classic texts from the present, revenge may be a discomforting topic for its potential clash with justice; without that insulation, it becomes harsher still.

The elements of this dissonance also bear on the relation between revenge and memory. In contrasting revenge and forgiveness, I have already referred to a temporal distinction between the two, as the past is erased for forgiveness and sustained and reiterated in revenge. "Instant revenge" may be logically possible, but in practice it would be identical to resistance; more typically an interval occurs between the occasion and act of revenge which thus also presupposes memory. (Although this interval need not be of long duration, its existence not only distinguishes revenge from resistance but also seems in its consequences intrinsic to revenge; the saying "Revenge is best served cold" epitomizes the conjunction of retribution and delay.) If one thinks of memory, furthermore, as a construct rather than as a natural faculty or repository waiting to be filled, then revenge can be well understood, with the temporal extension it presupposes, as a means of *creating*

---

[17] So Hannah Arendt speaks of the "chain reaction" of revenge; see *The Human Condition* (Chicago: University of Chicago Press, 1958), 240.

memory: not just a particular memory, but memory as such, and so also the sense of personal or communal identity for which memory is a necessary condition.

Revenge in these terms is *useful* for memory and identity—a function that is further reinforced in its future dimension: the sense that any particular act of revenge, far from bringing closure, may in turn be countered or superseded by another. This anticipation of the future in revenge is also arguably a condition of memory, one often ignored because of memory's more evident focus on the past. But memory involves, together with a look backward, the capacity to reiterate or "re"-present what is recalled there; that is, by a purchase on the future. Without the capacity for this projection forward, memory would be *in* the past as well as of it. Thus, another link in the unusual allegiance between revenge and memory—an allegiance that can be admitted even if we stop short of Nietzsche's radical claim that one central reason for the construction of memory is *to make revenge possible.*[18]

I do not with this mean to assert that revenge is a necessary, let alone a sufficient condition for memory; other emotive or moral conditions share some of the features cited: "promising," for instance, presupposes a consciousness that bases the present on the "promise" of a future act. But the fact that revenge motivates memory—and from the memorable starting point of pain (either directly or, in the pain of emotional loss, as reflected)—suggests a more common and important role for revenge in the construction of memory than is usually assumed.[19] At the very least, *when* revenge occurs, it would indeed foster memory: not exclusively, not necessarily justifiably, but nonetheless—with memory a crucial element of both individual and collective identity. Insofar as the impulse for revenge is repressed or displaced, moreover, a danger arises that affects all indirection or concealment—that its agent may lose sight of and so control of its transformations. In those circumstances, revenge may become something quite different, pointed in a different direction (either toward other objects or backward, against the agent himself). I have claimed that in some of its displacements this indeed has been the effect of the impulse for revenge in relation to the Holocaust.

---

[18] See, for example, *The Genealogy of Morals*, second essay, Sec. 3; and *Human All Too Human*, vol. 2, Sec. 33.
[19] Nietzsche emphasizes the role of "blood, torture, and sacrifice" in the making of memory (*The Genealogy of Morals*, second Essay, Sec. 3); a less sweeping but more concrete account appears in George Orwell's essay "Such, Such Were the Joys," in his account there of a schoolboy learning to the accompaniment of beating. (One analysis of the physiology of memory cites changes of body chemistry [e.g., the flow of adrenalin] as related to "lasting" memory; see *New York Times*, Oct 25, 1994, C1, C11.

In a world of perfect justice, where all wrongdoing was punished (and where there was reason to believe that it would be), revenge would have no place; if it did appear, it would have the quality of self-indulgence recognizable as spitefulness and finally as injustice. Even for those who believe that finally justice does rule in the world, however, and certainly for those who do not believe it, revenge seems yet to remain in practice an assumed means of expression and one among other instruments of identity and memory. Some of its manifestations are prima facie morally culpable; perhaps, as I have suggested, justifications for revenge remain at best faute de mieux—for want of a better alternative, with the clear implication that we can readily imagine what such a better alternative would be (although also that we *have* to imagine it, since it is not actual). To take this position commits one to the view that in the dissonance between revenge and justice, the former must finally give way to the latter. To reject this conclusion is to place revenge outside the purview of justice, thus also threatening the status of justice itself.

How do such general comments bear specifically on memory in relation to the Shoah? I revert here to the theme that surfaced earlier as hypothetical but which can now be asserted categorically. The impulse and act of revenge, displaced or overt, have in fact contributed to the shaping of memory and consciousness of the Shoah—as they should have been expected to. Displaced expressions have served to veil this role, and it is important for self-understanding and for the future shaping of memory that these displacements should be made explicit. The principal emphasis in the collective public consciousness of the Holocaust has been on commemoration (again, as the Holocaust Museum in Washington is a *Memorial* Museum)— recalling the loss of life, mourning it, honoring it. Revenge offers a very different perspective on the past, one that it is not necessary to advocate or to justify in order to recognize as having had an historical role. That this role may be more difficult to assimilate in the present than mourning or commemoration is not a justification for not attempting to do so. If "Zakhor" is an imperative, the need to know how memory works is no less pressing than the need to determine what it is that memory should remember.

11

Germany Reunified: The Stigma of Normalcy

The speed at which reunification of the two Germanies moved should not be allowed to obscure the misgivings which that event called up in 1990 and which in various forms have continued since—in the countries of Western and Eastern Europe whose most recent memory of a united Germany re-called the menace of invasion and occupation; among Jews in or outside those countries for whom Germany's restoration to "normalcy" seemed (per-haps would always seem) premature; in the two Germanies that had been divided and that became conscious in reunification of the fear—not only on the part of others, but also their own—that whatever had brought about the division in the first place might at some point, just as suddenly, reap-pear. All these, of course, were added to the mutual suspicions between the two "countries" that the division itself engendered.[1]

Admittedly, the strongest and most overt expressions of apprehension at the prospect of reunification in 1989 when the Berlin Wall came down have since become muted, almost dissolved in other tensions and difficulties that span the now united Germany; and if the differences in economic status be-tween the earlier two Germanies continue to demarcate a border between

---

[1] For a sampling of many accounts (and viewpoints) on the process and consequences of reuni-fication, see, e.g., Richard J. Evans, *Rereading German History: From Unification to Reunification: 1800–1996* (New York: Routledge, 1997); Marc Fisher, *After the Wall: Germany, the Germans, and the Borders of History* (New York: Simon & Schuster, 1995); Jeffrey Herf, *Divided Memory: The Nazi Past in the Two Germanys* (Cambridge: Harvard University Press, 1997); and (for a view through the lens of reunification of the claims in Goldhagen's *Hitler's Willing Executioners*), Dieter Pohl, "Die Holocaust-Forschung und Goldhagen's Thesen," *Vierteljahrshefte fur Zeitgeschichte*, 45 (1997), 1–48.

them (not as rigidly as before, but no less publicly), the surface of unification is almost unruffled ideologically even for its critics, if only because of the combined sense of historical irreversibility and inevitability which in politics is the equivalent of justice. It is clear in any event that whatever the world's other governments felt at the time about German reunification, no one among them and not even the group collectively was in a position to block it even if they had wished to; there too, the sense of inevitability—although probably a less confident sense of justice—prevailed. The decision and the act were thus in the hands of the two Germanies themselves. And for them, with the breaching of the Berlin Wall—its fragments turned immediately into souvenirs—the question of reunification was not, strictly speaking, a question at all. It was the division into the two parts that had been an artifice, an intrusion that required justification, not its demise. Outside the two Germanies, then, nobody *could* say no to reunification; inside, with rejection a possibility, the very question would not be admitted (at least on the right and in the center of German politics, the very large majority)—if only because to take it seriously as a question would have been tantamount to ratifying the conditions that led up to the division and an admission that the ideal of a unified Germany recalled from before that time had been forfeited.

In contrast to many claims of political or historical inevitability, however, the misgivings expressed openly at the time of reunification have persisted in a variety of forms, some displaced into other expressions, a few still openly asserted—but all of them representing a measure of concern which is more than only a prudential assessment of the practical difficulties that the new Germany, now neither West nor East, faces. This continuing question—partly symbolic, partly also practical—is no less important than the prudential one, as that calls attention to the still unresolved relation in German history between reunification and the Nazi past, of which the postwar division of the Germanies had been so visible and concrete a symbol that, for many, it obviated the need for any such analysis. This relation embodies the question of what conditions Germany collectively, as one, can be required to meet to win acknowledgment that the German past is indeed past—to settle, once and for all, that Germany and the Germans have sufficiently rehabilitated, for themselves and country, the Nazi past and that they have given sufficient assurance for the future, thus meeting those two unavoidable conditions for the restoration of normalcy, or even more radically, for forgiveness, again both within Germany and in the eyes of the international community.

The connection between the terms of forgiveness and the reunification of Germany may seem remote, but it becomes more readily plausible on the hypothesis that the division of Germany into East and West served a symbolic function that extended well beyond the material origins and the role of that division in the Cold War. The prospect of reunification brought to the surface an awareness that the divided Germany had been not only an expression of East-West tensions, but also was emblematic of Germany's own history—reflecting backward by symbolic displacement to the condition preceding the division, that is, to Germany as it had been unified under the Nazi regime and as it at that time exalted even a greater and larger unity. The barbarism of the Nazi regime itself thus brought also the post-Nazi period into German history but still under the Nazi rubric—this time, however, in the form of punishment.

The two Germanies, in short, signified at the level of nations a verdict on the Third Reich—a symbol immediately intelligible to anyone who took seriously the Nazi past and even to those, inside or outside Germany, who disputed that verdict or would in their own minds have ignored it. The analogy here is difficult but pointed: like the original bearer of the mark of Cain, Germans in their divided country would go among the nations identified by the labeled directions they wore: "East" or "West." The line of demarcation between them (unlike others within the "same" country, as between North and South Korea) had been imposed from the outside, not by a "civil" war or internal decision; even if not designed as this, it stood as a judgment—exacting a material penalty from the people "divided" by it and evoking the symbolic associations of subordination and physical punishment (boundaries, after all, are nothing if not physical) as a continuing reminder to observers outside the two "countries."

If the division of Germany had this symbolic character, moreover, reunification would then also be a symbol—implying restoration and the return to normalcy. As division was a penalty for Germany's past, reunification would mean that the terms of the penalty—assessed by the society of nations as they enforced the division or even if they only "recognized" it—had been fulfilled; the "debt to society" had been paid. Only this conclusion, it seems to me, accounts for the uneasiness, beyond practical anxieties, roused initially by the prospect of unification and continuing to this day in reaction to the place assumed in Europe by the united Germany. To be sure, there is a difference between the moral act of forgiveness and the legal standing of someone who, duly convicted and sentenced, has "served" the terms of the punishment imposed. In the latter case as well, however, the slate is in some sense wiped clean—and if the prospect of Germany's legal restoration has produced concern about the opening of a path to its economic or political dominance in Europe, the prospect of moral absolution or forgiveness for Germany's past has for many been just as unsettling.

Again, to link forgiveness and the restoration implied by international recognition mingles moral and legal considerations. But in practice those two domains are inseparable, and the judgments embodied in the Nuremberg trials and the United Nations Convention on Genocide make clear how close that connection must be in any retrospective view of Germany: "genocide" as a concept in international law emerged from the vaguer and ad hoc concept of "crimes against humanity" that discloses its moral origins; both of these were brought to international notice and recognition by the "thousand-year" Reich as it was instead compressed into only twelve years and then stood before the International Military Tribunal at Nuremberg in 1945. In relation to forgiveness, however, the misgivings stirred by the prospect of reunification have a weight absent from the legal concept of recognition by itself. The main impediment here is implicit in the principle that forgiveness can be granted (among human agents) only by those who have been wronged. On this principle, since the wrong to Nazi victims was genocide (or in some cases, "only" murder), the possibility that the German past should be forgiven would on this view be precluded; the only people who could forgive are unable to do so because of the act for which forgiveness would be sought. If it was.

It may be objected, however, that even if this condition of forgiveness holds among individuals (and we saw, in Chapter 9, that there, too, the matter is open to dispute), it hardly applies to corporate bodies or groups, especially, as in present-day Germany, when new generations who could not have been causally responsible for the Nazi regime constitute the largest part of the populace. Even this qualification, however, does not alter the importance of ascertaining what the Germans can now do that, however it falls short of achieving full forgiveness, would so far meet the requirements of a national "making good" as to move the Holocaust from being an open wound—where renewed gestures of repentance can be constantly demanded—to a synthesis of history and memory that honors the past but is yet able to present it *as* past. What can be asked of Germany and Germans that would amount to national restitution or "making good" in the realm of what is possible? Not for the purpose of erasing the historical record but to reach a point at which Germany's Nazi past is removed from the reach of external demands on the nation and its citizenry because of that past. (This would still leave open the possibility of demands and the sense of responsibility that the Germans might impose on themselves.)

Formally, the two conditions already referred to remain even with the transition or passage of generations: acknowledgment—more precisely, incorporation—of the past and its character and, related to that, assurance about the future. Words alone, as in any other aspect of the political or moral domain, are insufficient to meet these conditions. The question then becomes what, in the way of specific actions, can demonstrate that normalization or, so far as the term applies to international relations, forgiveness, was warranted? Or, what can Germany *do* to show that the Nazi past is indeed overcome, after which no further demands related to that past, from the outside if not from the inside, could reasonably be made?

As I have suggested, one function that the division of Germany served was to avoid this very question. So long as the country for which "oneness" had been an aspiration and ideal (the concepts of "Ein Volk!" and "Ein Reich!" long preceded the call for "Ein Führer!") was divided, that mark of past transgression would be constantly present, adding the weight of irony to a quite literal reality; memory would thus be preserved. As in the most compelling symbols, moreover, this one had come into existence and been recognized in the absence of any formal or conscious decision about its role as symbol—a fact that intensified the Dantesque justice of its inversion of the Nazi myths of unity and totality. As long as the stigma of division remained, furthermore, specific attempts at restitution (in the form, for example, of monetary compensation) for the Nazi past by the two Germanies—in practice, of course, attempts by the Federal Republic alone—could be acknowledged and even accepted noncommittally by their beneficiaries. Always remaining beyond such exchanges was the mark of division, judged even by the Germans who might think of it or of *some* national punishment as justified, to be "unnatural." (And who, after all, better than those who suffer punishment can measure its weight?) Admittedly, this understanding of the ultimacy of the symbol of division did not persuade everybody; so, for example, the fierce struggle in Israel in 1952, led by Menachem Begin, against Knesset ratification of the reparations agreement between Israel and West Germany, on the grounds that such an agreement, whatever disclaimers accompanied it and whatever other symbolic reminders remained to the contrary, would carry with it the effect of forgiveness and normalization.

With reunification, however, the question that had been deferred by the symbolic presence of the division came forcibly and explicitly into view. If erasure of the mark did not signify restitution and normalcy, what further, beyond what had already been required, could other nations or groups or individuals demand of Germany—and when would such demands end? The conclusion seems unavoidable that in the absence of either literal or symbolic requirements imposed at the time to replace the division, unification might indeed have been taken to signify a full return—with no more to be subsequently required of Germany in practical terms than would be asked of any other nation. This implication was not stated in so many words, nor do I mean to suggest that the divided Germany stood alone as a reminder or penalty (symbolic or otherwise) of the Nazi past. Numerous other "moments" in the more than forty-year history of the divided Germany served both those functions—and indeed they continue now as well, a decade after reunification. The current struggle, which has become an open political debate—and a factor in the 1998 national elections—over exactly what would be a suitable German monument marking the Holocaust, epitomizes these moments: on the one hand, pressure from both inside and outside Germany to establish this "official" means of respect (and apology); on the other hand, the issues of extent and magnitude which, even beyond the questions of moral or aesthetic quality, reflect the question of how much *else* in the way of obligation is represented by assent to this. But in comparison to the image of a house—a country—divided against itself, riven by an imposed boundary, even these other pointed and evocative reminders remain subordinate.

One response to the question of how and when the tabulation of past wrongs might be considered erased moves to the extreme of rejecting that question itself, asserting rather that the unification of Germany changed nothing in respect to the past or the future because no national or collective (a fortiori, no individual) act could: the Nazi past will not and should not be allowed to go away, and symbols carry no more weight in this balance than attempts at material reparation. Certainly it is arguable that no specific act of restitution, irrespective of how large or extensive, could fully lift the onus of that past, nothing that in literal terms would even approximate the "Wiedergutmachung"—"making good again"—that such reparations aim for. Not necessarily for any lack of will, but because of its intrinsic impossibility. As certain individual acts may be unforgivable, so too corporate or national acts may be similarly judged—with the difference that individual responsibility dies with the individual and is thus limited to that predictable span, whereas corporate or national life has no similarly "natural" extent, not even a nominal statute of limitations. The implication of this claim that by it other national crimes than those of the Nazis also become unforgivable—and the culpability for them enduring—is not itself an objection; for anyone who accepts the premise, the latter conclusion would only add to its weight.

But as other differences distinguish individual and corporate responsibility, so too a verdict of what amounts to permanent national condemnation—in contrast to the certain end of individual culpability—is also open to objections. The most obvious of these is that insistence on an unending German obligation to the past must increasingly be addressed to Germans who themselves had no part in that past, who in ever-growing proportions (and in the not-too-distant future, altogether) were born after 1945. Even without assuming a notion of collective guilt, it is generally accepted that the moral obligations of one generation—no less, for example, than its financial obligations—can in some circumstances be transmitted to another; the question remains of what the extent and detail of that transmission can or should be. And here a second issue gains force—as demands are specified for compensation and/or punishment for an act believed (by those making the demands) *always* to exceed the possible response to those demands; that is, where no punishment or compensation is adequate. In confronting this basis for expectations or demands, even groups or individuals who accept responsibility for the act at issue would find reason to balk. It is, after all, a verdict of metaphysical not historical guilt to judge that acts of reparation that are demanded will nonetheless *always* remain insufficient.

The reaction against such a conception of limitless obligation—in effect, the limitless burden of the past, where "ought" does not imply "can"—was not the only reason for the Historikerstreit or for the dispute preceding it between the "intentional" and "functional" interpretations of the "Final Solution." But it was an undercurrent in those analyses, and one that is understandable even if one rejects the interpretations of Nazi history (e.g., by Nolte or Hillgruber, or as turned into practical politics by Austria's President Waldheim) that thought to replace the limitlessness of German obligation by denying any obligation at all. (On this view, the end of culpability comes quickly—since there was no reason for it to have begun.) When those who accept responsibility for the past in terms set by the victims or their inheritors hear that nothing they do can overcome that past, others who deny all responsibility gain an additional pretext for arguing that "the past that will not pass" should simply be denied *as* the past. To accept national responsibility for a limitless obligation is in effect to forfeit the claim of legitimacy as a nation; more immediately, such acceptance would leave Germany hostage to any demand made on it that was based even indirectly on the Nazi past and the national responsibility allegedly transmitted from that time.

Even the severity of these consequences, it has to be recognized, has not dissuaded those who argue against the possibility of German restoration. But it is also clear that the latter view in its extreme form usually appears at a personal, not at a political level—for example, among the ever-smaller group of people who still, symbolically, refuse to visit Germany or to buy products manufactured there. (I say "symbolically" here not to deny force to the practice, but to suggest that it rarely comes at any greater practical cost than momentary inconvenience and is thus in effect *only* symbolic.) To generalize this position in political terms would entail the permanent isolation of Germany, a continuing role for it as a pariah nation. And quite aside from the improbability that any such policy could win widespread formal or even informal acceptance, not even those committed personally to ostracizing Germany have proposed that their view should be generalized in this way. The existence of an Israeli embassy in Bonn (soon in Berlin) and of a German embassy in Tel Aviv may not settle the rights or wrongs of the matter, but its practical implications and *their* moral grounds cannot be ignored—any more than can the imagery of then-Chancellor Kohl delivering an address at Brandeis University or being shown on German television wearing a yarmulke in attending the funeral of the German Jewish communal leader Ignaz Bubiz.

At the other extreme, it is obvious that for many countries and people, the ratification of normalcy suggested by a unified Germany only made (and makes) explicit what they were quite ready to believe anyway: that World War II is long past and that the enormities of Nazi Germany have been requited or (what amounts to the same thing) that nothing more can be done about them. Germany reunited, on this view, is Germany restored; the international playing field is once again level, with Germany now to be counted as a full participant, indeed, because of its economic and intellectual strength, as a central "player" on the world stage.

But this conclusion, it might be argued, comes impelled by a combination of material considerations and the passage of time, not by moral reason or a verdict of justice—and the surest basis for raising this objection is precisely the reaction of unease that surfaced with the prospect of reunification and that persists even as the memory of the divided Germany itself dims. Admittedly, the formulations expressing this uneasiness have often pointed to the future: Will German history repeat itself? But this formulation, too, refers to the past still more than to the future, to doubts about Germany's response to its history as measured by what it ought to have done (or do yet) to make good on it. It is in this sense, then, that German reunification articulates a question that had been frozen, submerged in the divided Germanies and that having been brought into full view by unification, continues to reassert itself: What can be required of Germany and the Germans that would, in the eyes of others, overcome the Nazi past—those others viewed as a collective, beginning with the victims and survivors of the Nazi genocide (and those who now speak for them) and extending even to those who might now choose a role as "bystanders"?

In the early postwar years, the avoidance of this question could be explained by a combination of factors, including the need to determine the individual responsibility of Nazi leaders and, in making provision for the survivors of all nationalities (whatever side they had been on) to repair the damages of war. West Germany's agreement in this context to pay reparations to individual Jewish victims and, as a collective gesture, to Israel was related, beyond the moral issues involved, to West Germany's remarkable economic recovery and the role that the country assumed in the Cold War (where East Germany had an opposing if less than equal role). In 1955, the three powers with responsibility for formal oversight of West Germany renounced that role (with the exception, for example, of the prohibition on German manufacture of atomic, bacteriological, or chemical weapons). Since then, of course, the question of whether the past is indeed past has been forced into the open in various settings—in 1985, for example, when President Reagan and Chancellor Kohl visited the military cemetery at Bitburg in which SS men had been buried together with men of the Wehrmacht, provoking a controversy that reached a climax with the Bundestag speech by then-President von Weizsacker on the failure of German sight and memory;[2] or in the subsequent challenge by Jürgen Habermas to the German historians attempting to realign the proportions of the Nazi past that then ignited the Historikerstreit.

Certainly there is this evidence and more that the question "What is to be done?" was, even if repressed, consistently alive for the Germans of Germany divided, however sharp their differences in responding to it. And although the Germans are beyond the point—with reunification, irrevocably—where requirements of international law or treaties reacting to the Nazi past apply to them in any corporate way, and although they are not bound by anything that non-Germans as individuals may in the future demand, the expectations formulated by others will no doubt continue to figure in their discussions. Even if this were not the case, however, it would be important for other groups and nations to confront the issue from their side of it—in part, because to remain silent on this question is also to speak: Is there to be *no* national statute of limitations? And in part, for the sake of moral judgment itself: What are the extent and depth of corporate responsibility? It is not only that justice should both be done and seem to be done on these matters as elsewhere, but also that closure is itself a value in the context of such issues. The reasons for this last claim resemble the justification for regarding forgiveness too as a value: that by it, the agents previously divided and at odds, together with the community generally of which they are part, are enabled by integrating the past and the present to move into a common future, reaffirming the possibility of solidarity and the institutions required

---

[2] See on the Bitburg controversy, Geoffrey Hartman, ed., *Bitburg in Moral and Political Perspective* (Bloomington: Indiana University Press, 1986).

for it. (The standing of this claim as a value, again, does not mean that it overrides all others; here, as with any value, it faces the prospect of conflicting obligations and rights.)

It may be that even sympathetic responses to this demand for a formula of reconciliation will seem arbitrary or partisan in whatever they propose— to that extent also missing the mark of justice. As the Nazi past did not involve or affect all groups and individuals equally, the requirements that various groups or individuals may express to bring an *end* to such requirements (assuming they accept this idea in principle) will almost certainly—like memory itself—also be contextual, particularistic. But that some such judgment should be made becomes more and more pressing, not mainly for practical reasons but—strained as this may seem—for the sake of justice. To be sure, history dissipates no less than memory, and there is little question that with time the now still sharp edge of the twelve-year Third Reich will dull, no matter what decisions or actions are now taken in respect to the actions for which it was responsible. But the temptation to leave the matter to history or forgetfulness—that is, to forgo taking a position—has obvious liabilities even if what is asserted instead were to remain (as it surely would) more notable in principle than in its detail.

Not to speak of an end to the demands that can be set for Germany, given the symbolism of its unification, would have the consequence of producing exactly the opposite effect; that is, of accepting unification as the restoration of normalcy and also then, in itself, as the rejection of all further requirements or demands. Even the latter judgment stated explicitly, however, would in my view be preferable to the acquiescence implied by silence, since the former would assert the justice of now erasing that past for its victims and perpetrators alike. This claim was what the ceremony that brought together President Reagan and Chancellor Kohl at the cemetery of Bitburg, with its graves of SS men as well as Wehrmacht soldiers, intended (although failed) to confirm. As in parallel lines seen from afar, the distance between victims and perpetrators was represented there as diminishing over time; at some point—and the leaders of the two countries declared it to have been arrived at then—the moral differences between victim and perpetrator hardly matter. The two belong alike to the past—perhaps not equal as judged, but with all their once extreme differences in the past having no special significance for the present. But justice cannot, *should* not be equated simply with the passage of time—which seems to have been the principle applied there.

At the other end of the spectrum of responses to the prospect of national restitution would be found the insistence on reaffirming, more literally than before, the mark that the divided Germanies previously imposed symbolically. This amounts to the claim that nothing Germany can do, divided or unified, warrants the concessions of normalcy or forgiveness—in effect, that Germany's fate and future are as unconditional as was its surrender, entailing its permanent status as a pariah nation. The latter verdict is as harsh as the judgment at the other extreme is remissive—but neither of those implications is in itself a reason for choosing one or the other. And indeed the "harshness" of assigning to Germany the status of eternal pariah is probably not even the principal reason of those who might favor it. For even observers who reject that extreme option may well find themselves troubled by the alternative, as it implies that once certain conditions have been set for normalization or international "forgiveness" and once those conditions are met, normalization or "forgiveness" is indeed entailed: no further conditions can be added. The conditions set, in other words, could be neither limitless nor open to later revision. And once met, they would signify a new normalcy; that is, an end to special German obligations as imposed from outside for the German past.

To those non-Germans—Jews and others—for whom reverberations of the German past have hardly diminished since the end of World War II, this last and obvious step has been a stumbling block that has caused them sometimes to avoid the issue entirely. That response is not difficult to understand: few precedents offer guidance, and the enormity at issue challenges the common formulas of "probationary" conduct. Always, it seems, for every stipulation, the same question can be raised: Would *these* conditions, if the Germans met them, be sufficient? So, for example, consider the vagaries of this minatory statement, which is meant in fact to be friendly, by Michael Lerner, the editor of *Tikkun*: "It will take a massive effort of German creativity and a commitment by the entire German people to figure out how it can begin to rectify these wrongs. . . . Only a German people that accepts responsibility by dedicating its intellectual and economic and political resources to healing the pain it has created has any right to ask to be accepted amongst the family of nations."[3] On the one hand, the possibility of restoration for Germany—normalcy—is implied here; on the other hand, the vagueness of the conditions stated works against the very possibility. How would anyone ever know if the conditions had been met? That the cause of such dissonance is understandable, however, does not diminish the need to resolve it in terms as definite as the cause itself; that is, in the belief that at *some* point, Germany's past may justly cease to constitute its present.

As the Germans have a past that has so far refused to go away, those who are not Germans but remember the German past have a *present* that will

[3] Michael Lerner, *Tikkun*, July-August, 1990.

not go away: the question, namely, of what they require of the Germans, whether as based on their own historical relationship to the Nazis (as it may be) or as "disinterested" judges of an extraordinary crime. The division of the two Germanies quickly took on the form of a symbolic response to that question; the reunification of Germany formulated the question again not symbolically but literally and, if not for the last time, more dramatically than it is likely ever to reappear. And if the question set in this context is not at some point explicitly addressed, the return to normalcy implied by re-unification, attended as it has already been by the swift integration of Germany into the New Europe, will encourage forgetfulness of the particular past for which the mark of division and now normalization or restoration— or forgiveness—are proposed. The issue will be settled not by being confronted but by looking away. There will be forgetting, in other words, without forgiving.

In any such process, the particular past of the Nazi genocide would almost certainly lose its identity, persisting if at all only as one among a large number of historical wrongs for which there are names or titles but no memory. History is replete with events that have undergone this change; we can recite the names as we have learned them—by rote, not because they are part of us: in Roman history, in the civil wars of European nationalism, in the colonial history of the Americas. Perhaps this outcome is inevitable for all history that is not sacralized or placed outside of time. But it seems too early for anyone, German or non-German, to agree to a future without memory for the German past; it also seems too late in this secular age to demand or expect the opposite alternative of a *sacred* history.

The need to find a third way, then, with the conditions of normalization explicitly set out, is clear. The one proposal I have to offer is the conventional and mild one of a probationary period—with no strong reasons for recommending one length of time for that period over others. But whimsy may at times be the only antidote for arbitrariness—and so also for the probationary term that recommends itself to me, adding an echo of the Jewish tradition to its length which ensures that I would not myself be alive to judge whether the conditions of probation have been met or not. This would be to count a period of 120 years—the Yiddish blessing for long life—beginning from May 7, 1945, the day of the Nazi surrender which marked both the end of the Nazi genocide and the beginning of life for Germans who had not shared the world with the criminal acts of the Third Reich. The length of this "sentence," if not its reason, is evidently arbitrary. No doubt, it is more extended than many would think warranted and too brief for others, certainly for those who believe in hereditary guilt transmitted not by the act but through the agent and thus to every succeeding generation. But guilt ascribed in the latter terms comes close—too close—to the sources of the crime it is meant to respond to, and how much does one have to know about either biology or ethics to recognize that guilt is no more a genetic inheritance than is moral conscience? On the other hand, 120 years *is* a long time—or term. But it is not, even so, as long as the consequences of the acts to which it is meant as a response. And however arbitrary this or any other limit must seem, the alternative to designating a specific length of time is worse than arbitrary, it is wrong. It would place an infinite verdict in finite hands—and justice does not lie in that direction either.

Afterword: Lessons to Learn,

or What Future for the Holocaust?

My concluding title here is, I realize, doubly offensive. On the one hand, it speaks about the "lessons" of the Holocaust—as though that enormity should be viewed as a school for study, as if together with the horror of that event as it persists in our awareness, we ought also, at the same time, to observe it with a detached and calculating eye that looks ahead to future contingencies and opportunities in our own lives and in those of others— students—whom we hope to teach. Furthermore, not only this wary split-consciousness is troubling (don't give *all* of yourself even to that moment), but the casual optimism supporting it suggests, in effect, that in this instance as any other, no matter what the occasion, there is always some profit to be gained, an "up" side somehow joined to its malevolence. And the swift objection must come here that for certain historical moments, it should be only the event itself that is "learned," nothing beyond it—from respect for the human dignity violated in it which imposes a continuing obligation, but also because the sheer weight and density of the event clash with any move to abstraction or reflection. Would we dare to ask someone who was dying what "lessons" his experience promised for us, the living? And what would we expect to "learn" from the response if we did venture the question?

And then the question of what future for the Holocaust—an oblique way of asking whether the Holocaust *has* a future—adds from its side the crassness of a wager, implying that it is not enough for us to have experienced or revisited history even in its extreme reaches, that also here we are encouraged to calculate how we would experience that history when the present is past and the future is present—that is, when our own sense of that extremity is past. To be sure, there is at times good reason for taking a "long" (that is, an understanding) view of the past, but the nature of the specific events must, it seems, affect any such undertaking—as does the question of how long the "long view" is supposed to be. Once again, for most occurrences, truly long views seem humanly irrelevant; in even the shorter long runs, memories dim and histories blur, and for the longer ones, much more sharply, as Keynes put it, "we are all dead." That death includes, of course, not only individuals but history and memory as well.

Within this broad framework, then, there seems little more to be said about the "future of the Holocaust" than what has already become obvious and present: that the process of historical encapsulization and distancing— at times contested but unavoidable—will continue on its steady way. Admittedly, a second and third generation of memories—those of the children and grandchildren—have since added their identities to the event itself; but also these identities show the effects of normalization and historicization, an increasing remove that renders the Nazi genocide a subject for discourse among other genocides, an incentive for art and reflection (these to be placed then among other artifacts of memory), even for politics and ethics, but all of them beset (how could it be otherwise?) by the expanding networks of historical detail and nuance that encroach on the distinctive moral space that "the Holocaust" would rightfully claim if only we could make the images of history stand still. Suffering and pain are the surest incentives for memory, more even than guilt (suffering once-removed) and certainly more than the scholarly or disinterested observations of science. Thus it will be in Jewish history if anywhere—followed at some distance by German history—that the future of the Holocaust will have its principal "site." But if the destruction of the two temples in Jerusalem and the Exiles that followed them can be economically conflated into a single day of mourning and fasting, one can without risk predict the general and ritualized outlines into which the Holocaust will come to be fitted in its own institutionalization. (Proposals continue to this day to compound this historical marker by urging the commemoration of the Holocaust on the single day of Tisha B'Av.)

The more palpable memorials—the physical sites of memory in the camps, the more artfully composed tributes at Yad Vashem or at the Washington "Memorial Museum"—may endure, but even a "surfeit" of such specific memory will almost certainly give way to the law of the conservation of collective memory on which the retelling and writing of history impose their own constraints. Official visitors to the State of Israel who had as a matter of course, after 1967, been expected to pay their respects at the Western (not so long before, the "Wailing") Wall were, after a transition period, directed to Yad Vashem instead—the Holocaust thus becoming an official emblem of Israel at least vis-à-vis the world outside it. But also that require-ment has now been (officially) weakened, and one need not look only to post-Zionism's antihistory to expect a continuing diminution in this cere-monial role. That role, after all, had always had an awkward place in Israeli culture. The fate of the Jewish victims (and even of the survivors) which was clearly a problem in Israel during and immediately after the Holocaust (Were their fates not themselves proof of the Zionist claim that Jewish exis-tence was impossible outside a Jewish state?) subsequently was accorded tol-erance and eventually something more. But also this accommodation has remained uneasy, troubled in equal measure by the difficulties the Holo-caust has posed for the religiously Orthodox community of belief (Where, after all, was God in the camps?) and an otherwise disparate group of secu-lar nationalists for whom the ideal of a "greater Israel" assumed a histori-cally transcendent status. God might well then be in the land, and so it could hardly be surprising that at times the other sharp lines between these two groups would disappear.

The issue is somewhat different from that of commemoration for the question of what lessons can be learned from the Holocaust. To a certain ex-tent, the offense in that question is unavoidable; yet there are also differ-ences among the answers that can be given to it. I do not mean by this the differences between historical lessons, on the one hand, and religious or moral or philosophical lessons, on the other, since those differences are all too easily exaggerated and so also misrepresented. There is, for example, a considerable historical irony in the "lesson" posed by the Holocaust for re-ligious or theological commitments, since in those terms (whether in the context of Judaism or not) there can be nothing novel or even unusual in what the Holocaust "teaches." The classical problem of evil becomes no more severe or instructive when evil is magnified millions of times than when it is encountered in its minimal form. The crude vulgarity in "expla-nations" of the Holocaust as punishment for religious transgression on the part of the victims or (still worse) by the waywardness of others for whom the victims then vicariously suffer hardly warrants comment. And even the subtler response according to which the value represented in the human freedom of will must take responsibility for the consequences to which that freedom may lead—or the subtlest of all responses (so subtle, that it virtu-ally disappears) that God is supposed to have temporarily withdrawn, hid-den: these, too, only postpone the conclusive question of how, in the face of God's beneficence and omnipotence, he would yet find sufficient reason to acquiesce in, if not to cause, such an occurrence. There is no confuting the claim that if the Holocaust were seen as only God can see it—in the context of the larger whole of which it is part—that "whole" would somehow dis-close itself as better with the inclusion of the Holocaust than without it. One need not be able to confute this claim to doubt it, however, and not only because of the unfathomable good that it requires to balance the two sides of the scale.

Even in non- or extrareligious terms, where the stakes of rationalization are slighter and serve no institutional or hierarchical interests, some of the lessons that have been assigned to the Holocaust stretch banality or vacuity to an extreme. To be sure, only to identify the phenomenon of genocide in the Holocaust as the clearest, most deliberate expression of which there is record is indeed a "lesson": the actuality itself expands the space of moral history by an addition that those who deny to historical events a moral form will then have to rediscover—more harshly, to reinvent—for themselves. But this fact and even its corollary which asserts the concept, and then also the heinousness of genocide, remain lessons in the abstract—a severe reminder that learning, finally, is concrete; that also the ancient and largest God is in the detail, with the particularity of sight itself.

The lure of abstraction is only one aspect of the dangers encountered in pointing the lessons of the Holocaust; indeed what has emerged as the largest common denominator in such accounts—the "lesson" most frequently cited—is that the Holocaust demonstrates, points to, *exhibits* what man is capable of doing to man, people to people; that is, what the combination of human malevolence and ingenuity can accomplish when turned toward its most natural object—man himself. And of course, this conclusion is warranted by the evidence and, in a limited way, perhaps also edifying although not surprising. So the conclusion is warranted and instructive in the way that historical commonplace ever is, indeed as any finding from the expanse of human history will be; everything that happens, after all, represents what is in the capacity of human beings to do to others (and themselves). The instructor who points to such a "lesson," however, not only distances but also skews the Holocaust and whatever might be more pertinently found in it. For it was not as human beings alone that the Nazis initiated the "Final Solution," and it was not as human beings alone or even first that the Jews were made its object. On both sides history worked with—from, to—particularity. The Nazis, as they enacted what they believed to be their "destiny," sought to deny existence to the Jews in theirs—not, on either side, as members of a common humanity but on the basis of deliberate principles of exclusion. And if the latter, quite specific principles—in their sources and in what they signify—are lost or obscured in what we teach or learn from the Holocaust, it is not clear how much light any other lesson of the Holocaust can shed except, again, as tautologies reiterate what they have already assumed.

What is required then in speaking about lessons of the Holocaust is that they should stand at the verge between contingency and necessity, between the concrete and the abstract, between the particular and the general, between the past and the future, even also, as I have suggested, between history and memory. These prescriptions, too, smack of the generalized abstraction they are meant to contest, and I would not claim, in these essays, to have escaped that danger myself; that is, to teach concretely and sequentially when reflection and even history itself seem so often to resist or violate all such order. But might not something in *this* be the first lesson bequeathed by the Holocaust? Few personal narratives among the countless diaries, memoirs, testimonies from the Holocaust fail to assign a central place in their retelling to the element of incredulity: the sense that what in the Holocaust became actual was viewed, even as it unfolded, as impossible— that it simply *could not* be happening. Primo Levi's record of his astonishment at the camp at Fossoli, that a German guard would strike someone not out of anger but with no reason other than that of the person's person, his existence, may seem now—as it soon did for Levi himself—a moment of notable naiveté: who now, with what we know about the Holocaust, would spare a moment for surprise at *that*?

But this small instance was emblematic of an element of the human constitution so deep-seated as to be biological, not a matter of learning at all: the belief in a "normal" order of practical and moral experience which, for the sake of self-preservation or sanity itself, resists admission to deviations or "surprises." Virtually all Holocaust testimonies speak repeatedly of this incredulity—the inability to credit the enormities that all the evidence pointed to: such disbelief coming not as a measure of the future (since at these moments, the future was not even contemplated), but as an indication of the present, what was taking place right before the eyes that doubted it, at times what was happening *to* the eyes themselves. The experience of denial in respect to the future—hoping for the best when evidence and reason argue for much less—is familiar enough: in the presence of personal illness or misfortune, against institutional turmoil or economic and political stress. For them all, avoidance has the immediate attraction of apparent security, of believing that, whatever hardships it held, at least the continuity of the past cannot simply, in a gesture, be dismissed or overturned. All this in respect to the *future*. How much more difficult to understand such incredulity when it is not the future but the *present* that is in this way placed in doubt, seen at the moment with one's own eyes? Yet the evidence from the Holocaust indicates that this too occurs, incapacitating and debilitating at the very time one's faculties are most intensely called on to act. The eyes that saw and understood in ordinary circumstances did not, in *those* circumstances, see and understand, not even what was happening immediately before them or to them. Numerous accounts, from both the victims and perpetrators, record this sense of incredulity and the practical reactions to which it led and to which it now, in retrospect, contributes an explanation.

We may well ask, to be sure, what sort of lesson this provides. Is there a way, the question here would go, of preparing oneself or others for this: for the unexpected, for the *impossible*? Certainly if such preparation could be learned, it would be a lesson that the Holocaust had indeed taught, but the very terms of the project suggest its improbability. Perhaps one might speak here more restrainedly, although even then with doubts: "Don't be surprised if history surprises you," or "*Do* believe what you see, even if you can't imagine it" or "Don't assume that because you have not experienced something before this, you cannot be experiencing it now." The problem with any such caution is that the believing or understanding they assume as a basis for future action is not always (perhaps ever) distinct from the act of seeing in the present, shaped by expectation not only in prospect but also retrospectively; each depends on what we already know of the unknown or the unexpected or the impossible—which is precisely what makes them *un*known, *un*expected, *im*possible.

The only way of taking such contingencies into account, it seems, would be by consistently attaching the most malign construction to each historical moment or event—conscientiously anticipating the worst imaginable outcome at every moment. This perspective would in effect be an inversion of theodicy (the belief in divine and thus also earthly goodness); in human terms it would be—is—so unusual that it does not even have a name ("pessimism" or "fatalism" only begin to capture it). And of course, this view too, even in its purest form, makes no allowance for the limits of the human imagination: the "worst imaginable outcome" is itself tied to the past. But the price exacted by this perspective would itself be unbearable, elevating the Holocaust in the imaginative expanse of evildoing to a norm that excludes the possibility of goodness or value in human experience except by accident. It would thus add a further wound to an already terrible one—proposing that history as a whole should be viewed in the shape and quality of the Holocaust; that is, preparing us to face the Holocaust at every moment.

Perhaps, in terms of individual response, no preparation for cataclysm could shape a sufficiently strong response to it, one that might indeed alter its course. Furthermore, every "lesson" drawn from history will always be a lesson by analogy; and since analogies are endless (everything resembles everything else in some respect), what can be learned from analogy cor in the end to a decision on what one *decides* to learn from analogy; thus, back to the beginning.

And yet, if we look underneath the grounds of analogy, there may indeed be a lesson not only from but of the history of the Holocaust, one that makes anyone now alive and future generations as well the beneficiaries of those with roles in that genocide, whether as victims or perpetrators or bystanders.

This is the simple conclusion—simple but not to the point of tautology: "If the Holocaust happened once, it can happen again." To be sure, the "it" in this declaration, like the Holocaust itself, can be variously described—so narrowly as to apply only to the war of the Nazis against the Jews or, at the other extreme, broadly enough to implicate man's inhumanity to man, the potential inhumanity of humanity. Neither of these, for reasons already mentioned, points exclusively and fully to the Holocaust—a requirement that has the additional burden, I have suggested (in Chapter 5), of avoiding the claim of uniqueness as that claim rules out the possibility of a second occurrence. This lesson, then, could not be learned (it would be false) if the Holocaust were indeed unique; that fact is one among other misrepresentations (and dangers) implicit in the Uniqueness-Claim.

It is not even necessary, on this formula, to assert that the Nazi genocide was the first instance of genocide, although if it is not the first, it is surely the most clearly articulated in historical and causal—and moral—terms. All that this lesson as drawn teaches is that because such an event occurred once (that is, in the historical circumstances that it did and with the historical consequences that it had), it can occur again. It is the prospect of repetition in the event, not in the circumstances (since no one has proved those circumstances, the causes of the Nazi genocide, necessary) that points the lesson here—but a lesson that would be quite empty if one did not know what occurred historically to constitute the "it," that is, what and how it happened.

So: "If it happened once, it can happen again" presupposes knowledge of the "it" and the "happening." And the conclusion drawn from that knowledge would then, as a lesson, shade and shape the future, casting forward an understanding of its possibilities and so also, however difficult to detail, anticipation and preparation for it. A considerable body of evidence shows that in January 1933 almost nobody—Jews or Nazis or anyone else, in Germany or outside it, politically sophisticated or political naifs or ideologues—predicted an outcome of Nazi rule that concluded in the "Final Solution." Notwithstanding this failure of anticipation, "it" occurred nonetheless. Some features of that shared misconception were perhaps indefeasible: the few who did see through it, who predicted what would happen, were usually alerted as much by chance or ideological conviction—rather than by insight—as those who did not. If there was logic in the historical development, it was a logic that no texts had taught and hence the difficulty of translating "If the Holocaust happened once, it can happen twice" into a practical warning when its status seems more that of moral principle standing on the verge of a philosophy of history than a straightforward historical claim.

Perhaps the most that can be inferred here are certain practical cautions, *negative* lessons. Among these, an obvious one would be that the ideologically laden concept of "high culture," so often cited as distinguishing Germany even among the nations of Western Europe, proved to be no impediment to the transformation effected by Nazi Germany; certainly the rule of law there was no obstacle, any more than were other honored codes of conduct in the esteemed professions nor any more than were the institutions of religion or secular learning, both of which constituted a formidable presence in Germany. At least one considerable set of future expectations can thus be ruled out on the basis of Germany's history: the belief that the distinctive features of a high culture immunize it against the lure of barbarism. We also see, conversely, that nominal historical circumstances—and personal decisions—are capable of overcoming even deep-rooted and valued foundations of "enlightenment." (Those who object that the very fact that Germany accommodated itself to Nazi designs is proof that the culture was not "enlightened" find themselves in a circular argument that leaves the relation between Nazi Germany and the Germanies before and after it inexplicable.) To observe pre-Nazi German culture in its distinctive features, then adding to it the technological changes since the Holocaust which make "industrial" warfare still more feasible an option for any national group, is to see that there is *no* "here" of which one can say with assurance, "It can't happen here."

Admittedly, this conclusion—and so, warning—is related to a general principle not specifically related to the Holocaust; namely, that claims for the historical impossibility of *any* occurrence—like the contradictory claims for historical necessity—presuppose something more than only historical evidence. On the other hand, to admit the possible reoccurrence of a Holocaust reflects not only the premise that anything we can imagine (and many things that at the moment we cannot) can happen—since, in the case of the Holocaust, although it must still be imagined (as possible), there is the historical event itself. Since that was actual, it must have been possible—itself an unexpected lesson that challenges the traditional order of actuality and possibility.

Furthermore, nothing in that one-time occurrence and possibility precludes the recurrence of either (as would hold, for example, in the Creation: once and only once). Thus, more than only in principle, the possibility is implicit—actual—in the doctrine "If it happened once, it can happen again." This does not mean that it *will* or *must* happen again; nor does it mean that history must now be viewed continuously, from moment to moment, as verging on a "New Holocaust." It does mean, however, that Holocaust, or its species, genocide, is now a constant—it is not too much to say, permanent—option in world history and politics: a possibility so extreme that nobody, from the most powerful political figures to the least, can look at or act in the world without assuming responsibility for the awareness of it as a possibility. Ignorance may morally and in the law be a pertinent excuse where that plea concerns a sequence of events for which there was no precedent experience and/or where the harm caused is remediable. Nobody could claim either of these in the event of a new Holocaust. The possibility of its reoccurrence—*another* time—should, it seems, be lesson enough.

THIS ONE, very general and near-tautologous lesson might, in addition to other liabilities, seem to contradict my emphasis earlier in this book and elsewhere on the historical particularity of the Holocaust: that we do not understand even as much as can be understood about that occurrence if we analyze it exclusively in world-historical terms or as evidence of what is "humanly" possible. Indeed, the historical character of the Holocaust points also to a number of lessons that if they too remain generalities (in some measure, this is intrinsic to any inference as it projects from the past to the future), are more concrete than the single large abstraction claiming the possibility of its reoccurrence. Here we encounter the systematic difficulty of inferring from one instance a more general claim, but this is no more than the risk faced by any contention about the characteristic features of the Holocaust as they have indeed been actual.

One such claim seems hardly less obvious than the larger one previously cited: that the likelihood of genocide increases under the cover of general war. In the case of the Nazi genocide, this implication seems clear. Nazi antisemitism was an important element in its ideology from the beginnings of the Nazi movement; there can be no doubt of its presence in Hitler's *Mein Kampf*, written when Hitler was imprisoned (1923) and at a time when he himself did not imagine even the possibility of the "Final Solution" that would, twenty years later, be his to implement. The intensity of his *passion* then is undeniable and perhaps would never grow stronger; nonetheless, even he could see no further, among the many extreme statements he would make there, than to suggest, as he conceived of harm to be inflicted on the Jewish enemy, that "if ten or twelve thousand Jews might have been given a whiff of gas," they might then have learned the lesson they deserved. Twenty years later, these numbers would be beneath notice because they were, comparatively, so trivial; by that later time, *they* were unimaginable.

It is a harsh but often ignored fact that until 1941, eight years after the Nazi assumption of power in Germany, official Nazi policy at least in respect to German Jews called not for their extermination but their forced emigration. The invasion of Poland in September 1939 initiated a change in what the Nazis conceived of as both possible and necessary in respect to the "Jewish question"—a change more fully (that is "finally") actualized with the declaration and initiation of war against Russia in June 1941. It is true that other factors also contributed to the planning of the "Final Solution," but the cover provided by a general war which could then be represented as posing an undeniable threat to the German "homeland" was preeminent among these. The shifting nature of modern warfare, given impetus by the "industrialized killing" that World War I had made part of the order of battle, obscured in a general way the traditional distinction between combatants and noncombatants. And although civil conflicts, within a particular nation, might be genocidal (even in their primary motivation), for the Nazi genocide it was the expanded field of general warfare that provided a means that antagonism or hatred within a nation, even within Nazi Germany, would have realized only with greater difficulty or perhaps not at all.

To be sure, given the technology available for modern warfare and the growing material interconnections among nations, the conclusion that the occurrence of international war provides a ready ground for genocide may appear quite beside the point; certainly any "lesson" learned from this seems feeble beside the larger issue of how such wars themselves can be anticipated or prevented. But this does mean that both within the warring countries and as the conflict between or among them crosses each other's boundaries, the potential for genocide—even when the latter goal appears subordinate to the "reasons" for the conflict—increases. The consciousness of this potential in the warring countries and in other countries not directly involved ought itself to be a warning.

A second aspect of this same phenomenon, evident also in the Nazi genocide, is that the intention for genocide may be—in terms of national or corporate intentions, virtually must be—incremental. That is, not even the aim of genocide, let alone its implementation, is likely to appear (perhaps, *cannot* appear) in the "original intent" that is politically expressed. The division of opinion about intentionality among historians of the Holocaust on this issue in respect to the "Final Solution" seems in fact one issue in that history that has indeed been resolved (so, at least, one part of the argument in Chapter 4). The claim that Hitler or the Nazis more generally had, from the beginnings of their political strategy, envisioned—intended—the "Final Solution" is refuted by the evidence of an evolutionary process by means of which that purpose emerged gradually and in response to a sequence of contributory factors (including the reactions to various initiatives on the part of the Nazis by the "bystander" nations or groups). It is theoretically possible, of course, that the idea and even the act of genocide could be instantaneous—individually or even collaboratively, as the push of a button might result in the annihilation of a *genos*. In that event, little could be done to avert the outcome; also, under a cloak of absolute secrecy, any prediction of its occurrence might, by hypothesis, be impossible. But systemic constraints, except in virtually impossible instances, argue against such a scenario. The likelier sequence of events would be akin to that which led up to the "Final Solution" in the plans of Nazi Germany, a movement by stages which responded to specific circumstances along the way: social and institutional reactions inside and outside Germany, battlefield developments, international and intranational responses.

This argument against the historical necessity of the Nazi genocide also points a rudimentary lesson: that responses at the several stages in the incremental process make a difference in the process itself, potentially with the power to deter it entirely, but in any event to constrain, delay, or minimize it. This may seem to amount to no more than a general caution that evil on a large scale sets out initially from lesser—small—events and decisions and thus with the warning that to turn a blind eye to individual acts opens the way, invitingly, to larger and corporate wrongdoing. In the case of an outbreak of fire, the symptom and the phenomenon are one and the same: there can be no doubt of its occurrence, its likely consequences, and so also of the need to react. Few social phenomena come close to this transparency, however, and genocide is a complex social phenomenon. There are indicators that, although not in themselves genocidal, foreshadow it—with the Holocaust here again providing a model. Well before the "Final Solution" was formulated as a plan, the Jews of Germany, many of whom considered themselves Germans first and Jews second (or sometimes not at all), were disenfranchised; the Nuremberg Laws of 1935 radically altered their status and rights as citizens. If any warning of a likely outcome is noteworthy, one finds it here, where the formal protection of law, previously observed, is—legally—withdrawn.

Admittedly, this overt limitation of rights may be unusual, a distinctive irony of Nazi Germany's wish, in its early stages at least, to preserve the semblance of legality. It assumes, moreover, that the rights of citizenship had been granted in the first place—and that is not always the case. Even the possession of formal rights does not mean that serious abuses in practice may not be ordered or sanctioned, with the effect of leaving the formal rights meaningless. But again, we are speaking here about what can be learned from the Holocaust, *that* event; and this one indicator, which was recognizable and known both externally and internally, was also largely ignored on both sides of Germany's national boundaries. It was one moment in a series of incremental steps which, if they were not all so definitive or openly displayed, were also recognizable as an indicator of what was to follow. Thus, even an act as dramatically horrific in outcome as genocide need not announce itself; for its own reasons, it almost certainly *would* not—but it may nonetheless and despite itself provide foreshadowing.

And a third point, rooted historically in the same phenomenon: where genocide is concerned, there *are* no bystanders—supposedly disinterested parties who as onlookers may choose or not, with equal justice, to maintain their neutrality. To some extent, this third point is a version of the general, even metaphysical claim that everything that happens is in some way related to everything else—a contention that in its moral version would impose responsibility and thus obligations on every person for wrongs committed anywhere and everywhere. And surely it is difficult to argue with the claim that, morally, there should be no difference between the discovery of someone starving to death on one's own doorstep—which presumably would produce an immediate reaction—and knowing that thousands of miles away, someone—or some millions—are starving to death. But if this is true on an individual scale, the issue on a corporate scale is still larger, not only because of the numbers involved, but also because in genocide the element of intentionality is more clearly evident and also more readily open to collective action.

No doubt, for any particular event or action, certain individuals or groups will bear a greater measure of responsibility than others. This is clearly the case for the Holocaust even if we cannot draw fixed lines among the degrees of responsibility. But if any one implication emerges from the incremental development of the Nazi genocide, it is that the individuals and groups who at the time or even afterward regarded themselves as bystanders have discovered that they did indeed have a role and thus a measure of responsibility in its mechanism. This applies not only to the so-called neutral countries at a time when other countries took sides with the Axis or with the Allies, but also among both the nations and citizens constituting those two warring factions. It includes—the evidence increasingly demonstrates—the governmental institutions and individual citizens of the Allied powers (even among Jewish groups outside Europe, in the United States and the then Palestine) who at times acted as though they too were bystanders, as if they had a choice—with something to be said on either side—between remaining disengaged and becoming involved. The point here is that anyone close enough to see such a "choice" is by that fact implicated. A decision at that juncture to be "disengaged" is already an engagement, with determinate, and in this case severe, consequences. It might be argued that where genocide occurs in the new "global village," there simply are no bystanders.

It might be objected that these several, in some ways peripheral lessons share the defect of the first, larger one—that they too are so general as to obscure any specific reference to the Holocaust. The need here, once again, is to reflect the particularity of the Holocaust in whatever we say about it or infer from it. Since that particularity is tied fundamentally to Jewish history, on the one hand, and to German history on the other, the implication is that if there are any lessons to be learned, we should find them first in one or the other or in both of these—and that if there are no such lessons, the particularity of the Holocaust itself, on which I have placed such emphasis, might reasonably be disputed in favor of the more universal view of its import that has been criticized here. To be sure, reference to "Jewish" or to "German" (or indeed to any such national or ethnic) history has sometimes been criticized as presupposing an essentialist subject. But it is certainly possible to speak of such histories without making this presupposition, if only by recognizing that substantial numbers of people have, over long periods of time, identified themselves (that is, from the inside out) as Jews and Germans—and that certain events associated with those groups, now including the Holocaust, have entered the histories of both.

This is not the place to address the question of how historians decide whose history they are writing or even the more specific question of what difference it makes to the writing of "a" history as to who does the writing. Certainly some of differences in versions of Holocaust history are due to attempts to write German history within the context of Jewish history and to write Jewish history within the context of German history. "*Some*" of the differences, I say, because quite fundamental differences occur also when the provisional boundaries cited are carefully observed or, otherwise, when the boundaries themselves are flatly denied (that is, when historians write on the larger scale of European or world history). But the narrower issues that come under these general headings are evidently large enough.

The writing of German history in respect to the Holocaust has gone through the stages of silence, of guilt and apologetics, of denial and displacement, and—in the past two decades—a struggle which will no doubt continue for normalization. The latter term need not be pejorative. If German history has any conceptual reference, there could be no reason for excluding the Holocaust from it. The struggle—represented initially in the intentionalist-functionalist debate and its successor Historikerstreit—is over what shape normalization can reasonably take without making the Holocaust simply disappear (that it *should* disappear is one view in the struggle). The complexity of whether and how this can be accomplished—even in theory, let alone in practice—is underscored in the notable recent advances in the historiography of the Third Reich. When obstensibly "neutral" countries such as Switzerland and Sweden turn out to have had a significant role in the economic sustenance of Nazi Germany, for example, this might seem to argue for a dispersion of responsibility—and even if the claim is made that this amounts to an addition to the burden of guilt, that the burden is shared becomes itself a metaphor for normalization.

It seems fair to predict even now, however, that whatever course such normalization follows, the bare fact of the Holocaust—the genocide and the brutality exercised in it—will not "go away." The numbers and identity of the dead and the means used which led to that end remain as given. If it is impossible to infer exactly what should or will follow from this datum for post-Holocaust (and future) German history, present evidence is sufficient to conclude that it will not amount to a justification. And if we hear (as we have) that in its search for "what happened," the writing of history need not even consider questions of responsibility or justification, the Holocaust stands as a significant item of evidence against that view. Insofar as historians exclude that consideration, this would mean only that the burden of writing moral history would be taken up by others and that the writing of history "as such" would place itself in question. In either event, that the Holocaust represents a large-scale moral failure in German history remains a basic element. It seems patently implausible to sustain the claim advanced by some historians (and much popular opinion) that this failure reflected an essential "German" trait or a determinant causality in German national history: the conclusion that "if it happened once, it can happen again" also argues against such claims. But it remains a matter of fact that it was Germany as a nation and not some other that initiated the "Final Solution"; and if it is unclear how that will or ought to translate into German history— what this past imposes on post-Holocaust and future German generations— the question itself persists as a distinguishing legacy from that past. The question itself thus becomes a lesson.

The efforts to draw lessons for Jewish history have been more various although no less contentious, beginning with those attempts at religious or theological rationalization which, I suggested earlier, belong to the more general, not peculiarly Jewish, response to the problem of evil. The most immediate reaction in historical terms has been the attempt to place the Holocaust in relation to Zionism and the Diaspora, inferring—from sources on both sides—that it constituted evidence, even proof, of the Zionist claim for the necessity of a Jewish state. The premise of this claim is that a Jewish state would have averted the "Final Solution," either by the power it would have been able to exert in international affairs or, if that failed, as a place of refuge. At times this line of argument reduces to the tautology that if the Jews of Europe had not been in Europe at the time of the Nazi rise to power, there would have been no Holocaust; but neither this nor the accompanying irony that the Holocaust itself contributed substantially to the establishment of the State of Israel dispels the narrower claim that the existence of a

Jewish state would have made a difference—and the lesson then sometimes drawn from this for Jews who live *now* in the Diaspora, which is that they too will live in insecurity unless they return to the Land.

The historical basis for this very broad claim may have some force, although as a counterfactual, it has to take its place alongside numerous others, both sharing their hypothetical (and unprovable) character and competing with them. It seems no less likely, for example, that if the early reaction to developments in Germany after Hitler's assumption of power had been stronger and more concerted—on the part of the Germans, but also in other countries and in the Jewish communities outside Germany—this too would have made a substantial, even a sufficient difference. Quite aside from the fact that the State of Israel has its own vulnerabilities, furthermore, the "lesson" thus asserted about the necessity of Israeli nationhood for Jewish identity or survival is part of the traditional "negation of the diaspora," which assumes the unqualified benefits of political autonomy as incomparable to any alternative, and—as part of that—a denial of the creativity and life of the Jewish diaspora as a whole. The continuing relation, and to some extent the dependence, of Israel on the diaspora is one complicating factor in assessing this judgment; others include the fact that even now, with the occurrence of the Holocaust and the establishment of the State of Israel clearly in historical view, antisemitism remains a persistent force that affects Israeli Jews as well as Jews outside Israel. The expulsion of Jews from Arab lands after 1948 is one aspect of this, although with rather a different genealogy from that of the European persecution—and even there, of course, neither the Holocaust nor the existence of the State of Israel has laid that disposition to rest. (In present-day Poland, with a Jewish population of as few as 15,000 of a total of 39,000,000, it seems that only the *memory* of Jewish existence is a sufficient basis for antisemitism.) The question of the relation between Israel and Jewish communities outside it is too large to be addressed here, but there can be no doubt that this remains a point at which the Holocaust will continue to impinge on Jewish history— perhaps epitomized, although in a contrary way, by the revival of a German-Jewish community which has grown from zero at the end of the war to approximately a quarter of the size of the prewar community.

If the Jewish "return into history" frames the largest lesson for Jewish history emerging from the Holocaust, it is not the only one. So, for example, on the "lachrymose conception of Jewish history" as Salo Baron titled it, the Holocaust would have been both predictable and substantiation of the view itself. Again, Fackenheim's "614th Commandment"—his prohibition against giving the Nazis a "posthumous victory" and thus a precept for continued Jewish identity—amounts to a version of this "lachrymose view," in which persecution is seen not only as strengthening Jewish identity, but as a (even, *the*) ground for that identity. This seems to me only a less blatant version of Jean-Paul Sartre's misrepresentation in *Reflexions sur le question juive* of Jewish identity as defined essentially by *anti*semitism: no antisemites, no Jews.

None of the latter "lessons" is in my view convincing or adequate to the event from which they are drawn. In part their defects reflect no more than the difficulty of inferring general lessons from a particular history. It is not only that for every mistake that we recognize and for which we propose a remedy, other, new mistakes become more likely—but also that to think retrospectively about any particular change that would have altered the historical past opens the question of what else would have been altered as a result of that change. This reservation is still another reason for distinguishing present memory and identity from specific predictions about the future. The certainty of *some* place for the Holocaust in Jewish history can hardly be doubted; equally compelling, however, is the expectation that over time, the perspective on that place in Jewish history will alter. As the continuity of Jewish identity and history before the Holocaust had many and more positive grounds than only those of the collective trauma of exile and persecution, the memory of the Holocaust itself may itself be all the lesson it provides for Jewish history—the more so as that history includes a substantial involuntary element. To this extent, the response of Yudke in Haim Hazaz's novel *The Sermon* who asserts "I want to state that I am opposed to Jewish history" is an exercise in futility; by the same token, the commandment in its several Biblical versions of "Zakhor!"—"Remember!" or its variant which came out of the Holocaust: "Never again!"—are redundant. No doubt, choice is involved in the shaping of identity and memory, but the most constant lessons that either of these commandments holds for the future may take shape irrespective of individual or even collective decisions. In this sense, that the Holocaust occurred remains, by itself and alone, both the first and the last lesson of the Holocaust.

WE NOW—whoever we are, however the time or space of history locates us—represent the post-Holocaust. This is not merely a chronological marker, because at some point in the future, other events or perhaps the elongation of history itself will almost certainly make that reference obsolete: not mistaken (since its literal sense will be warranted indefinitely), but irrelevant. What the designation means is that for the first and second generations, extending already to the third after the Holocaust itself, the more than half century since the Holocaust "formally" ended yet remains a bearer of its consequences. This historical aftermath itself might have been different from what it has been or now is. But lessons would have little to reflect on (and no purpose) in a world of necessary or deterministic events; contingency alone—in the events, in the teachers, in the students—provides grounds for reflection, sending out affective lines that may then be informative, that may at times alter or even save lives.

Like other truths so rudimentary that they go without saying, that we utter only with embarrassment, it is the fact of the Holocaust's occurrence that remains its primary and most concrete lesson. Only imagine someone reviewing the detail of that occurrence without showing *some* evidence of reaction or change. And yet, of course, that lesson too has been turned aside—revised or even denied. It is as though here, if anyplace, one finds confirmation for Hegel's dialectic as intrinsic to the structure of thought— the antithesis appearing, with no need for evidence or further reflection, almost at the moment that the thesis shows itself. The formulations of Holocaust-denial, furthermore, have set out not only from this logic of consciousness but also from the related logic of morality, the will to violation that figures as an element—prior as well as posterior to—moral truth. There is, of course, a sociology and psychology as well as a logic of this denial as it in effect continues the common will, during the Holocaust itself, to refuse to credit that occurrence. It is also clear that the public voice of Holocaust-denial has been consistently marginal and stigmatized, but that voice has nonetheless been consistent, audible since the moment that the physical act of the Nazi genocide ended; there is no reason to believe that whatever initially motivated that denial will itself disappear. Indeed, the phenomenon has by now a tradition of its own—history and memory—to build on, linking up with other like-minded claims, often inside although sometimes outside the laden tradition of antisemitism. Responses to expressions of Holocaust-denial have included their legal prohibition in countries such as France, Canada, and Germany; elsewhere the attempt has been made to impose an informal boycott of silence—a refusal to afford it the dignity of a reaction, as a number of Holocaust scholars advise. Such tactics may have a certain symbolic value, but it seems to me that the most efficacious *practical* response will be found in the principle on which historical analysis and reflection are based, whatever their subject; that is, by building a network of evidence and inference that will stand against anything else that might be asserted (or denied) about its subject. In this sense, a cloak of silence or even legal prohibitions are subverted by the practice of history itself, and even the symbolic force of such other reactions falls short of the efficacy that speaking about—that is, speaking *for*—the Holocaust will have.

Beyond and apart from this, moreover, there is something to be gained— also a lesson to be learned—in public recognition of the phenomenon of denial, which is in any event impossible to avoid. Part of this lesson is a general one for which the occurrence and history of the Holocaust serves as an occasion; namely, that historical representation—history in its chronicles and narratives—has a moral as well as a cognitive component, and that the two are intertwined. This is to claim more than the truism that historical descriptions or accounts can be appropriated for a multitude of purposes open to moral judgment. Like any other act, interpretation too reflects decisions of the interpreter that express a scale of values. But more—and more important: historical descriptions themselves, in their articulation and thus through the criterion of truth or falsity to which they answer, have a moral ground. The conventional distinction between lies (falsehoods consciously asserted) and mistakes (unintentional falsehoods that omit or misconstrue items of evidence) introduces a moral component to putatively descriptive discourse. That moral component, however, also enters the realm of historical discourse even earlier in its formulation, through the connectives that give coherence to the most "neutral" description, and even earlier still, in the very selection of a subject for historical reflection.

Historical subjects do not depend for the reality of their reference on the act of description. But what a subject is represented *as*, even—as "the Holocaust" clearly demonstrates—in the name assigned it, involves more than only a "descriptive" citation. This moral origin applies also when the subject has no evident ethical implications (as in the idealized discourse of the natural sciences); where the subject as designated conveys an ethical implication, the moral weight of that initial articulation becomes heavier still. The truth or falsity of Holocaust descriptions would then have a moral character even if—as Holocaust-denial claims—the event itself were much diminished from what it is generally held to be. In this sense, Holocaust-denial raises a moral issue even as it denies that the Holocaust raises any specific moral issues because (on its claims) that event never took place. Thus Holocaust-denial furthers the very ends it would subvert.

The other part of the lesson of Holocaust-denial is more specific, attached to the history of antisemitism. That history, as in many other histories of prejudice, has been imaginative in its working, typically presenting itself not as prejudice at all but as scientific analysis or cultural reflection or—as in the case of Holocaust-denial—as straightforward historical representation. Insofar as Holocaust-denial is presented—and criticized—as a historical representation, it also claims immunity to the charge of antisemitism, as though even if it should prove to be mistaken, its errors would be only additional missteps in the generally fallible process of the writing of history. Holocaust-denial qualifies *at least* as this, but that association is not a reason that it may not also be judged antisemitic. One has only to analyze rhetorically the specific statements of Holocaust-denial to recognize in them almost always, if not necessarily, standard features of the antisemitic tradition: a double standard of evidence, the introduction into putatively objective descriptions of ad hominem and tendentious explanations, the claim of invidious comparisons (as between the Holocaust and other genocides) where no such comparisons (like the Uniqueness-Claim) are integral to the bare assertion of historical occurrence. It is not inconceivable that the Denial-Claim can be asserted in the absence of such accompanying motives or motifs, and at least some authors who make the claim also deny the charge of antisemitism. But denial of the charge is not, of course, proof against the charge itself, and the prima facie evidence, beginning with the effort of denial, almost always points in the opposite direction. The imaginativeness of antisemitism, in other words, extends within that tradition also to the narration and analysis of its single most blatant expression.

To be sure, much greater emphasis has been placed in the attention given the Holocaust since 1945 not on its denial but on its recognition, in analysis as well as in commemoration. And together with this, the varieties of representation have been fully represented themselves. The institutionalization of the Holocaust has been accompanied by diverse kinds of "deformation"—ranging from politicization to sentimentalizing to bombast to vulgarity and, as a last indecent touch, to a genre of pornography. Even if, as many commentators have suggested, the more written about the Holocaust, the better—since what is crucial is that the Holocaust should be a focus of attention in history and memory (in effect, better that anything written about the Holocaust should exist than not)—this would not be a reason for ignoring the differences in the forms or manner of its representation. Historical and cultural discourse arguably provides a stronger proof that nature abhors a vacuum than physics—in effect that everything, every view that *can* be imagined or expressed will be. There should be no surprise, then, in the fact that the diversity of Holocaust discourse extends to denial or to the shadings that verge on it. What this argues for, however, is the importance of more, not less discussion; of heightened, not silenced discrimination in judgment; it is the price—and in the end, the value—of a liberal society to which the Holocaust stands in antithesis.

A commitment to pluralism and tolerance does not, however, imply that differences do not matter—any more than it implies that differences do not occur. It is commonplace in theories of representation—cultural, artistic, historical—that there is a connection between content and form, that the two are closely interrelated. There is no reason to exempt the subject of the Holocaust from this constraint; if anything, one might suppose that the constraint should gain in importance in proportion to the significance of the particular content in question. It is likely that for some aspects of the post-Holocaust, the issues of expression are so complex and difficult, or that by their character (as in the process of commemoration or ritualization) they so require the test of time, that even judgments made in good faith will prove to be mistaken or "deformed." But also these possibilities argue for, not against, the process of judgment, of continually testing what is said about the Holocaust, of seeing how it is represented and of disputing its misrepresentations both in the most immediate historical sense and in their aestheticization or politicization when that occurs—that is, on moral grounds. One consequence of the enormity of the Holocaust has been that the very utterance or representation of the term has come to command the space around it. There is good reason for this, but also danger, since it opens the way to exploitation of various kinds—the devaluation of a "currency" assumed to be so strong and compelling that no devaluation seems possible. It is clear that this view—that so long as its representations come with good intentions, the Holocaust cannot be abused or deformed—is mistaken; that representations that act not by denial but by affirmation may also be open to these charges and should be willing, especially because of their subject, to face them—refuting them when that is possible, admitting them when it is not. Here as elsewhere, high-minded motives by themselves are not enough. This aspect of the "future of the Holocaust" originates in lessons learned from the *post*-Holocaust, rather than from the Holocaust. But we would not find ourselves in the one if it had not been for the other— and *that* remains a lesson of both.

Index